AF813467

ECHOES OF THE TRAUMA

This book discusses the echoes of the trauma that are traced in the relational narratives that the sons and daughters of Holocaust survivors tell about their experiences growing up in survivor families. An innovative combination of the Core Conflictual Relationship Theme (CCRT) method with narrative-qualitative analysis revealed common themes and emotional patterns that are played out in the survivors' children's meaningful relationships, especially in those with their parents. The relational world of the second generation is understood in the context of an intergenerational communication style called "knowing–not knowing," in which there is a dialectical tension between knowing and not knowing the parental trauma. In the survivors' children's current parent–adolescent relationships with their own children (survivors' grandchildren), they aspire to correct the child–parent dynamics that they had experienced by trying to openly negotiate conflicts and to maintain close bonds. Clinicians treating descendents of other massive trauma would benefit from the insights offered into these complex intergenerational psychological processes.

Hadas Wiseman is Senior Lecturer in the Department of Counseling and Human Development, Faculty of Education, University of Haifa, Israel. She is a member of the Society for Psychotherapy Research (SPR) and of the International Association for Relationship Research (IARR). She works in Israel and spent a sabbatical year at Simon Fraser University, Vancouver, Canada. Wiseman is also a certified clinical psychologist in private practice in Tivon, Israel, and is coauthor of *Conversation as Method: Analyzing the Relational World of People Who Were Raised Communally.*

Jacques P. Barber is Professor of Psychology, Center for Psychotherapy Research, Department of Psychiatry, University of Pennsylvania, Philadelphia, Pennsylvania, United States. He is president of the Society for Psychotherapy Research. He coauthored the *Handbook of Brief Dynamic Therapies*, *Handbook of Dynamic Psychotherapy Research and Practice: A How-to-Do-Them Guide* and *Dynamic Therapies for Psychiatric Disorders (Axis 1).*

Echoes of the Trauma

RELATIONAL THEMES AND EMOTIONS IN CHILDREN OF HOLOCAUST SURVIVORS

Hadas Wiseman

University of Haifa, Israel

Jacques P. Barber

University of Pennsylvania

CAMBRIDGE
UNIVERSITY PRESS

CAMBRIDGE
UNIVERSITY PRESS

Shaftesbury Road, Cambridge CB2 8EA, United Kingdom

One Liberty Plaza, 20th Floor, New York, NY 10006, USA

477 Williamstown Road, Port Melbourne, VIC 3207, Australia

314–321, 3rd Floor, Plot 3, Splendor Forum, Jasola District Centre, New Delhi – 110025, India

103 Penang Road, #05–06/07, Visioncrest Commercial, Singapore 238467

Cambridge University Press is part of Cambridge University Press & Assessment, a department of the University of Cambridge.

We share the University's mission to contribute to society through the pursuit of education, learning and research at the highest international levels of excellence.

www.cambridge.org
Information on this title: www.cambridge.org/9780521879477

© HadasWiseman and Jacques P. Barber 2008

This publication is in copyright. Subject to statutory exception and to the provisions of relevant collective licensing agreements, no reproduction of any part may take place without the written permission of Cambridge University Press & Assessment.

First published 2008

A catalogue record for this publication is available from the British Library

Library of Congress Cataloging-in-Publication data
Wiseman, Hadas, 1956–
Echoes of the trauma : relational themes and emotions in children of Holocaust survivors / HadasWiseman, Jacques P. Barber.
p. ; cm.
Includes bibliographical references and index.
ISBN 978-0-521-87947-7 (hardback)
1. Children of Holocaust survivors – Mental health. 2. Children of Holocaust survivors – Psychology. 3. Holocaust survivors – Family relationships. 4. Psychic trauma – Transmission. 5. Transference (Psychology) 6. Holocaust, Jewish (1939–1945) – Psychological aspects. I. Barber, Jacques P., 1954– II. Title.
[DNLM: 1. Psychoanalytic Therapy – methods. 2. Holocaust – psychology. 3. Jews – psychology. 4. Parent-Child Relations. 5. Survivors – psychology. 6. Transference (Psychology) WM 460.6 W814E 2008]
RC451.4H62W57 2008
618.92'8521–dc22 2008007584

ISBN 978-0-521-87947-7 Hardback

Cambridge University Press & Assessment has no responsibility for the persistence or accuracy of URLs for external or third-party internet websites referred to in this publication and does not guarantee that any content on such websites is, or will remain, accurate or appropriate.

In memory of my beloved parents
Esther and Gdalyah Wiseman

In memory of my father, Leon Barber, and my in-laws, Irena and John Auerbach, who each survived the Holocaust in his or her own extraordinary way

CONTENTS

FOREWORD

The Internal Echoes of Holocaust

Dan Bar-On, Ben-Gurion University of the Negev

This book makes an important contribution to the growing literature on the aftereffects of the Holocaust on the families of its survivors – mainly the second generation. Its special focus is on the intergenerational relations between the members of these families. To study these relations the authors applied the Core Conflict Relational Theme (CCRT) method to interviews that focused on interpersonal relations within these families. By doing so, the authors avoided unnecessary assumptions about "pathologies" in these families. Their qualitative approach also avoided the tendencies of some recent quantitative studies that claim that there are no such aftereffects within families of survivors, studies that undermine what voices within the second and third generations tell us and the echoes these stories have within us. Wiseman and Barber tell us how the echoes of that horrible period still resonate among hundreds of thousands of its survivors, their children, and their grandchildren.

In a certain sense, the variety of studies and their sometimes contradictory results represent the different assumptions researchers make about the human beings they study, more than the phenomena they study itself. Just as economists make assumptions about the possibility of predicting human behavior based on the expressed wishes of these people to purchase certain products, some clinical psychologists used uncritically psychoanalytic terminology related to "pathologies" of survivors of the Holocaust; this terminology was developed by

Freud to depict abnormal reactions to normal situations (Bergmann & Jucovy, 1982). The present book suggests that survivors' reactions to the Holocaust were mostly within the normal range of reactions to an extremely abnormal situation. Still, these reactions had echoes in the relationships among the survivors, their children, and their grandchildren, echoes that need our attention and the systematic analysis that is provided in this book.

Some quantitative researchers recently claimed that there are no such aftereffects (van IJzendoorn, Bakermans-Kranenburg, & Sagi-Schwartz, 2003). They remind me of a student I had in the mid-1980s at Ben-Gurion University in one of my workshops, "The Psychosocial Aftereffects of the Holocaust on the Second and Third Generations." This student, during the opening circle of self-presentations said, "I belong to the second generation, but I do not believe there is such a phenomenon, so I came to see what you are talking about." Although some students wanted to jump on her (feeling that she undermined their own feelings as the second generation), I tried to defend her right to feel differently, which probably had its special Israeli roots in being ashamed, in earlier years, of belonging to a Holocaust survivors' family (Bar-On, 1995). We know of major generals in the Israeli army who disclosed their childhood Holocaust roots only after they were out of their active military service. So deep still was the stigmatization of the early years that they had to present themselves as Israeli-born and hide their true origins for many years.

Perhaps also the claims to no aftereffects represent researchers' own personal inclinations that such aftereffects should not be "put on" survivors. They may have reacted to the assumption that relational aftereffects can be seen as some kind of accusation of the survivors, who suffered so much and who were stigmatized enough, and that the survivors should not be burdened with any unnecessary additional stigma. This approach puts the survivors' assumed need of protection above those of their children and grandchildren. In my view, there is also a methodological flow with quantitative studies that compare samples of families of survivors with families of "control groups." In many cases these control groups are families of Jewish European descent who did not live under Nazi occupation (this is the legal definition of Holocaust survivors). Still, if one looks more closely into the stories of members of these control groups, one will find that although they succeeded in fleeing from the Nazis to Russia or to Israel or the United Kingdom, many of their family members were still murdered in the Holocaust. As a result, they go through processes of mourning, of silencing these losses, but they "have no right to feel effected" in the eyes of the survivors, or in their own eyes, and in my view therefore cannot be counted as a control group in any deeper psychological meaning.

The ambivalence of researchers in this domain can be understood, as we study a complex phenomenon many years after the original occurrences, effected by several simultaneous processes: what happened to the protagonist before, during, and after the Holocaust, specifically the process of immigration, which was the fate of most survivors and which has its own psychological toll; the dynamics of the family; and the personality of the protagonist.

The analysis in this book, however, goes beyond the ambivalence of the researchers of previous clinical or quantitative methods. Wiseman and Barber allow us to listen to voices of children of survivors, who are by now parents themselves, along with the voices of their own adolescent children. Unlike the earlier studies that depicted the second generation as dependent and in the shadow of their survivor parents, here we listen to them also as mature adults trying to navigate their way between their aging (and sometimes deceased) parents and their own adolescent children. Such a navigation is difficult, as they are very attentive to the needs of their own ailing parents while they try not to repeat the mistakes their parents have made with them (mainly of excessive emotional control), but also not to go too far in the opposite direction (of emotional neglect). This study also tells us about a different period within the Israeli-Jewish culture. By the 1990s – the time of this study – the original silencing by the Israeli society of the stories of the survivors was finally broken. That silencing was based on the somewhat cruel bias of the absorbing Israeli society of the 1950s and 1960s, which maintained that the survivors "did not fight for their lives" according to local standards and therefore were not "good enough" (Bar-On, 2006).

However, within the families of the survivors, the echoes of the original social silencing is still present, as many survivors had their own subjective needs to not tell their children about what they went through "to save" them from that past. This phenomenon suggests their lack of psychological thinking; they did not understand that silencing is one of the most effective ways of transmission of trauma. In many of these families the grandchildren were the ones who opened windows in the "double wall," which I formulated as an image of the inability of survivors and their descendents to talk openly on the burden of the past (Bar-On, 1995).

Grandchildren have new ways to ask their grandparents questions, to let them tell what they went through. This is probably true in general (I can testify now as a grandfather myself), but in the shadow of the Holocaust this sometimes played a special and important liberating role: the grandchild is the one who travels to Poland, visiting the sites where his or her grandparents survived, while other family members do not. In this book, we hear how the grandchildren can more openly express their feelings, sometimes in contradiction to those of their own parents, something that members of the second generation could not afford in relation to their parents.

Wiseman and Barber give us a positive perspective for the future, which they call "the music of knowing and not knowing." The echoes of the past create a special kind of music, and when one learns to listen to this music, it resonates as a combination of what one knows and does not know. This could be important general advice about life stories told and untold concerning earlier traumatic life events. In light of the Holocaust, it has some special additional value. I would like to add here that I have experienced lately that some survivors have new and warm recollections of their family life prior to the Holocaust (Litvak-Hirsch & Bar-On, 2006). These recollections may have been hidden under the enormous burden of the tragic fate of family members during the Holocaust. Now that they again have a big family, during festivities and gatherings they can recall the good old times and tell their descendents about them. Unfortunately, their own children have no such recollections, as they were usually born into the Holocaust, and, therefore, in terms of relational patterns, I am afraid that the second generation will remain with the psychological price of that period, hopefully thereby this price will be saved from their own descendents. This could become their own consolation.

PREFACE

Sixty years after the end of World War II and the liberation of the Nazi concentration camps, the study of the long-term psychological effects associated with the Holocaust remains of interest to both social scientists and clinicians. The focus for the last three decades or so has been on the intergenerational transmission of the Holocaust trauma to the children of the survivors, often referred to as the "second generation." Psychological trauma, especially massive traumas such as genocide, may have long-term effects, not only on the victimized generation but also on the next generations that did not endure the traumatic events directly. The question of whether the trauma of the Holocaust has been transmitted to the second generation has been the topic of much clinical and empirical research, as reflected in the large numbers of articles and books. Our book, however, addresses the more specific issue of what psychological sequelae, if any, have been transmitted from survivors to their children. We answer this question by exploring scientifically the relational world of the second generation as it unfolds in the narratives they tell about their experiences growing up in families of Holocaust survivors. Much of the material integrated in this book is based primarily on a research project that we conducted in Israel to study the transmission of the relational themes, as well as the main psychological issues and sensitivities that may play out within those families.

In developing this research project on offspring of Holocaust survivors we were inspired by the position of the late Hillel Klein (1980), an analyst whose work and writings were influential in the understanding of the survivors and their children.

> Research has shown that we can no longer speak of the transmission of psychopathology from one generation to the next, but rather of the transmission of common motifs, mythologies, issues, sensitivities within families and between the generations. (p. 553)

Klein's position resonated with our clinical impressions as psychotherapists working with children of Holocaust survivors, suggesting that common themes and sensitivities are evident in these high-functioning and accomplished adults. Consequently, instead of the focus on psychopathology, which characterized the early studies, the focus we chose was the interpersonal themes and patterns manifested by children of Holocaust survivors. This new focus led us to search for the best conceptual framework and methodology to shed light on such complex dynamics.

On the very hot summer day that we met in Israel to discuss our potential research collaboration, the idea of applying the Core Conflictual Research Theme (CCRT) method (Luborsky & Crits-Christoph, 1990) to the study of the second generation was born. Thinking over vivid examples of the narratives told to us by second-generation patients, clinical case studies we had read, stories in books written about the experience of the second generation, and movies, we were excited by the possibility that the CCRT method would help us uncover the interpersonal themes and sensitivities experienced by the second generation. It seemed to us that applying the CCRT method, an established method in psychotherapy research, to study relational narratives that we would collect from children of Holocaust survivors could provide a unique way to stay close to interviewees' personal experiences and be highly relevant to clinical practice. Our collaboration brought together expertise in qualitative-narrative methodology (Hadas Wiseman) and in the CCRT method (Jacques Barber). To trace the "Echoes of Trauma" we integrated the innovative method of the CCRT with the qualitative-narrative analysis of themes, emotions, and intergenerational communication patterns that emerged in the relational narratives told by children of Holocaust survivors.

Another aspect of our research that we would like to underscore is that the majority of the narratives presented and analyzed in Chapters 3 to 10 (Parts One and Two) were collected from a random, nonclinical sample of children of Holocaust survivors from a national database. Instead of relying on a convenience sample, which has been common in studies on the second generation, we sampled our Israeli-born participants from lists provided by the Israel Population Registry. The sample consisted of fifty-six participants (thirty men and twenty-six women) across an age range of 30 to 49 years (at the time of data collection in 1996–1997). The mothers of these men and women were all survivors of Nazi concentration camps, and two-thirds of the fathers were either survivors of concentration camps or had been in Europe during the war. (See Appendix for demographic details.) In addition, we include a preliminary exploration of change and continuity in the child–parent dynamics that transpire between survivors' children and their own children (the survivors' grandchildren). This exploration of past and current parent–adolescent relationships was derived from narratives collected recently from a school-based sample of second-generation parents and their adolescent children. (See Appendix for demographic details.)

We hope our book gives voice to the subjective experiences of men and women raised by parents who had survived the Holocaust by portraying the common themes and sensitivities in their relational world. We also believe that the book pays tribute to the remarkable resilience of the survivors and their descendents in the aftermath of the Holocaust. Finally, we hope that what we have learned from these adult children of survivors can be generalized to descendents of other populations of victims of trauma who have also experienced violent and enduring atrocities.

ACKNOWLEDGMENTS

This book is the fruit of a special collaboration between our research teams at the University of Haifa and at the University of Pennsylvania Center for Psychotherapy Research.

We wish especially to acknowledge our former and current graduate students and research assistants for their invaluable help and input at various stages of the Second-Generation Project. Among these, we are especially grateful to Idit Yam and Alon Raz for their outstanding role in coordinating the major study during 1995–1998 in Israel and to Carol Foltz at the University of Pennsylvania. Special thanks go also to Alon Goldberg for his help and diligence in coordinating the study during 2002–2005 on parenting adolescents. Sharon Snir, Einat Metzl, Nurit Gur, and Dafna Hadar contributed greatly to the narrative analysis of the relational stories and of the specific emotions. Brian Sharpless carefully edited Chapters 8 and 12.

Our major study titled "Central Relationship Patterns in Second Generation Holocaust Survivors" was supported by the United States–Israel Binational Science Foundation (BSF Grant 94–00199 to Hadas Wiseman and Jacques P. Barber). The more recent study titled "The Experience of Parenting Adolescents among Second Generation Holocaust Survivors" was funded by an Israel Foundation Trustees Grant (2002–2004) to Hadas Wiseman. We also appreciate greatly the support we received from the Faculty of Education of University of Haifa and from the Department of Psychiatry of the University of Pennsylvania.

We were fortunate to enjoy the important and supportive involvement of colleagues at the University of Haifa, especially Ruth Sharabany, Avi Sagi-Schwartz, Ofra Mayseless, Miri Scharf, and Anat Scher. We were influenced by the work of Lester Luborsky and Paul Crits-Christoph on the CCRT, and by the work of Amia Lieblich and Ruthellen Josselson on narrative research. We are deeply grateful to Gaby Shefler, Yael Desheh, Orya Tishby, Tova Weisman, and Dorit Ringart for their clinical insights and continuous professional and personal friendship. We are also indebted to the Society for Psychotherapy Research and especially to Irene Elkin and David Orlinsky for providing us the springboard from which we could develop our collaboration, and to Eric Schwartz from Cambridge University Press for his trust and professional support.

Finally, *Echoes of the Trauma* could not have been voiced without our many interviewees, who are presented under pseudonyms. We hope that in this book we have depicted their interpersonal world in a way that resonates with their experiences. Last but not least, we would like to express our love to our families – Itzik, Adi, and Uri and Smadar, Natalie, and Adam – for their ongoing encouragement and patience, each in their own unique way, throughout the process of this collaborative project and the writing of this book.

Hadas Wiseman, Haifa, Israel
Jacques P. Barber, Philadelphia, United States
December 2007

1

Introduction – A Narrative Approach to Bridging the Gap between Clinical Case Studies and Empirical Research on Children of Holocaust Survivors

CHILDREN OF HOLOCAUST SURVIVORS – THE "SECOND GENERATION"

The term "second generation" has become an accepted shorthand phrase that refers to adult children of Holocaust survivors. The term has not only been part of the professional literature, but it has also made its way into music, film, literature, and other arts (Solomon, 1998). In North America, as in Israel, children of survivors define themselves as a group of adults who share certain issues in common due to being the sons and daughters of surviving parents and have formed self-help groups.

In Israel, until the 1990s the term "child of Holocaust survivors" was an ambivalent one. It was assumed that identifying oneself as having parents who were Holocaust survivors suggested that their trauma had been transmitted from them to their children. That is, children brought up in families of survivors were affected by the parents' trauma, which attested to negative psychopathological consequences. Statements such as "I am not from a typical family of survivors" or "I never considered myself as a child of survivors" or "the Holocaust has not affected my upbringing in any way" attest to the emotionally laden nature of the term and to the need to define oneself as free from the psychopathological consequences that this term may imply. For some sons and daughters of families of survivors the very fact of having parents who suffered the Holocaust has been downplayed or not acknowledged at all by the parents or by themselves. An Israeli colleague in her mid-40s recounted that only when she watched a documentary made for Israeli TV about her father's story as a child survivor did she grasp for the first time his (and her own) connection to the Holocaust. Reading the subtitle of the documentary on the screen, *The Story of a Holocaust Survivor*, the realization suddenly hit her fiercely and she burst into tears. Until then, although she knew her father was in Europe during the Holocaust she never considered herself the daughter of a Holocaust survivor, that is, one of the second generation.

Another example I (HW) encountered of late realization of a family's Holocaust background was the case of one of my graduate students in winter 2000, in connection with a course assignment that included the topic of the second generation of Holocaust survivors. This student, in her 30s, first discovered through the course assignment that her own parents were Holocaust survivors. It came as a great surprise. She had always had the impression that because they came from Rumania they had not personally experienced the Holocaust. Five years later, in winter 2005, I developed a graduate course that focused on psychological aspects of the memory of the Holocaust. Interestingly, the timing of the course coincided with much of the attention then being given in the media worldwide, and especially in Israel, to commemorating 60 years since the liberation of the Nazi concentration camps and the end of World War II. At least half of the students who enrolled in the course had some Holocaust background in their family. This time it was the third generation who were surprised to find out how little they knew about this background and how much more there was to know and uncover. The very fact of considering oneself as second generation is apparently complex, probably involves certain changes in one's awareness, and needs to be considered in the context of personal development and the sociohistorical context.

The more recent social-cultural-historical context, as the survivors grow old and many second-generation children have lost one parent or both, creates a fresh surge of interest in making their experience known to themselves and to others. Lately, children of survivors, following the death of the parent(s), have set out to trace their parents' past and to write about their own experience while growing up, either in scholarly work (e.g., Wajnryb, 2001 – *The Silence*) or in literary writings (e.g., Guttfreund, 2000 – *Our Holocaust*; Miron, 2004 – *A Tale of Life and Death*). In our book we will discuss the complex processes of the echoes of the Holocaust and the emotions and conflicts of the second generation in knowing and not knowing the Holocaust trauma.

"BECAUSE OF THAT WAR": TRANSMISSION OF TRAUMA FROM PARENTS TO THEIR CHILDREN

In referring to the term "second generation" Solomon (1998) suggested, "The assumption of all who use the term *second generation*, is that it is more than merely a biological marker and that somehow or other the trauma of the Holocaust has been transmitted from the survivors to their children" (p. 69). Numerous publications in the last three decades have attempted to investigate *whether the trauma has been transmitted*, and if so, *what has been transmitted* from the survivor parents to their children. Before we turn to provide an overview of this literature, we would like to consider a certain duality regarding the possibility of transmission of the Holocaust trauma to the next generation. We suggest that both the *subjects* themselves and the *researchers* experience a duality or ambivalence about confirming or disconfirming the transmission assumption.

As for the subjects, as suggested earlier there may be variability in the extent to which they feel that defining themselves as second generation is part of their identity. On the one hand, these sons and daughters may feel obliged to acknowledge their parents' suffering, and that if they do not acknowledge the aftereffects of the trauma on themselves, as stemming from their parents' traumatic experiences, they are possibly belittling their parents' suffering (Felsen, 1998). Moreover, they may indeed feel strongly that they continue to carry the scars of their parents' trauma. As one of the participants in our study indicated: "I, as a second generation, should also be entitled to compensation" (referring to the monetary compensation that the survivors received from Germany). These sons and daughters of survivors may themselves have a need to receive acknowledgment of their own experiences, which they view as related to their parents' traumatic past experiences. On the other hand, confirming the assumption of intergenerational transmission might be perceived as blaming the surviving parents for being responsible for their children's problems, which may arouse guilt feelings in the children (Felsen, 1998). The children may feel that disavowing the transmission assumption, namely showing that they are no different from children of nonsurvivors, is part of their parents' victory over the perpetrators, who failed to damage the next generation (Danieli, 1984; Felsen, 1998). Thus, depending on their affective and cognitive attitudes toward their experience of being children of Holocaust survivors, some sons and daughters may view themselves as being highly affected by their parents' Holocaust trauma ("because of that war . . . "), whereas others may feel that "there is no such thing as second generation" (Hazan, 1987). This duality is relevant to the methodological issues around subject selection and measurement tools that we describe later.

As regards researchers of the second generation, they may also feel caught up in the duality toward the transmission assumption. Like their subjects, they may lean toward focusing on vulnerability by confirming the long-term effects of trauma on the subsequent generations. By contrast, they may focus on evidence of adjustment and resilience that disputes the transmission of trauma to the second generation. Among researchers, however, much of the controversy surrounding the findings from the numerous studies on the children of Holocaust survivors (for reviews see Bar-On, Eland, Kleber, Krell, Moore, Sagi, Soriano, Suedfeld, van der Velden, & van IJzendoorn, 1998; Felsen, 1998; Kellermann, 2001; Rieck, 1994; Solkoff, 1992; Solomon, 1998) centers on methodological issues. Next we survey these issues.

CLINICAL CASE STUDIES VERSUS EMPIRICAL RESEARCH ON CHILDREN OF HOLOCAUST SURVIVORS

The study of the second generation began with clinical reports by psychiatrists and psychologists who were treating the children of the survivors (Rakoff, 1969; Sigal, 1971, 1973; Trossman, 1968). On the basis of their clinical observations, research clinicians proposed that the psychiatric distress of these youth reflected a "survivor syndrome" (Niederland, 1968), transmitted and perpetuated from one generation to the next (Barocas & Barocas, 1973). Researchers became interested in studying whether a "children-of-Holocaust-survivor syndrome" existed, and sought to understand the process by which the parents' Holocaust experiences may have affected the emotional development of their children (Danieli, 1983; Sigal, Silver, Rakoff, & Ellin, 1973).

In 1974 Kestenberg formed a study group to investigate the effects of the Holocaust on the second generation, utilizing psychoanalytic source material (Kestenberg, 1982). The purpose of the investigation was "to learn whether survivor parents, as a result of their own traumatic experiences, can influence certain aspects of development, conflicts and psychopathology of their children, as well as the adaptive capacities of their offspring" (Jucovy, 1992; p. 270). This study revealed characteristic conflicts and recurrent patterns in offspring of survivors who had sought analysis. The investigators suggested that these patterns and symptoms should not be labeled a "syndrome" but a "complex" or "profile," because many of the features did not contribute to the formation of psychopathology, and some even constituted expressions of strength (Jucovy, 1992; Kestenberg, 1982).

Psychoanalytic clinical case studies further portrayed characteristic conflicts and recurrent patterns of Holocaust Survivors' Offspring (HSO), such as depression, guilt, aggression, problems in interpersonal relationships, separation-individuation conflicts, and identity issues (Freyberg, 1980; Gampel, 1982, 1992; Kestenberg, 1982; Kogan, 1995; Pines, 1992; Wardi, 1992). Researchers generally attributed these to the survivors' parenting styles. The survivors perceived their children as a source of new hope and meaning, and expected them to be a form of restitution for the families, goals, and communities that were destroyed in the Holocaust (Nadler, Kav-Venaki, & Gleitman, 1985; Russell, 1980). Hence, the second-generation children were overvalued and overprotected (Jucovy, 1992). Analyses of clinical material suggest that the children's sensitivity to their parents' suffering may lead to guilt-ridden protectiveness of the parents. Acting out of aggression toward the parents becomes problematic, as does the acknowledgment of aggression and conflict in general (Wanderman, 1976). "To the child of the survivor, death guilt (i.e., guilt relating to having survived the Holocaust) is communicated as ever-present and unexplained guilt. The child is frequently forced to take on the burden of having to fulfill not only his own developmental needs but also his parents' unrealistic expectations in that he must compensate for the parents' sense of worthlessness" (Barocas & Barocas, 1973; p. 821). Clinical reports suggested that particularly during adolescence, survivors' children had difficulty achieving autonomy, partly because their attachment to their parents was so tenacious (Jucovy, 1992). The parents, it was argued, only exacerbate the problem, because for them the issue of separation seems to reactivate their memories of separation from their own parents and siblings, a separation that meant loss (Shiryon, 1988).

A major methodological issue regarding the clinical accounts of the transmission of Holocaust trauma to the second generation is subject selection. The subjects in these case studies were HSO who presented for psychotherapy. These individuals may have grown up in families with depressed members and disturbed patterns of relating, which could have led to the transmission of the scars from one generation to the next. Thus, it is not surprising that findings from clinical reports suggested that psychopathology was more prevalent and more severe in the HSO population than in the general non-Holocaust-related population. In light of the duality we mentioned earlier, it is possible that these HSO were those who indeed attributed their distress to their parents' Holocaust background.

In contrast to the picture portrayed by studies of clinical samples, studies based on nonclinical samples did not generally support the clinicians' bleak descriptions. The majority of studies that empirically investigated the postulated transmission in nonclinical samples of HSO reported no significant differences between HSO and comparison groups on various aspects of personality, family atmosphere, and mental health (Keinan, Mikulincer, & Rybnicki, 1988; Leon, Butcher, Kleinman, Goldberg, & Almagor, 1981; Rieck & Eitinger, 1983; Rieck 1994; Sigal & Weinfeld, 1987, 1989; Weiss, O'Connell, & Siiter, 1986; Zlotogorski, 1983). For example, in one of these studies in the United States, Leon et al. (1981) compared a nonclinical sample of survivors' children with a matched group of Jewish children whose European parents emigrated to the United States before World War II, and found no significant differences in personality factors on the Minnesota Multiphasic Personality Inventory (MMPI). A controlled study conducted in Israel found that HSO achieved higher academic success and higher economic success than control subjects (Rieck & Eitinger, 1983).

Although controlled studies of nonclinical samples overcome the problem of bias toward those who suffer from the transmission of trauma, the methodological problems of recruitment of subjects and what constitutes the HSO group and the appropriate control group remain. First, recruitment of subjects often relies on those who volunteer or belong to some organization that defines them as HSO so most studies are based on so-called convenience nonclinical samples of HSO. Very few studies have relied on random sampling of HSO from the general population. These studies are easier to conduct in Israel through lists provided by the Israel Population Registry (by special approval for the purposes of research), as was done more recently in studies by Sagi-Schwartz, van IJzendoorn, Grossmann, Joels, Grossmann, Scharf, Koren-Karie, and Alkalay (2003) and ourselves (Wiseman, Barber, Raz, Yam, Foltz, & Livne-Snir, 2002). Second, regarding the definition of the HSO, some studies have defined them broadly as children of parents who were in occupied Europe during

World War II whereas others have focused on the descendents of Nazi concentration camp survivors. Third, with regard to what constitutes an appropriate control group, it has been argued that the difference found between second-generation survivors and control subjects can be attributed to HSOs' immigrant status rather than to their parents' concentration camp experiences (Weiss et al., 1986). For example, a study comparing children of Holocaust survivors, children of other European immigrants (non-Jewish), and children of American-born parents found no significant differences in mental health or in feelings of anomie among the three groups (Weiss et al., 1986). The study suggested an immigration effect in that offspring of American-born parents showed greater alienation, less religiosity, and a tendency toward feelings of guilt. Specifically, in studying HSO in Israel and comparing them with non-HSO, it has been argued that those immigrating to Palestine before 1939 may a priori differ from those who stayed in Europe (Nadler et al., 1985; Nadler, 1987; Silverman, 1987).

The aforementioned striking discrepancy in the findings that emerged from clinical case studies compared with nonclinical controlled studies and the largely equivocal findings on the second generation have been documented in major reviews of the research in this area (Bar-On et al., 1998; Felsen, 1998; Kellermann, 2001; Rieck, 1994; Solkoff, 1992; Solomon, 1998). These reviews, which were conducted mostly in the 1990s, were based on the common qualitative review method, namely counting studies that support and refute the intergenerational transmission of the parents' traumatic experiences to their offspring. This method of reviewing the evidence has been criticized for not taking into account the highly heterogeneous quality and the size of samples in the reviewed studies. Most recently, van IJzendoorn, Bakermans-Kranenburg, and Sagi-Schwartz (2003) conducted a highly sophisticated meta-analytic investigation addressing the question: "Are children of Holocaust survivors less well-adapted?" Meta-analytical procedures facilitate a quantitative analysis (i.e., computing average effect size across studies) that can take into account study characteristics (e.g., sample size). From their series of meta-analyses (on 32 samples involving 4,418 participants), van IJzendoorn et al. (2003) concluded that there was no evidence in nonclinical samples of the influence of the parents' traumatic Holocaust experiences on the children's adjustment. These researchers defined adjustment broadly, as including indicators of posttraumatic stress, other symptomatology, and general mental health. We contend, however, that in studying intergenerational transmission we need to reconsider the focus of our research, and seek the realms in the life of the second generation in which it is relevant to search for the impact of parents' traumatic experiences on the second generation.

SEARCHING FOR THE ECHOES OF TRAUMA: ASKING THE RELEVANT QUESTIONS

Much of the early focus of studies on the intergenerational effects of Holocaust trauma has been on psychopathology (Solkoff, 1992). Such studies on nonclinical samples often concluded that the second generation scored in the normal range. Interestingly, when subjects who participated in such a study were later informed of such findings their response suggested that they felt that the researcher had "missed the point." Blumenthal reported that the participants' reaction was that "they *did* suffer from emotional difficulties, which they ascribed to their being offspring of Holocaust survivors, yet the questionnaire was irrelevant to their specific problems" (Blumenthal, 1981, in Rieck, 1994; p. 650).

In trying to consider such difficulties and sensitivities from which the second generation may suffer, we contend that the search for the echoes of trauma should focus on the realm of the relational world. Indeed, one of our interviewees, while trying to recount a relational episode (following the instructions of the Relationship Anecdotes Paradigm interview, to be described in Chapter 2), indicated after some effort to recount an episode: "I can't quite find the words to recount the interaction that I am telling you about. You know I am a medical doctor and I am also involved in research, though a totally different kind of research, and I am not familiar with your methods, but I know *you hit the real issue right on the head.* It is probably something to do with the way I am in my interpersonal relationships and the way I communicate with others."

A NARRATIVE APPROACH TO BRIDGING THE GAP BETWEEN CLINICAL CASE STUDIES AND EMPIRICAL RESEARCH

Given the considerable consensus that investigation of the intergenerational effects of Holocaust trauma should focus on various developmental-social-emotional domains, researchers (Bar-On et al., 1998; Sagi-Schwartz et al., 2003; Wiseman et al., 2002) considered what might be a suitable framework and methodology to explore the relational world of the second generation.

Recently, attachment theory and its research methods have been suggested as an appropriate conceptual and methodological framework to integrate clinically and qualitatively based methods of clinical case studies with empirically based group studies. First, it has been suggested that attachment, separation, and loss are highly relevant concepts for understanding the psychological aftermath of the Holocaust. Second, attachment theory stresses the continuous and cumulative nature of favorable and unfavorable child-rearing circumstances, and in that respect it transcends the gap between clinical and nonclinical observations (Bar-On et al., 1998; Sagi-Schwartz et al., 2003; Scharf, 2007).

The conceptual and methodological framework that we have suggested is based on contemporary adaptation of psychodynamic theory (Freud, 1912/1958; Luborsky & Crits-Christoph, 1990) involving central relationship patterns (Barber, Foltz, & Weinryb, 1998; Luborsky & Crits-Christoph, 1998). Central relationship patterns refer to characteristic ways of relating to others and are thought to be the product of highly ingrained patterns or schemas of relationships with important others (Barber, Foltz, et al., 1998). It is assumed that these relational schemas, which are initially constructed from emotionally laden interactions with parental figures in the earliest years of life, are carried forward into subsequent relationships (Bowlby, 1988). To study central relationship patterns manifested in the second generation we used the Core Conflictual Relationship Theme (CCRT) method. We maintain that the CCRT approach, which is rooted in the psychodynamic tradition, provides us the kind of framework and methodology that is appropriate to capture intrapersonal and interpersonal dynamics in the relational world of the second generation. Our adaptation of the CCRT method (Wiseman & Barber, 2004) provides a promising way to bridge the gap between the clinical and empirical research on the second generation. In this book we use the CCRT method to study relational themes and communication patterns in the narratives of the second generation in close relationships. Thus, once the relevant questions have been formulated, researchers are faced with the challenge of finding sensitive research tools for revealing what our interviewee referred to as "hitting the real issue right on the head."

OUTLINE OF THE BOOK CHAPTERS

Following the presentation of the CCRT method in Chapter 2, the remaining chapters are organized in three major sections. The first part includes the major relational themes that we identified in the second generation's relational narratives. The chapters in this part are organized according to the CCRT components. Chapter 3 refers to the major Wishes, namely the wishes for closeness and autonomy. Chapter 4 ties together the three components of the CCRT: the need to protect (Wish) the vulnerable parents (Response of Other) and to avoid conflicts (Response of Self). Chapter 5 (which ends Part One) goes beyond the identification of the CCRT components of the previous chapters to themes of intergenerational communication of trauma as expressed in the narratives. We suggest that the patterns of familial communication of trauma that we identified form the context for understanding the emotions in the narratives that are presented in Part Two of the book.

The chapters in Part Two are organized according to the emotions that appear in the relational narratives of the second generation. The emotions that are most discussed in the clinical literature on survivors of major traumas and their children are anger, guilt, shame, anxiety, helplessness, and loneliness. In Chapters 6 to 9 we consider these negative emotions; in Chapter 10 we present narratives that refer to positive emotions, such as feelings of joy and pride. In each of the chapters in this part we emphasize how the nature and quality of trauma-specific interpersonal communication between the survivor parents and their children (discussed in Chapter 5) play a role in the sons' and daughters' emotional experiences.

In Part Three we consider the healing of trauma in the chain of the generations. Chapter 11 is based on a recent study on "the experience of parenting adolescents among second-generation Holocaust survivors" that explored continuity and change in the relational themes in parent–adolescent relationships. The narratives in this chapter illustrate the complexity of the dynamics that we refer to as *the quest for corrective parenting.* Chapter 12, the concluding chapter, integrates the interpersonal themes and emotions that make up the narrative picture that we portrayed of the interpersonal world of the second generation. We consider how understanding the picture we described of the relational patterns and "knowing–not knowing" familial communication processes can inform clinicians working with intergenerational long-term effects of trauma.

2

Studying Relationship Narratives with the Core Conflictual Relationship Theme Method

THE CORE CONFLICTUAL RELATIONSHIP THEME METHOD

The Core Conflictual Relationship Theme (CCRT) method was developed by Lester Luborsky in the late 1970s (Luborsky & Crits-Christoph, 1998) as a way to formulate and formalize core conflicts or central issues. These formulations can then become components of a larger and more comprehensive dynamic formulation of the patient's problems. Since that time, this method of assessing central relationship patterns has received a great deal of research attention. In fact, some of the original research was compiled into a book edited by Luborsky and Crits-Christoph.

The origins of the CCRT method are firmly rooted in clinical experience and close observation. Luborsky (1977) realized that the data he used to formulate the patients' central conflict was derived from patients' spontaneous narratives about their interactions with other people. He also noticed that his formulation of the central relationship pattern contained three components: What the patient wanted or desired from the other person (*Wish*), how the other people reacted (*Response of Other* – RO), and how the patient, or "self," reacted to their reactions (*Response of Self* – RS).

The following example of a CCRT formulation is provided by McAdams: "A man's first memory was that of being held in his mother's arms, only to be summarily deposited on the ground so that she could pick up his younger brother. His adult life involved persistent fears that others would be preferred to him, including extreme mistrust of his fiancée" (McAdams, 1990; p. 441). In this man's narrative recollection of an early interaction with his mother, the Wish expressed might be "wanting to feel securely loved by mother," the mother's response (RO) is "rejection," and the boy's response to this rejection (RS) is "mistrust" (Thorne & Klohnen, 1993; p. 227).

The recurrent appearances of the specific CCRT components (Wishes, ROs, and RSs) across relationships serve to form the person's overall CCRT. The assumption is that these recurring themes capture the central relationship patterns or schemas that underlie a person's characteristic ways of relating to other people. These central relational patterns are thought to be the product of highly ingrained patterns or schemas of relationship with significant others. It is assumed that these relational schemas, which are initially constructed from emotionally laden interactions with parental figures in the earliest years of life, are carried forward into subsequent relationships (Bowlby, 1988). Thus, CCRTs can be considered components of dynamic character structure.

The Use of Narratives

The material needed to formulate the CCRT is obtained from the narratives that patients typically tell during therapy. The CCRT focuses on these narratives that discuss interpersonal relationships; therefore they are called *Relationship Episodes* (REs). Such episodes are often described in stories, anecdotes, and other interpersonal recollections that are expressed during psychotherapy sessions as well as during many everyday conversations. For a narrative to be considered an RE, it must include reference to an *identified person* with whom the patient is interacting and some *description of the interaction.* These relational narratives have the quality of a story with a beginning, middle, and end, and most often have the form of "this is what happened when I wanted him/her to . . . and he/she reacted . . . and as a result I felt . . ." The therapist listens to these specific interpersonal narratives to identify the CCRT in the patient's life. Although the patient may talk about several people in an RE, clinicians and judges are usually able to agree who is the main person with whom the patient is interacting in that RE (Luborsky, Barber, & Diguer, 1992).

An important aspect of the narrative is the amount of detail that the patient provides about his or her interaction with the other person. This is referred to as the degree of the "completeness" of the relationship episode. A relatively complete relationship episode is one in which the narrator describes the exchange between him or herself and another person in terms of the wishes and the responses from the other person and of the self, as well as the outcome of the event. The more specific the description, the easier it is to use the RE for deriving the three CCRT components. In other words, when deriving a CCRT, we are more interested in the detailed account of each specific interaction rather than the way in which the individual generalizes across different situations

In general, research has shown that it is easy to obtain four to five detailed relationship episodes in a typical dynamic therapy session (Luborsky et al., 1992). Possible reasons for their ready availability are that REs are convenient ways for patients to provide specific information to the therapists about their troubles. Relating to the therapist REs also provides the patient an opportunity to express, process, resolve, and integrate personal and sometimes difficult experiences. The telling of the RE in a therapy context may also be indicative of the patients' hope that once the therapists fully hear and understand the patients' experiences and circumstances, the therapists will be better able to help them. Luborsky et al. reported that the narratives obtained from a study of open-ended dynamic therapy included mostly events that had occurred recently. Not surprisingly, many of the narratives were about intimate relationships and problematic relationships.

Examining the content of the REs in open-ended dynamic therapy, Luborsky et al. (1992) found that the average RE included a mean number of three different wishes, four different responses from others, and four different responses of self. Studying the wishes found in open-ended dynamic therapy, the most commonly expressed wishes in the narratives were "to be close and accepted" (40% of patients), "to be loved and understood" (36%), and "to assert self and to be independent" (33%). The first two, the wish "to be close" and "to be loved," possess many similarities. In fact, it seems that these wishes are expressing the fundamental conflict in life between wishing to be close and loved versus wishing to be independent and autonomous. These two main sets of wishes are not only the most common, but they also carry much theoretical weight (Blatt, 2004; Luborsky, Barber, Schaffler, & Cacciola, 1998; McAdams, 1985). The most frequent responses from others were "rejecting and opposing" (42%) and "controlling" (36%). The most frequent responses of self were "disappointed and depressed" (45%), "unreceptive" (42%), and "helpless" (36%). In many narratives, it is quite clear that the negative responses of self are often a product of negative responses from others to the patients' wishes.

In CCRT research, the responses are defined as *negative* if they could be seen as such from the patient's point of view. That is, these are responses that reflect an interference or expectation of interference with the satisfaction of the narrator's wishes. Similarly, a *positive* response is defined from the patient's point of view as a response that reflects noninterference or expectation of noninterference with the satisfaction of the narrator's wishes. Using a sample of patients in open-ended dynamic psychotherapy, Luborsky et al. (1992) reported that the ratio of negative to positive responses in REs was five to one for the ROs and almost eight to one for the RSs. In a different sample that only included patients diagnosed with Major Depression, a similar ratio was found. Indeed, it is likely that individuals in psychotherapy wish to discuss problematic interpersonal situations and, as a result, often talk about negative responses in which their wishes were met with frustration from significant others. In their review of studies that compared positive and negative CCRT patterns, Gryner and Luborsky (1998) concluded that children's narratives (i.e., those based on completion of fictitious family stories by using dolls) are far more positive in both the RO and the RS components than the narratives that normal adults tell. Narratives of psychotherapy patients are even more negative. This was attributed partly to the different conditions under which the narratives were collected. Regarding normal adults, a study conducted in Germany found that only 35 percent of the RS components were positive (Cierpka et al., 1992; in Gryner and Luborsky, 1998).

The Relationship Anecdotes Paradigm Interview

Although the CCRT method was developed using transcripts of therapy sessions, materials needed to derive the CCRT have also been gathered from a specialized interview called the Relationship Anecdotes Paradigm (RAP) interview. In a RAP interview, an individual is asked to tell stories about actual events in their meaningful relationships. These stories are treated as Relationship Episodes that are collected outside of therapy sessions.

The original set of instructions for the administration of the RAP interview is as follows:

> Please tell me some incidents or events, each involving yourself in relation to another person. Each one should be a *specific* incident. Some should be current and some old incidents. For each one, tell: (1) when and where it occurred, (2) who was the other person it was with, (3) some of what the other person said or did and what you said or did, and (4) what happened in the end. The other person might be anyone – your father, mother, brothers and sisters, or other relatives, friends or people you work with. It just has to be about a specific event that was personally important or a problem to you in some way. Tell at least 10 of these incidents. Spend about three, but no more than five, minutes in telling each one. I will let you know when you come near the end of

> five minutes. This is a way to tell about your relationships. Make yourself comfortable and engage in this RAP session as you would with someone who you want to get to know you (Luborsky, 1998; p. 110).

We used the RAP interview method in our research for the purpose of collecting interpersonal narratives from children of Holocaust survivors by using a nonclinical sample. We translated the original RAP instructions into Hebrew and slightly adapted them for the purposes of collecting narratives on the relationships with significant others in the lives of the second generation. In asking for stories of meaningful relationships, the instructions of the RAP are usually to tell ten episodes with the narrator being free to tell any incidents about any person. Theoretically speaking, the narrator can choose to tell all ten episodes about the same person, for example, incidents with his or her intimate partner. To collect a meaningful number of stories about our interviewees' interactions with specific different people in their close relationships, we asked them to tell two stories about each of five specific relationships. The five people they were asked to narrate were: mother, father, spouse/intimate partner, close same-sex friend, and one of their own children (nephew/niece or another person, if they did not have children of their own). In addition, as we were interested in the sons' and daughters' recollections from childhood and adolescence, we asked them to tell one story that occurred recently and one that occurred in the more distant past. The narratives presented in this book were collected and analyzed using this interviewing method.

Scoring Relationship Episodes

Whether the material is obtained from therapy sessions or from a RAP interview, it must be transcribed and delineated into clear relationship episodes. Delineating relationship episodes is easily done by one judge or research assistant. Once the REs are well defined, the material is usually scored by two or more judges. Historically, the CCRT judges had to decide how to score each Wish, RO, and RS by using the judge's own *tailor-made categories.* In this method, each clinical judge uses his or her own language for describing the component of the patient's central relationship pattern. If one intends to use the CCRT in clinical practice, then this is the preferred method given that it attempts to capture the idiosyncratic aspects of the participant.

An example of a "tailor-made CCRT" clinical formulation follows. It was derived from the analysis of an interview with a patient referred to as Ms. Smithfield (Luborsky & Barber, 1994) and was written in the first person:

> I wish to resist domination and not to be forced to submit or to be overpowered. But the other person dominates, takes control and overpowers me. Then I feel dominated, submissive, helpless, and victimized (Luborsky, Popp, Luborsky, E., & Mark, 1994; p. 178).

For purposes of quantitative research, however, there are drawbacks to the tailor-made method because each judge uses her or his own language. This requires a large investment of effort to compare the terms used by the two judges for the purpose of calculating reliability. For instance, if one judge uses the wish to be loved, whereas the other uses the wish to be close, one needs to make a decision if these categories are similar or not. To solve these problems, standard categories have been developed that can be used by any trained judges. The CCRT standard categories themselves were derived empirically from the most frequent categories tailor-made by judges. Three of these standard category lists are described in Barber, Crits-Christoph, and Luborsky (1998). Only the second and third list remain in use. The second included approximately thirty categories for each type of component. These standard categories were then cluster-analyzed, resulting in the creation of what are now called "clustered standard categories." Barber et al. (1998) published the list of eight standard clustered categories for the wishes, eight for the responses from other, and eight for the responses of self.

If one analyzes Ms. Smithfield's interview by using the standard clustered categories, one would likely come up with the following formulations for each of the three CCRT components:

> Wishes (W): *to overcome the other person's domination; to assert my independence and autonomy.*
>
> Responses from Others (RO): *dominating, controlling, interfering, intimidating, and intruding.*
>
> Responses of Self (RS): *passive, submissive, dominated, compliant, deferential, and gives in to the power of the other* (from Luborsky et al., 1994; pp. 178–9).

One of the important and sometimes difficult requirements for scoring the CCRT is to keep the degree of psychological inference at a relatively concrete level. Inferences at a higher level of abstraction (such as the patient is struggling with oedipal issues) are discouraged. Rather, judges are asked to stay closer to the material and therefore to increase the likelihood that their ratings will be reliable.

Reliability and Validity of the CCRT

Reliability is an attempt to assess the extent to which one's score is reproducible. That is, the extent to which the scores given by one CCRT judge could be reproduced by another CCRT judge. In addition to demonstrating that it is possible to decide reliably on the main persons involved, Crits-Christoph, Luborsky, Dahl, Popp, Mellon, and Mark (1988) and Crits-Christoph, Luborsky, Popp, Mellon, and Mark (1990) demonstrated good reliability for the specific delineation of the REs. Finally, Crits-Christoph et al. (1988) reported good reliability for the scoring of the CCRT standard categories. Overall, the

CCRT formulations have shown moderate to very good reliabilities (Luborsky et al., 1994).

In our application of the Hebrew version of CCRT standard categories, which were used for the purpose of a quantitative analysis of the interpersonal patterns in the nonclinical Israeli sample, we found acceptable to good levels of interjudge reliability indices (Raz, Wiseman, & Barber, 2002; Wiseman & Barber, 2000; Wiseman & Barber, 2007; Wiseman, Metzl, & Barber, 2006).

The validation process of any psychological construct is a long-term, complex endeavor. "Validity" of a measure generally refers to *what* the measure actually measures and *how* well it does so.

Correspondence with the Concept of Transference

Luborsky was very much impressed by the idea that the CCRT could be used as a measure of transference. In his view, the CCRT covers some of the same territory that Freud (1912/1958) had staked out in his definition of the transference template (Luborsky et al., 1994, p. 172). To illustrate their view of the clinical correspondence between the CCRT and measures of transference, Luborsky et al. provided a CCRT account of the transference pattern in Freud's famous Dora case (1901–5). Dora expressed a *wish* for love from her father (and from Herr K.) followed by her experience of the *response from the other person* (her father) who was more interested in Frau K than in her. This was followed by *her responses from self* of feeling rejected *and* experiencing dissociative symptoms (Luborsky et al., 1994).

Further similarities between the two concepts are evidenced by a series of observations and studies (Luborsky et al., 1994; Connolly, Crits-Christoph, Barber, & Luborsky, 2000). We will cover only some of the most important parallels between the two concepts: First, there is evidence that the transference can be conceptualized as involving the patient's CCRT with the therapist. Fried, Crits-Christoph, & Luborsky, (1990) and Fried, Luborsky, & Crits-Christoph, (1992) showed a significant degree of resemblance between the CCRT derived from narratives involving the therapist and the CCRT derived from narratives involving other people. Another finding is that the transference pattern is expressed both within and outside of the psychotherapy. Barber, Luborsky, Crits-Christoph, and Diguer (1995) showed that the CCRT components derived from narratives told to the therapist during psychotherapy are highly consistent with CCRT components derived from narratives told to a research assistant in a RAP interview conducted prior to the beginning of psychotherapy. This finding suggests that in studying relational narratives obtained from RAP interviews, we are simulating, to some extent, the kind of relational narratives that may be told in psychotherapy (Wiseman & Barber, 2004). A final aspect of the relationship between the CCRT and transference that has received some empirical support is the issue of awareness level. Luborsky, Crits-Christoph, Friedman, Mark, and Schaffler (1991) have begun to show that less conscious aspects of the CCRT may be reliably judged by following a set of guidelines for identifying such aspects.

The use of the CCRT method for research purposes in developmental psychology studies was originated by Thorne & Klohnen (1993) as part of the landmark longitudinal study of personality development initiated by Jack Block (1971) and Jeanne Block (1993). They applied the CCRT method with a nonclinical sample to test CCRTs in processes of personality consistency and change. The RAP method was used to elicit the subjects' personal memories at age 18 years and again at age 23, and the themes that emerged were traced to their antecedents. In planning our research on relational themes in children of survivors in adulthood, we felt that the Thorne and Klohnen (1993) study offered a compelling case for the analysis of personal memories as a key to understanding the course of themes in personality development. Furthermore, we believe it also demonstrated the validity of using the RAP method with a nonclinical sample.

Further discussion on the CCRT can be found in numerous articles published over the past 15 years. These include more than hundred studies in which the CCRT method is used in psychotherapy research, as well as studies in which applications of the CCRT method in personality (e.g., Thorne, 1995), developmental psychology, and psychopathology are examined. These studies have been conducted at research centers worldwide, including the Center for Psychotherapy Research at University of Pennsylvania in the United States, as well as at sites in Germany, Sweden, and other countries (e.g., Barber, Foltz, De Rubeis, & Landis, 2002; Waldinger, Diguer, Guastella, Lefebvre, Allen, Luborsky, & Hauser, 2002; Waldinger, Seidman, Gerber, Liem, Allen, & Hauser, 2003; Wilczek, Weinryb, Barber, Gustavson, & Asberg, 2004; Wiseman, Hashmonay, & Harel, 2006).

In the subsequent chapters, we apply the CCRT conceptualization and method as a way to study the relational themes and emotions that emerged in the narratives that were collected by means of the RAP interviews that were conducted with our nonclinical sample of adult children of Holocaust survivors. For information on the procedure of the CCRT ratings and the narrative qualitative analysis in the Second-Generation Study, see the Appendix.

PART ONE

RELATIONAL THEMES IN THE NARRATIVES

This part addresses the major relational themes that we identified in the second generation's narratives. Its chapters are arranged according to the three components of the Core Conflictual Relationship Theme method (CCRT). Chapter 3 considers the two major Wishes, namely the *wish for closeness* and the *wish for autonomy.* Chapter 4 combines the themes in the three CCRT components that were identified as most prevalent in the narratives of survivors' children about relational encounters with their parents: *the need to protect the other* (Wish), the other *is vulnerable* (Response from Other – RO), and in response to the other the self *avoids conflicts* (Response of Self – RS). Chapter 5, which ends Part One, goes beyond the identification of the CCRT components of the previous chapters to cover the *themes of intergenerational communication of trauma* expressed in the narratives. The identified patterns of familial communication of trauma provide the context for understanding the emotions in the narratives that are presented in Part Two.

3

Wishes for Closeness and Autonomy

The wish for autonomy and the wish for closeness are two central dimensions of personality development and relationships according to psychodynamic theorists and attachment theory (e.g., Blatt, 2004). Human beings have innate needs for individuation and self-definition and for establishing and maintaining relatedness with others (Bakan, 1966; Buber, 1936). In this chapter we present first the themes of *closeness, care,* and *intimacy* that were depicted in the relational narratives of the second generations about parents, spouses, and children. Second, we present the themes of *autonomy* and *control,* which often appeared in diverse forms in the relationships of the second generation with significant others, especially the survivor parents. We recount separately particular narratives in which either the wish for closeness or the wish for autonomy was distinctly identified in our analysis as the central wish even though both these themes appear in some narratives. Much has been written about the conflict between the need for relatedness and the need for autonomy, and their dialectical relation (Aron, 1996; Blatt & Blass, 1990, 1992; Safran & Muran, 2000). On an intrapsychic level, personality development entails negotiating the need for agency versus the need for relatedness (Aron, 1996; Blatt, 2004). On an interpersonal level it involves negotiating the needs of the self with the needs of the other (Safran & Muran, 2000; Safran, 2003).

In considering the most commonly expressed CCRT wishes, Luborsky, Barber, & Diguer (1992) and Luborsky, Barber, Schaffler, &

Cacciola (1998) found (in a sample of neurotic patients) that the three most frequent wishes were "*To be close and accepted*," "*To be loved and understood*," and "*To assert the self and to be independent*." The first two wishes pertain to the wish for closeness or relatedness, and the third concerns the wish for autonomy and independence. These two fundamental wishes or needs are also prevalent in our nonclinical sample of adults.

THE WISH FOR CLOSENESS: THEMES OF CARE AND INTIMACY

Striving for interpersonal closeness is fundamental in human development (Bowlby, 1969/1982, 1980). The sons and daughters in our study, overall, described their parents as caring and greatly involved in their lives. Their experience, indeed, was more often that of feeling that their parents had difficulty in gaining what they themselves would consider a comfortable distance from their parents (as we will see in the narratives on the wish for autonomy, and in Chapter 4 on the parents' overprotection). Some of the salient narratives in our analysis were, however, those in which the wish for closeness, love, and support from the parents was accompanied by a sense of emotional distance from them. The son or daughter seemed to find it difficult to overcome, or reduce, this felt emotional distance.

Hanna's story stood out particularly in its description of a daughter's *wish to connect* to her mother. Its expression in the narrative is idiosyncratic, and it sparked our curiosity. From repeated readings there emerged, somewhat condensed, many themes that are presented in the different chapters of the book. These themes are wishes for closeness and care, as well as wishes for autonomy. We analyzed this story, which we call the *Thirst Story*, first according to the CCRT framework as illustrated below. Hanna, married and a mother of four children, recalled from her childhood the following interaction with her mother.

Wish for Connection: The Thirst Story

HANNA: *I remember once, I was a little girl, don't remember how old – 8, 9, 10, and I was very thirsty in the kitchen and my mother was busy with something, and she did not want to give me something to drink. And, I stood there and made all sorts of faces, with all the "poor me" in the world so that she would give me some water. I suppose that in the end she did, but I remember that I stood and I did this with my mouth [moves her lips to demonstrate to the interviewer] so that she'd realize that I was very thirsty. I guess that in the end she did give me (a drink of water), but it's interesting that I don't remember that, but instead I remember the bit about me standing there, asking for it, and I remember that she got mad at me; I don't remember the part where she brought me the glass of water.*

INTERVIEWER: Do you remember how you felt in this situation with mother?

HANNA: *I don't remember being hurt, or anything like that. I just simply really wanted to drink; maybe I even wanted more to annoy her just by standing there, and maybe I wanted to get a madder response from her. I don't . . . don't remember myself as pitiful. I remember I always wanted to stand on my own, and I never dared to do so with my mother. There was no such thing as saying NO or anything like that that kids do nowadays. But for me to say NO to my mother! That word never came out of my mouth, never once with my mother.*

Analysis of the thirst story using the CCRT framework:

Wishes: Hanna's primary wishes are to get from her mother what she wants and needs, to get attention, and to be responded to by her mother. Her secondary wishes are to annoy her mother, to defy her, and to assert herself.

RO: Her mother is perceived as rejecting, not understanding Hanna, and being annoyed and irritable.

RS: Hanna feels not responded to, ignored, and as a result, she tries deliberately to annoy her mother.

Perhaps symbolic of their relationship, the narrative begins with Hanna describing her mother as busy and herself as thirsty. This opening defines the major themes played out in Hanna's recollection of the interaction between herself and her mother. Hanna *wishes for a connection, for a response from mother, and to get her attention*; but Hanna perceives her mother's response as ignoring her, and later being annoyed with her. In response Hanna intensifies her attempt to get what she wants (to have her mother give her a drink of water), even to the point of desiring conflict with her mother, if only to generate some contact with her. Asked by the interviewer if she remembers what she felt in this situation (asking for RS), Hanna denied feeling hurt or pitiful. Her thought about her wanting to annoy her mother is followed by the statement that she never dared stand up to her. The wish to get attention or to connect with mother and the wish to assert the self both appear in this narrative. We took Hanna's wish for connection, or her wish to be taken care of by her mother, to be the primary wish; Hanna's secondary wish, arising out of the frustration of the primary wish, is to assert her self, or the wish for autonomy in her relationship with her mother.

Hanna's thirst is first and foremost a story about the need to be taken care of and nurtured by her mother. Being able to say to mother what she wants, or what she does not want, is enacted in this narrative around a most basic and primary experience, feeling very thirsty. Members of different audiences before whom we presented this story (e.g., Wiseman, 1999; Wiseman & Barber, 2001) were often puzzled. They asked, "Why couldn't an 8- or 10-year-old girl get a glass of water by herself? Why did she have to ask her mother for it?" This puzzling aspect of the narrative suggests an early relational schema of the daughter centered on her wish that her mother respond to her and her most basic needs. She wants mother to read her nonverbal signs of thirst, and to be available, responsive, and empathic. Instead mother is portrayed "as busy with something" in the kitchen and Hanna, trying to engage her, describes the sense that this can be done perhaps only by annoying her mother. Perhaps the mother herself fails to respond because she does not understand why Hanna cannot act more independently.

Wish to Be Understood and Supported

The wish to be cared for and to be understood is evident in Liora's early recollection from preschool age. She recalls wanting her mother to support her need for more time to grow up by staying on for another year at kindergarten. In contrast to Hanna, Liora recalls herself voicing her wish to mother out loud:

> LIORA: *Because my birthday was in December, I had the option of staying on another year at kindergarten or going to primary school the next year. One evening I went to my mother and I told her that I wanted to stay another year at kindergarten. I don't remember if as a child I even knew there was some uncertainty about my going to primary school; I simply told her that I want to stay in the kindergarten because my friends were staying. (The kindergarten had younger children, who would stay on for another year, and older children, who were to go to primary school.)*

Without the interviewer's asking, Liora goes on to explain the personal meaning of this recalled event:

> LIORA: *You know why I remember this event with mother? Because of her listening and being attentive to me. She really related to me at the same level of an adult. Like I felt she looked into my eyes and it felt that we're equals. She really listened, and after that she spoke to the kindergarten teacher and told her what I said, and as a result I stayed on there for another year. I felt it was due to my telling her what I wanted, and it gave me a very good feeling to know that you can express something you want and it is attended to. The attention was very meaningful.*

This recalled experience, then, involves the daughter's ability to voice her wish, but also the experience that the mother is responsive to the expressed wish and accepts and supports the daughter. The historical truth of this story, of course, is not as important as the narrative truth (Spence, 1982). Perhaps because of Liora's younger age (born in December) the kindergarten teacher recommended that she stay on for another year (in Israel this option is available to children born after mid-December). Be that as it may, what is meaningful, as Liora also explains so clearly, is her experience of being active in asking for what she wanted; no less important is the experience that mother was empathic to her daughter's need. The "outcome" in this relationship episode (RE) was *positive*, namely Liora's wish was fulfilled.

Wish for Closeness That Is Fulfilled

In some examples of the good experiences of closeness with parents during childhood, the son or daughter describes the parent as paying special attention to him or her. Some of these experiences occurred at times of special needs of the child (e.g., when feeling ill). Jonathan recalls the time he had a high fever, and remembers that nevertheless he had a good feeling of being cuddled when his mother took his temperature: "*I felt her arm and it was cool and I was boiling hot, it was very pleasant. That's what I remember.*" In this narrative Jonathan does not recall any verbal exchange – just the pleasant physical coolness that he felt from mother.

Sarah has pleasant childhood memories with her father (he too a Holocaust survivor), which she locates before adolescence:

> SARAH: *The neighborhood where I grew up in those days was surrounded by fields. From winter to summer we would go out with father and pick wild flowers (in those days it was not against the law). On weekends it was fun, as father would go into the kitchen make fresh juice – carrot juice so we'd see better and orange juice for our health. It was really fun. Hardly anyone had a car in those days, so we would walk and have a picnic for hours.*
>
> INTERVIEWER: What was it like for you?

SARAH: *I remember this as a pleasant feeling. We learned about the flowers, and we talked a lot. I remember him paying attention and showing interest in us. Later there was less time.*

INTERVIEWER: Paying attention to you specifically?

SARAH: *I don't remember us going by ourselves; I remember him paying attention to all of us, my brothers too. We would go together and he would explain things to us. He knew the names of all of the stars and of all kinds of insects in the fields, and how to take care of a goat that we once found in the ravine [laughs].*

Because the interviewer notices that Sarah refers to herself as one of a bunch (she and her siblings), she asks specifically if she felt singled out for attention. For Sarah this is a pleasant memory of *togetherness* with father, and she is not worried about her exclusivity. Moreover, father is described as "wiser and stronger" (he even knows how to take care of the goat), which is consistent with his being an attachment figure for Sarah (Bowlby, 1973).

Wish to Be Helped

The wish to be helped was also evident in some of the narratives about the sons' and daughters' current relationship with their parents. Women especially expressed a wish that their mothers be available to help them with their own young children. In a way they expressed the wish that their mothers would help them in their caregiving role.

Rivka starts her narrative by explaining that when her own children were born she had anticipated that her mother would help her much more than she actually did. With every child that was born she realized that this expectation was not to be fulfilled; in her narrative she tries to explain her experience of this frustrated wish.

RIVKA: *I don't know what to attribute it to, because after all there is a lot of love, and a lot of willingness, but there is this feeling that there is some kind of alienation. I don't understand it, and she (mother) denies it. If you ask her to do something specific for you she simply tells you what she'll be foregoing at that moment in order to help you.*

> *It bothers me a lot. So now, nowadays, I just avoid asking her (for help) unless I have no choice. I just manage in a way that I won't need to ask for her help. I used to ask for it much more.*

Rivka talks about this experience referring to herself in the second person (*she tells you . . . in order to help you*). This is perhaps as an expression of the distance she felt from her mother in those frustrating recurrent situations. When the interviewer then asked her specifically about her feelings in response to mother, she replied (using the first person):

> RIVKA: *I feel hurt, disappointed, and angry. It depends on the type of request, the kind of need. If it really puts me on the spot and I really need her help because I have no alternative, it makes me very very angry and it really hurts me very much. I just didn't understand why she couldn't help. I see the way I (unlike her) am always willing to help my own children.*

Rivka states at the beginning of the narrative that she feels her mother's love. On the other hand she seems puzzled by her mother's unwillingness to provide her with the help she asks for at times of need. At these moments, Rivka feels mother puts herself first, and not her. She is confused by her mother's behavior, which seems inconsistent and unlike the way Rivka responds to her own children when they need her to help them. She does not understand mother's unwillingness. Her frustration over her mother's not showing understanding of the help Rivka needs (it appears to focus on instrumental help) leaves her feeling a certain sense of alienation from mother. Moreover, her disappointment does not gain any recognition from mother ("*she denies it*"), which causes her to ask for less help and to feel a lack of caring and involvement on the part of her mother.

Wish to Feel Togetherness: The Wedding Story

The frustrated wish to feel togetherness with mother and the family is forcefully expressed in Zvi's *Wedding Story*.

ZVI: *At our wedding – yes, my mother had been for many years on bad terms with her family. I don't know the reasons. In principle I don't get into all these things . . . But when it came to my wedding we did it at a reception hall. Mother is totally anti-religious . . . she doesn't observe Yom Kippur [the holiest day of the Jewish calendar] . . . We didn't even have a bar mitzvah [Jewish religious ceremony for boys when they reach 13, usually also observed by nonreligious Jews], nothing. When she understood that the wedding was to be in a hall, and there would be a rabbi to perform the ceremony and everything, it was very difficult for her. When we arrived at the hall, I saw her. . . . I could tell that she had taken a number of tranquilizer pills, and she was really out of it. I was very, very worried that there would be some kind of blowup with somebody, that things would get out of hand. The part with the rabbi we managed to overcome; the part with her family we also managed to get over, up to the point of the music, which was actually relatively soft compared with what you hear nowadays. It bothered her. She went over to the band and shouted at them to lower the volume of the music. They tried to explain to her that it was impossible to play the music quietly. Until we managed to calm her down – but she was in such a state that it wasn't possible to talk to her.*

INTERVIEWER: Do you remember your feelings . . . ?" (Asking for the RS)

ZVI: *I was terribly hurt that she isn't really with us at the wedding. The minute she was on pills and all that I realized that she is not with us at all. And the part that all the time I had to be afraid and worry, and watch and look out to see what she is doing, so that nothing should go wrong, that there wouldn't be some kind of explosion that would ruin the whole simcha [happy event] for us. So I was very angry . . . I didn't understand. Until this very day I don't understand the . . .*

INTERVIEWER: What did it mean for you that she will be with you at the wedding?

ZVI: *That she'd be happy with us, that she'd enjoy herself, that she'd act appropriately, and she'd be with the entire family. I thought it would be an opening for some kind of togetherness with the whole family. But it didn't happen . . . We did not know anything about the Holocaust, we did not know about the whole connection . . . She wrote a diary and she didn't translate it into Hebrew. She left it in*

> *her mother tongue. Only when I was 18, at the request of my eldest niece (the oldest granddaughter), she translated it for the first time into Hebrew. Only then did we understand and learn what she'd been through. Until then we did not know anything, she did not tell us anything. We only knew that she had been in the Ghetto.*

In Zvi's sad story about his wedding night he describes his mother as *disconnected* from the event and from himself; Zvi feels her pill taking impairs her ability to take part and be connected to him and the others around her. Due to his mother's unpredictable behavior, Zvi is anxious for things to go smoothly. The music, which is part of the expression of joy and entertainment in this event, is too noisy and unbearable for her. Zvi wants his mother to feel happy for them and with them and to be connected to the family, so that there will be *some kind of unity and togetherness.* This wish is painfully frustrated as he is unable to get through to her and there is a sense of a communication breakdown. One could speculate that the wedding may have aroused certain associations for Zvi's mother that made it painful for her. Feelings of sadness and grief about the loss of loved ones, not there to share the joy, are often connected with such family events. For Holocaust survivors, such feelings of grief are amplified by the trauma of their massive losses.

Interestingly, unlike some other stories we have heard, Zvi is not unremittingly apologetic about his mother's behavior but emits the sense that he is angry that what should have been a night when he and his bride were the center of attention became one on which he had to worry about his mother not ruining their great occasion. Yet like some of the other sons and daughters he tries to understand mother's surprising behavior by attributing some of the responsibility to her traumatic Holocaust story. Throughout his narratives about his encounters in close relationships, told in other parts of his interview, it is similarly evident that he expresses the subjective feeling that he has been directly affected by his mother's traumatic past.

Wish for Family Cohesion

The narrative that Naomi told focused on a relatively recent problematic interaction with her mother that evolved around a movie on the "trip to Poland" with her mother that she had been making for some time.

The Movie of the Trip with Mother to Poland

A number of years ago Naomi went with her mother, her mother's sister (Naomi's aunt), and her cousin (the aunt's daughter) to Poland on a trip to the sites of the concentration camps. Naomi explains the family dynamics involved in this trip and those who went on it:

> NAOMI: *My extended family on my mother's side underwent the Holocaust together and they are especially connected to each other. No way only our nuclear family does something together. So I thought about this trip, I thought it over a few times – to go or not. It was a group of friends who as children had all gone through the Holocaust together. Each of them brought with him, or her, a family member from the second generation or from the third. Some came with children and some with their grandchildren. All the first generation (the survivors) knew each other, and the children and grandchildren met only during the trip. Now, I'm a photographer, so I decided to make some kind of movie about the trip. I didn't know quite what kind of movie I would make, but we went on the trip and I took pictures. For the whole trip I deliberated and pondered about what kind of movie to make.*

Naomi explains to the interviewer that she deliberated particularly between making a movie about her family alone or one about the whole group. She took pictures over many hours, and says she felt "a lot of pressure during the trip from the group." Naomi's narrative does not clarify what she means by this sense of pressure. Does it refer to the dynamics in the group during the trip, or to her own feeling of pressure about what she wants to do with the movie, or what she thinks she is expected to do? She continues:

NAOMI: *I started to think about it and I decided that I would make a movie about the family, so it would be like a memento for us in the family. This was actually one of the aims I thought about in my considerations about going on the trip in the first place. Two days before the trip we had a talk among the nuclear family, as well as the extended one, and I interviewed all my cousins and my sister about why they decided to go on the trip or why they decided not to go. As for me, I said that one of the reasons I decided to go on the trip was that a testimony of it would remain.*

Naomi further explains to the interviewer that it took her 3 years to edit the movie. During this time she felt great pressure from the group that went on the trip, who saw that she shot many hours of film, and also from her mother, who asked, "What's going on? Why is it taking so long to finish the movie?" She continues:

NAOMI: *My mother didn't understand that it takes time to make a movie. Time for the pictures and time to decide what to include, and I deliberated and stopped, and again deliberated and stopped, and then I did it. I finished editing the movie and I dedicated it to my mother and my aunt. It was a movie only for us, for our family. It showed only our side of the family.*

From the way Naomi related this narrative we see that making this movie carried an important personal meaning for her. She wanted the movie to carry a personal meaning for the closest family members too – her mother and aunt. The movie had to be something personal that she presented as her very own effort for the closest family.

The story continued, in her opinion, to an anticlimax when she finally invited the whole family to dinner and formally screened the film:

NAOMI: *When the movie was over my mother said that she was very disappointed. It was clear to me that she was disappointed because now she couldn't invite her friends from the group for the screening as she had imagined. When she saw the movie she realized that she actually had nothing to show her friends, because I wanted to make a movie of our family and that's all.*

This clash of wills, although unspoken, seems to enact a family drama. The interviewer asked Naomi if she and mother talked about it, and she replied simply that they did not. To the interviewer's inquiry about how she felt she replied:

NAOMI: *I was offended. From this whole story of the movie I came out feeling really hurt. I had put in so much effort, and had written the text for the movie. Every word I said in the movie I thought about a hundred times. And she didn't relate to it this way. Six months later a relative came from abroad and wanted to see the movie. I translated the Hebrew text into English for this relative, and I saw that my mother suddenly saw that I also talked in the movie. That she now noticed that I had something to say. At the first screening she hadn't even noticed me.*

The issue of the mother's not noticing that her daughter had something to say seems to suggest that Naomi wants to be noticed and recognized. Perhaps she seeks validation for her point of view, especially in relation to the Holocaust. There is a sense that Naomi is hurt by her perception that for her mother the group (her survivor friends) is more important than the nuclear family and even her own children. Naomi appears to be in search of more intimacy and belonging through the personal story of the close family. Naomi's attempt to join in the family story and to produce a movie that would be meaningful to her mother (and aunt) is not acknowledged by her mother. The mother is experienced as not appreciating her daughter's hard work in making this movie or some difficult decisions she had made, for which the daughter wanted her respect. In addition, Naomi is apparently left to guess what it is in the movie that disappoints her mother, or in what way she wanted it to be different.

This story can be seen as representing the daughter's wish for closeness, but also her wish for self-definition. Naomi wants the way she chose to make her movie to win the recognition and respect she longs for. There is a sense that she wants the movie to have a private meaning for the close family. Her wish for validation is tied to her wish to feel belonging and sharing with her mother and her aunt. The dialectical expressions of both needs – for self-definition as well as relatedness – are played out in Naomi's story that had begun before the trip to Poland, and ended 3 years later with the screening of the movie. Although Naomi ends the narrative with some kind of recognition from mother (she saw that Naomi spoke in the movie), she appears to continue to carry this story as unfinished business. We can speculate that it is representative of the daughter – mother relationship in the sense that Naomi's wishes are not reciprocated by her mother, and none of her efforts lead to greater closeness and family cohesion. Perhaps Naomi continues to feel excluded from her mother's Holocaust story, and her search for the "family story" rather than the "group story" is left unresolved.

THE WISH FOR AUTONOMY

The Wish to Be One's Own Person and to Assert Self

In the face of parents' attempts to channel the children according to their own expectations, especially around academic and security issues, the sons and daughters expressed their normative developmental need to make their own choices and to assert themselves.

The Wish to Be Free to Make One's Own Choices

Aharon recalls how at around age 16, he was at a stage that he called "anti" (negativism) in that he made oppositional choices, such as his decision to end his high school studies. He explains that he was expected to be like his two older brothers, namely a top student, and to go to university. He says he remembers he wanted to go against these set expectations of his mother. He wanted to defy her and to do exactly the opposite.

AHARON: *Mother was very upset by my opposition, my resistance. For her it was very important that I should be an excellent student, that I should do well so that I could advance along the academic path. She recruited her brother, my uncle, to come to our home, as he was a math teacher and he taught engineering at the university. He was a so-called authority on this issue. They both (my mother and my uncle) sat with me in the room and they both tried to explain to me how one can't manage in life, without the highest knowledge of high school math and physics.*

INTERVIEWER: Do you remember what mother said?

AHARON: *That without completing school and eventually becoming a lawyer or accountant, or some similar profession, there was no point, there was nothing else to do with your life. She said: "What will you be just a worker in the street, a street-sweeper, a plain blue-collar worker? NO. This is not appropriate." I tried to explain that you can enjoy life also without working like a dog and putting all this effort into studying high-level math and physics, and that I prefer to go to the youth movement, and to be involved in after-hours school activities and do things I like.*

Aharon describes how for several hours his mother tried, with his uncle's help, to persuade him to study "what they wanted." As he put it: *"To get me to give in, to break down my resistance on this issue. But they did NOT succeed."*

The wish expressed in Aharon's narrative is *to be free to make his own choices.* He wants to decide on his own direction in life, instead of making decisions conforming to his mother's expectations. His mother, who feels she must convince her son, brings her brother (Aharon's uncle) who can speak from his acclaimed academic position to influence the son to change his mind and to have him fulfill her expectations. Aharon further explains that his brothers chose the direction that accorded with their mother's expectations. Perhaps they were naturally inclined toward mathematics. It is also possible, however, that the two older brothers refrained from rebelling and they achieved what was expected of them. Aharon, the youngest of the three boys, seemingly acts out the wish to be independent. He may also wish to define his identity as separate from his successful brothers.

At the end of his narrative Aharon reflects on his mother's extreme pressure to achieve "as if it was a matter of life or death." He indicates that at the time of his struggle with his mother he did not seem to understand the reasons that underlay her pressure and insistence.

> AHARON: *At the time when this interaction occurred, when I was 16, at that stage we didn't know much about the Holocaust. Today when I look at it, after I understood more about what she went through during the Holocaust, I can understand her reaction better. I realize that somehow her pressure came from fear. From her need for us to succeed to do things that she didn't manage to do, so she could rest assured that we were settled in life. That she had given us her all, and that from then on we could continue on our own and she would know that we were secure in life.*

The interviewer asks Aharon if he perceived his mother as disapproving of him. He replied that for him it was just her extreme persistence that stood out. When the interviewer asked him how he felt at the time (probing for the RS), he especially recalled the good feeling of being able to assert himself and fulfill his wish to be autonomous and independent. Aharon ends this narrative, which exemplifies the wish "to be my own person," by telling the interviewer with a smile that later he actually chose on his own to complete a university degree and he in fact became an accountant; "*but at that stage (age 16) it was important to me to do what I want and not to go by what was expected of me.*"

The Electrical Hand Drill Story

Another narrative that illustrates the wish to assert oneself in relation to the surviving parent is the following relationship episode that we call the *Electrical Hand Drill Story.* Shaul, a man in his 40s, recounted the following memorable encounter with his mother that occurred when he was in his early adolescence:

SHAUL: *When I was aged 13 – 13 or 14, something like that... I was... also the one with the best technical skills in the house, to do small repairs, things like that and... the one who was always responsible for the tools in the house, the work tools. That was me, and I wanted to buy – I wanted them to buy me an electrical hand drill... I don't know why I wanted an electrical drill.... And then my mother responded in a way that was very surprising, that is, it seemed to me a very surprising response then. Later she explained to me why, but she didn't want to buy me an electrical drill. The noise – drives her crazy... She didn't tell me why the noise drives her crazy. Only much later – she said that during the Holocaust she did forced labor. She worked in a factory that built airplanes, or something like that and they drilled, her job was to drill all day long on metal sheets. This noise, she said, "I can NOT hear."*

INTERVIEWER: How much later did she tell you this?

SHAUL: *About a year or 2 years later – no, not immediately. She said that the noise, that she does not want... she bought me the drill in the end, but this was different... everything I wanted, I got.*

INTERVIEWER: "So there was here something different in that at first she refused to get you the drill?"

SHAUL: *Yes, because she said "NO, I do NOT want a drill in the house, I do NOT want to hear, I do not want this noise in the house." But I... I wanted a drill, I need it for my tools, I didn't think about it at the time, I insisted. I understood only later. I didn't really pay attention at that time; I would have done it much more calmly, but as a kid...*

Like in Aharon's narrative, Shaul's story is also about a conflict of wills between the mother and the son. In Shaul's case, the conflict centers on a very specific desire: his insistence on his desire that his parents buy him an electrical hand drill. The story starts with Shaul's sense of his own unique competence and his emerging autonomous identity in early adolescence; he is "the one with the best technical skills . . . the one . . . responsible for the tools in the house." As part of this responsibility he asks for a new working tool, namely an electrical hand drill. Much to his surprise this request to buy the drill is met by his mother's absolute refusal. He explains that mother's refusal was very surprising because he was used to getting whatever he wanted from her ("everything I wanted, I got"). Shaul does not give in easily; however, he continues to assert that he wants the drill and that he needs it for his tools. So in contrast to other sons and daughters that we interviewed who had great difficulty voicing their wishes to their parents (see Chapter 4 on the avoidance of conflict), Shaul voiced his request out loud and insisted on getting what he wanted.

The desire for a drill can also be viewed as having a metaphorical meaning. From a psychodynamic perspective, the wish for a drill may be interpreted as representing a symbol of Shaul's *wishes for independence and manhood.* Aharon's story is about the power of winning his independence by not giving in to his mother's academic expectations; Shaul's story, which also revolves around wishes to achieve his own desires and goals, has a caveat. Mother does not yield to his request and insists that she does not want a drill in the house and that she does not want "this noise in the house." Not only does he not get the drill as soon as he asks for it: In addition, his mother does not tell him *why* the noise drives her crazy. Shaul sounds frustrated through *not knowing why* mother cannot stand the noise. On the other hand, after knowing that what he wanted was related to his mother's traumatic memories from the labor camp, he appears in retrospect to feel guilty that he insisted on the drill. Although Shaul's story is one that radiates a sense that he is in control and is achieving his goals, mother's Holocaust trauma leaves him feeling somewhat guilty and embarrassed by his insistence in light of mother's painful memories of which she tells him only later.

Metaphorically, the noise of the music at Zvi's wedding was unbearable for his mother, as was the noise of the drill for Shaul's mother. Each man tries to understand his mother's surprising response in light of her Holocaust experiences. In Shaul's case, he describes a very concrete connection between his mother's specific response to his request and her experiences with drilling during the Holocaust. Although he does not express much affect while relating that connection, he alludes to his feelings of guilt about not knowing the connection. These themes of the style of communication about the Holocaust (silence about the "noise" of the trauma) and the feelings of guilt that stand out in this narrative will be explored in Chapters 5 and 7.

Wish to Overcome Parents' Control

In the narratives of recalled interactions with the parents, the daughters seemed to have greater difficulty in asserting themselves and not giving in to their parents. The frustrated wish for autonomy is common among adolescents and most often revolves around day-to-day dealings, such as what to spend money on, what to wear, and so forth. Although such conflicts as described in the narratives depict the well-known generation gap between adolescents and their parents, the specific recalled experiences of such conflicts that our interviewees related often involved the echoes of the parents' traumatic past. Judy's story below is a good example of the way these echoes were expressed in the relationship episodes.

The Burned Box Story

Judy begins her account of recalled relationship episodes with her mother rather puzzled about what she can tell about their interactions.

> JUDY: *I don't know what can I tell you about mother... what can I tell you? My mother and I didn't have conversations. There was a big gap between us; she's a different generation and I'm a different generation. I couldn't get to the point of a conversation with her.*

The interviewer tries to help Judy to manage the task of telling a relationship episode by suggesting that it does not need to involve a conversation in which one actually sits and talks.

JUDY: *You see I only know that she worried about me all the time . . . and whatever I wanted, and what I would want to buy, she would always oppose.*

So Judy replies with a general statement regarding the overriding experience of her relationship with mother: a mixture of mother's constant worries about her and mother's continuous opposition to her. The interviewer tries to get Judy to relate a specific encounter with her mother.

INTERVIEWER: Can you remember something specific?

Judy refers to mother's continuous opposition to Judy's preferences in buying clothes and her age-appropriate desire to dress like her other adolescent friends:

JUDY: *When I started to dress up she always said, "I don't want you to buy all kinds of 'shmattes' and all kinds of rags. What are you buying rags for?" I wanted to buy them; I wanted to dress like everybody else. But she would always say "NO!" So I had to dress like a modest Polish girl, and I wasn't allowed to wear fashionable clothes. Whenever I wanted to buy clothes for myself she'd say, "No you don't need it." That's what I remember. I wanted certain clothes to dress up and then she'd always shop for me according to her taste, and I'd always dress according to her taste.*

Judy explains that even when she started to work and earned her own money to buy her own clothes mother continued to oppose her: *Shoes she would oppose. She'd say, "Better that you buy good shoes that are important for your back, or that you save the money to take care of your teeth. Don't spend your money on rags, why are you spending the money?"*

Judy recalls that these exchanges with her mother would be followed by mother explaining to her why she needs to be careful about spending money:

> JUDY: *She used to say, "You don't know what can happen next." And she'd tell me about how her mother had a box or a case that she would save things for the "nedunia" [dowry]. When the war began my mother was a young woman. So then, during the war, the box with the things that her mother (Judy's grandmother, who perished in the Holocaust) kept for the future marriage of her daughter (Judy's mother) was burned. She always told me about the box that burned.*

From this point, Judy continues the narrative by relating the way her mother would continue the story about "the burned box" by telling Judy about her own mother's good deeds; she would help people, she would take care of children and look after poor people who had nothing to eat or drink. She would notice that people did not have Sabbath candles and she would put candles for them beside their door. She then went on to recount the story that her mother would always repeat about her escape from the Ghetto with her brother, and how only they survived while the rest of the family that stayed in the Ghetto all died: "*She always told me these stories and about what she went through in the war, that she was in the Ghetto, and that they escaped. Only she and her brother survived. The rest of the family – her mother, her younger sister and her brother who was married with children – they all stayed in the Ghetto and said, 'You'll see, it'll be OK'; but Judy's mother and the mother's brother said, 'NO, we're going.'*" They left and they survived and those that stayed all died.

The interviewer, adhering to the instructions of the RAP interview that require the narrator to focus on a specific interaction, takes Judy back to the specific situation of the mother commenting on the clothes, and asks her how she felt then as an adolescent (probing for the RS). Judy goes back to depict the interactions with her mother in relation to her wanting to dress like her girlfriends: "*I felt that I always had to dress differently from all the other girls, and I would go shopping for myself. But she would always disappoint me with her reaction. She'd never say that what I chose was beautiful; she'd never encourage me, or say, 'You've made a good buy.' She'd always say, 'You bought rags. These are rags.' She would prefer me to save the money, put it in the bank to save it, but I wanted to dress up. She didn't let me do anything."*

Through this story about the lack of freedom to spend money and to buy clothes according to her own taste, Judy expresses her frustrated wish to have freedom in light of her mother's restricting style. Obviously, she also wanted mother's approval for her purchases, but instead mother saw them as inappropriate and unnecessary. In her depiction of her experience with mother around her frustrated wish to dress as she wished, Judy interjects her mother's Holocaust story: the burned box and the dead family. This seems to be part of the story, and mother would always tell her this story in this context. The echoes of the past are heard in Judy's attempt to explain her mother's controlling behavior as stemming from mother's ever-present sense of impending disaster and traumatic losses. One can imagine how difficult it would be in face of these traumatic stories for an adolescent daughter to assert herself and to overcome her mother's domination.

The Diary Story

The developmental stage of adolescence appeared to raise anxieties in the surviving parents concerning their daughters' emerging sexual behavior. Again, although this is a normative stage that most parents need to deal with when their adolescent children begin to explore and experiment with their sexuality, it seems that for surviving parents this issue raised more anxiety than normally expected. In the following narrative we have an astonishing case in which the mother's anxieties over her daughter's potential sexual behavior lead to extreme intrusiveness on the part of the mother.

> NILI: *I had very difficult years with my mother during my adolescence. I remember that once she was apparently worried about me when I had my first boyfriend. He was a few years older than me and she*

seemed to be very nervous about what was going on. She took out parts from my diary. At the time I kept a sort of diary and she copied it. She copied out chunks from the diary, apparently, to show to a psychologist, and I found the pages with the passages she'd copied. I went to her and asked her if she had looked in my diary, and she said that she hadn't, and then I knew that she was lying. It devastated me; it was a crisis.

INTERVIEWER (Quite shocked by the story): You say that you actually came and saw the notes, you knew she had read it, and you asked her and she answered, "NO"?

NILI: *Yes.*

INTERVIEWER: How did you respond?

NILI: I *was boiling mad. I was angry, and I shouted.... I think I frightened her with my reaction. Today in retrospect I can say that...*

At this point Nili seems ready to shift her focus to her mother's reaction to her reaction (shouting at mother). Yet the interviewer is still interested in Nili's response to her mother's denial of the act of copying parts of the diary.

INTERVIEWER: Did you say to her, "You're lying"?

NILI: *Of course. I said everything to her, all the terrible things that you can think of. But, let's say, that really in retrospect... I think she did it out of her concern. I guess I worried her, because he was my first boyfriend and it seems that I was going through some changes, and she was anxious and concerned about me. She wanted to know that he wasn't hurting me, not harming me. I don't know.*

In recounting this remarkable interaction with mother, Nili perceives her mother's extreme intrusiveness and lack of respect for her privacy as caused by her mother's overriding anxiety regarding her daughter's new romantic relationship. Nili suggests that the mother feared for her daughter's safety and goes so far as to suggest that the mother was frantic because she was afraid that the boyfriend might be putting her in risk. She suggests that the mother was ill equipped to deal with her daughter's new stage in life and required an outside professional view. It is unclear if the mother in fact showed the diary to a psychologist, but Nili suggests this possibility as related to her mother's desperate need to gain control over the potential danger posed by her daughter's emerging sexuality.

INTERVIEWER: How did this interaction with mother end?
NILI: *It didn't end. That's the way it was.*

The interviewer, probably puzzled by this woman's understanding and forgiveness, while telling the narrative, persists.

INTERVIEWER: What did you feel when you found out that she was reading your diary?
NILI: *There was a minor crisis. You see, she read my diary without my permission; it was annoying. She could have simply come to me and asked me, but of course, we didn't talk about anything. As much as I tried to fish out things from her past, it was impossible to talk to her. There were people who could talk to her... but not I, I didn't succeed... to have heart-to-heart conversations, so we didn't talk. So I guess she felt uncomfortable about asking me. She wanted to know what was happening with me and this was her way... I learned to forgive her a lot of things after I got married and had children.*

It is interesting to see how Nili responds to the interviewee's insistent inquiring about how she felt in response to what would be perceived by any adolescent as extreme violation of privacy by the mother. In many ways a diary epitomizes private territory, and many adolescents, especially girls, keep a diary as a way to express their private experiences and feelings. These are things they most likely do not share with others, perhaps their parents especially. In the opening statement of her narrative Nili indicates that she experienced great difficulty as an adolescent in her relationship with her mother. Her diary presumably contained her private thoughts about these difficulties and her new experiences with the first boyfriend. Between the lines of the narrative we can infer (from Nili's initial angry response) that her wishes were to be free of mother's intrusiveness and to have her private territory respected. A striking aspect of this story, however, is the way Nili shifts quickly from describing herself as boiling mad to saying it was a minor crisis. This is related to the suppression of expressing any anger at the parent (see Chapter 6).

The narrative ends with Nili going on to describe the *lack of open communication* between herself and mother. From considering the mother's indirect way of finding out what her daughter may be going through (by reading her diary and copying parts of it), Nili shifts to describing her own lack of knowledge about her mother's past. Channels of communication were closed between them. She attributes her mother's behavior to this lack of open communication and sounds forgiving of mother's behavior. Whereas the interviewer seems much more disturbed by the mother's invasion of the daughter's privacy and dishonesty (copying passages from the diary and then denying it), Nili in retrospect views her mother's behavior as if it was the only avenue open to her, given their lack of open communication. From this we can infer that in addition to the wish that mother respect her separateness (related to autonomy and self-definition), another central wish in the relationship with mother is for greater mutual openness and shared understanding (related to closeness and intimacy), whereby mother and she could "have heart-to-heart conversations."

Wish Not to Submit to Parents' Overprotection

Parents who have suffered trauma desperately need to protect their children and themselves from further suffering. They try to protect their children, ensuring their safety and keeping danger to their physical well-being at a minimum. All parents face the need to learn how to allow their children greater distance from them, and to grant them autonomy; however, from our narratives it emerges that for surviving parents, allowing greater autonomy was extremely difficult. In many cases this difficulty was played out through not allowing the child to go on trips away from home. Many of the narratives revolved around this theme of the child wanting to go away on a trip, be it short or long, near or far. Frustration of a son's and a daughter's wish to take a trip away from home was usually defined by situations that involved normatively accepted age-appropriate granting of autonomy by parents to their adolescent children. In other words, unlike their peers, children of survivor parents were not allowed to engage in such activities away from home.

I Really Wanted to Go on this Group Trip Abroad

An example of the wish to join a youth group on a trip abroad is Gila's story about an overseas tour that she wanted to take when at high school, but her father objected to it.

> GILA: *This is a story that happened when I think I was about 16. I was at high school and a youth delegation was organized to travel as a group to France. This was a time when children like me had no other opportunities to go abroad, like we weren't like kids from rich families with the lifestyle of going abroad. There were a limited number of children chosen to go on this trip abroad and I was chosen, but my parents did not agree, especially my father (in Gila's case both parents were survivors). Father was the more dominant and I tried to really convince him that I wanted to go on this trip.*

After indicating her father's opposition to her going on the tour, Gila goes on to explain the unusual context of the trip abroad at that time, which her father argued was the reason for his objection.

> GILA: *Then the Lebanon war broke out [June 1982] and there was a meeting of the school principal with the parents regarding the planned trip to France. My father went to the meeting and the principal explained that we would go on the trip as planned despite the war; however, for security reasons the children were instructed to hide the fact that they are from Israel. This meant just some special caution in not having any signs that identify you as Israeli, such as not speaking Hebrew among themselves in public places, and avoiding wearing shirts with Hebrew lettering on them. After this meeting when we got home my father said, "Forget about the trip." He said, "I was willing to let you go despite all the worries, but I am not prepared for you to go with these special security measures . . . I cannot accept that you go*

> *abroad, and in an organized manner, and you are told to hide that fact that you are Israeli."*

Initially Gila was clearly extremely disappointed and she tells the interviewer that she remembers that she cried. But then she expresses acceptance of and identification with father's point of view.

> GILA: *Later I reached the conclusion that in some way he was right. That it annoyed me too to be in the situation of hiding and I decided to relinquish my wish to go on the trip... that it angered me to conceal my Israeli identity. Despite all the upset and my really wanting very very much to travel I accepted his point of view. I reached the conclusion that I really understood him, that he was right and that when I grew up I would understand even more. So for now I'll announce that I have reconsidered my wish to go and that I am not going with the group.*

To the interviewer's question of what happened in the end, Gila answers in a rather unemotional way: *In the end the delegation went on the trip to France and they took someone instead of me, but I did not go on it.*

Gila's story begins with her telling the interviewer about this special opportunity at age 16 in which she was chosen to go abroad with a youth group. From the way she describes the sequence of events, her father seems to have had some difficulty agreeing to her going in the first place and she really tried to persuade him (*"I tried to really convince him that I wanted to go on this trip"*). Gila's primary wish, up to this point in the account, appears to be the wish to assert her desire to go on the trip to France. Youth trips away from home, especially trips abroad, are part of adolescents' "rites of passage." Then the story line has a twist to it, in that due to the Lebanon war security concerns arose about this tour. The security instructions that the school principal gives give rise to her father's objection to the trip, and he tells Gila that he will not allow her to go. Father's rationale centers on the need to conceal Israeli identity. Gila doesn't explain what father means by this. We can speculate that perhaps there is extra meaning attached to these precautions in light of what it meant during the Holocaust to be forced to hide one's Jewish identity. It is also quite possible that the meeting regarding the need for security measures reawoke father's initial anxieties about the trip. In her narrative Gila first indicates her disappointment, but she quickly switches to acceptance of her father's opinion, the point of damping down her own initial enthusiasm about going (*I decided to relinquish my wish to go on the trip*). One can only imagine the disappointment in response to this missed opportunity to travel abroad as one of a youth delegation, but Gila does not dwell on this aspect; instead she identifies with father's point of view (refusal to have to hide her Israeli identity while traveling in France).

We could ask whether Gila's father's response was unusual compared with that of other parents whose children were to go on the trip. Other Israeli-born parents under these circumstances would probably have accepted the security measures (e.g., hiding Israeli nationality) as a reasonable solution to the security concerns. It is interesting to note that part of the pride of the youth delegations to Poland is marching with the Israeli flag and singing the Israeli national anthem.

The special dynamics involved in these parent–child interactions around the theme of the parents' difficulty in granting autonomy will be further addressed in relation to the way the sons and daughters perceived their parents' overprotection, and the way the children responded by avoiding confrontation with them (Chapter 4).

Wish for Separateness – Leaving Home and Marrying

Some of the sons and daughters described the wish to gain separateness from their parents, who were experienced as clinging to them. The parents' tight grip was experienced as a burden. It was described as easing somewhat once the children married and left the parental home. Others, especially women, described difficulties in achieving separateness that continued even into mid-adulthood.

To Be Free from Mother's Tight Embrace

In narrating a relationship episode with his mother, Benjamin refers to the point in life when he got married. He describes great relief in that he had finally got free of his mother's bear hug when he was growing up. He opens his narrative by indicating that his mother was tied to him very strongly.

BENJAMIN: *She thought that I was tied to her apron strings. Then when I began to date, for mother the thought that I would eventually be leaving home was very very difficult. We went through the difficulties – as she saw it – of her accepting that I was leaving her, leaving home, and she was left alone. Of all the siblings, I was the one who was mainly with her (Benjamin is the youngest). It was very difficult for her.*

INTERVIEWER: Can you think of a specific interaction?

BENJAMIN: *She created problems in that she didn't like my future wife, or for that matter any other woman who could potentially take me away from her.*

INTERVIEWER: What did she say?

BENJAMIN: *She (the woman he was dating) didn't seem right to her, or she was not younger than me by enough years. Things like that.*

The interviewer asks about Benjamin's reaction to mother's lack of acceptance. He responds: *Sometimes I was angry, and sometimes I would not respond.*

INTERVIEWER: What did you say?

BENJAMIN: *I told her, "Listen this is the woman (his future wife) who suits me. That's the way it is. You have to come to terms with it."*

INTERVIEWER: How did she respond?

BENJAMIN: *You see, in time she came to terms with it, but it was very difficult. As if I was leaving her and she was left all alone. Father would go out to work early in the morning and return home late in the evening. It was that way for years. So it was difficult for her to have me leave home. But me – I already wanted to leave... to be free... for me it did really good.*

INTERVIEWER: How did you feel in response to her not being pleased?

BENJAMIN: *I told her that time would work wonders. But she took it very hard. She threatened not to come to the wedding and things like that.*

INTERVIEWER: How did you feel about the fact that you made your own decision?

BENJAMIN: *A very good feeling from a psychological point of view and that's it.*

The traumatic separation experiences in the lives of survivors make the normative stage of their children leaving home extremely difficult for them. Benjamin's mother is greatly upset by her youngest son leaving home and marrying. For the son, he seems to feel that he is finally achieving some sense of separateness and a better emotional distance from his mother.

Parents' Overinvolvement in Their Adult Offsprings' Lives

Although most narratives in which sons or daughters experienced their parents' intrusiveness involved recalled interactions from adolescence (Nili), some narratives referred to current difficulties in keeping boundaries between their adult life now as parents themselves and their parents' tendency to be overinvolved in their lives.

Mother's Overriding Voice

The wish for autonomy from her mother is described by Shoshana as a battle between mother's overriding voice and her own inner voice.

SHOSHANA: *Even today, when I myself am a mother, I still find it difficult to go by what I want rather than by what she tells me about how I should raise my own children. She can call me and tell me things, but by now I don't do what she says. I say, "Yes, yes, yes," but*

> *somewhere it continues to echo in my head. I still can't turn off her voice within me and it still is heard in me, even if I don't go by her wishes.*

The need to obey mother's wishes and the difficulty in asserting the self in the face of them is part of the difficulty in achieving autonomy from parents, even in adulthood. This difficulty in "turning off" parents' voices is further explored in Chapter 4 in relation to sons' and daughters' special commitment to their parents.

4

The Need to Protect Vulnerable Parents and to Avoid Conflicts

Survivors' parenting style has often been characterized as overprotection of their children (e.g., Jucovy, 1992; Halik, Rosenthal, & Pattison, 1990). By applying the Core Conflictual Relationship Theme (CCRT) framework (described in Chapter 2) to the analysis of the recalled interactions between the sons and daughters and their parents we were able to go beyond the issue of the degree of parents' overprotection to describing a prevalent interpersonal pattern between the children and their parents. Common to this specific interpersonal pattern that we identified in the narratives is the dynamics of the child's experience of the parents' overprotection: It is up to the child to protect the parents, perceived as those who have suffered enough, and therefore they cannot be confronted with the child's own needs. In these encounters the child appears hypersensitive to the parents' extreme anxiety about losing him or her. In response to the parents' overprotection the child's script is to avoid hurting the parents and to protect them. The three CCRT components that play out in this pattern identified in our research involve the following relational themes:

Wish (toward parents): I need to protect my parents. Responses from Other (RO): My parents are vulnerable, hurting, and controlling me and at the same time they are losing control. Responses of Self (RS): I avoid conflict and confrontation.

In this chapter we describe this intergenerational pattern, which we call *mutual overprotection.* A fundamental aspect of this constellation of Wish–RO–RS is the children's hypersensitivities to the perceived actual, or fantasized, parents' vulnerabilities, and the consequences for the way they respond to their parents. In what follows, we present and analyze these dynamics between the children and their parents as expressed in the narratives.

THE BURDEN OF CARRYING THE PARENTS' ANXIETIES

The dictum not to cause the parent any "unnecessary" reasons to worry or to raise their anxieties was clearly present in the narratives that involved the constellation of the need to protect the vulnerable parents. We found a painful example of this dynamic in Yehuda's story of the broken arm.

Cycling Injury and the Broken Arm

At the start of the RAP interview Yehuda states the "should not" while growing up: "You are not allowed to tell father anything that may annoy or upset him." He recalls a memory from the age of 8 or 9. He came back home by bicycle from his music lesson in the conservatory, as he always did in the afternoon. This time, however, he tried to cycle "without hands'" and as a result he flew off the bicycle and broke his arm. Yehuda explains that his mother was always out at work in the afternoon. He got home and he describes the implication of the rule not to cause father any alarm.

> YEHUDA: *I broke my arm. There were five fractures. One of them was an open injury. When I got home mother was still at work, but I was not allowed to go into the house, where father was, so that he won't get upset, so that he wouldn't have to do anything. I sat and waited for 3 hours outside the house for mother to get home from work, and then of course she took me to the hospital.*

Yehuda tells the interviewer that this is an example of how he was not allowed to share with father things that may upset him, even though he wanted to. He never dared, however, as he was taught that he must not, that it was forbidden. Yehuda understands this specific, memorable event of waiting in pain with a multifractured arm outside the house until mother returned, even though father was at home, as stemming from the fact that at age 7 (about a year earlier) his father had suffered a major heart attack. Under the pressure of the anxiety over whether father would survive, he was taught that it could be life-threatening if father got upset.

This narrative may be more about growing up with a father vulnerable to health problems rather than Holocaust survivor, but it still sheds light on the child's experience that it is the parent who is in need of protection. Interestingly, Yehuda doesn't mention his mother's emotional response to coming home and finding her son in pain. She does take care of him, and takes him to the hospital; yet there is no reflection on how due to his father's health condition and the rule not to cause him worry, the son made no attempt to get the immediate attention that his relatively serious cycling injury required. As to Yehuda, his RS involves pain, avoidance, and extreme self-control. He does not even consider bothering his mother or calling on anyone else, and remains alone in this painful situation.

It is unclear in this case whether the father's being a Holocaust survivor added weight to his health problem. In our study (Wiseman & Barber, 2000), the fathers particularly were perceived as more ill by the offspring of Holocaust survivors than the offspring of nonsurvivors, and perhaps this was their actual situation. In any event, the question of whether these are traces of that Holocaust trauma, or the echoes of the more recent trauma of father's heart attack, cannot be answered. Perhaps being a child of survivor parents means that the child is particularly aware of the possibility of losing his or her parents. Nevertheless, the dynamics in the parent–child relationship described here may be relevant to various kinds of parental trauma (Bar-On, 1999).

What is the experience like for the child who is forbidden to aggravate his or her parents' anxieties? When analyzing the narratives in our study we often found ourselves going back to books and stories written by second-generation authors. In this literature one finds ample vivid descriptions from the child's viewpoint of the experience of living with the burden of his or her parents' worries. One striking example of this experience can be seen in the following excerpt from a novel titled *Transparent Child* by Jacob Buchan (1998), who dedicated it "to the second generation."

> On Purim [a Jewish holiday that involves outdoor social events and dressing up – akin to Mardi Gras] you went with a few friends to Dizengoff Circle [in the heart of Tel Aviv]. An enormous stage was set up there. It was huge and decorated, with lots of music coming out of hidden loudspeakers, and the massive crowd, shoving and being shoved, closing in closer to the stage; and the costumes and the noise and tumult and the shots from the toy pistols; a real pleasure. It was all there. On the top of the stage, built on massive scaffolding, towering high above the people, the different bands and dance troupes began to appear. And the party began. Suddenly, all at once, it happened in front of your eyes: the great scaffolding started to collapse, to move, to shift here and there, and the screaming of the dancers and singers and musicians, and as if the earth had opened its mouth. Everything fell in on itself. In an instant, and you can't see anything. An earthquake. A haze and dust. Total disaster. You were a child, nearly a teenager. At the sight of the sudden destruction, which slowly unfolded right there, in front of your eyes, in the middle of the Purim holiday, the first thing that comes up in your mind is: when will your parents hear about this. And how can you let them know as soon as possible that you are not among the injured. For this purpose you are bound to do one thing only. And urgently: to present yourself to them. To get home as fast as you can. Get home! You turn your back on what's happening and begin to run.
>
> Your parents are sound asleep. You wake them up and tell them what happened, and they, still sleepy – your mother sits up resting

> on her elbows, your father lies on his side – tell you each in turn:
> You shouldn't have gone. These kinds of places aren't for you.
>
> Why don't you stay home?
> In these kinds of situations something can always happen.
> You can count on it – we know.
> We've already been through one or two things in life.
> And heaven help you if you cause us such worry ever again.
> Now go to bed and be happy you're still alive [Buchan, 1998; pp. 96–7; translated by the authors].

The description of this Purim event could be viewed as a relationship episode (RE). It is of a specific recalled encounter between the son and his parents and the episode has a beginning and end. The story is told in third person, as if the narrator is describing the child's experience from an observer's standpoint. The son who went to have fun with friends and enjoy the Purim holiday is faced with a sudden turn of events: What begins as an exciting although crowded event ends in disaster. The boy is frightened by the sudden turn of events, but first and foremost what besets him is the possibility that his parents will hear about what happened at the city center celebration and they will worry that he has been hurt. His aim and need is *to save them* from this intolerable thought. He races home to reassure them by them seeing with their own eyes that he has survived. One can speculate that the action schema described here so vividly is evoked in the child due to early experiences in his relationship with his parents.

The parents' reaction in this story appears extremely insensitive to what the child has just experienced. This "transparent child" is met by parents who do not see him, and moreover, they warn him not to worry them. This warning confirms his perception that his mission is to safeguard them from any worrying thoughts. Although such a bleak picture of extreme insensitivity on the part of the surviving parents was rarely found in our nonclinical sample, the dynamics of the need to protect the parents, even at a high cost for the child, was clearly apparent in the narratives. Sometimes the message that the parents cannot bear the worry about their child was explicit, as in Yehuda's story, and other times it was more complex and subtle. In Yehuda's narrative the encounter involved a situation in which he was actually physically wounded. In most narratives the sons and daughters are not hurt in any physical sense, yet they compromise their desires so as not to hurt the parents and to avoid confrontation with them at any cost.

YIELDING TO THE PARENTS' WORRY

Joseph tells the interviewer that from around the age of 13 years a serious issue arose. His mother, under no circumstances, would agree to his going away on trips [which involved his not sleeping at home for a few days]. He refers to the trips issue as problematic because it sparked many of his mother's anxieties.

Her Words Completely Paralyzed Me: The Trip to the Sea of Galilee

Asked to relate a specific encounter with his mother, Joseph tells the following story about the time he wanted to go on a trip to the Sea of Galilee.

> JOSEPH: *There was a time I came home and I decided that this time I had got to convince her to let me go on a 4-day trip to the Sea of Galilee. The minute I walked into the house, she spoke her usual sentence: "It's good thing you're home. I was already starting to worry about you." And all the while I was saying to myself over and over: "You've got to convince her that you're going on this trip." I sat down with her in the living room, and I started carefully to say that today they told us about the Sea of Galilee. She looked at me and said: "Really? It's very far. It's very dangerous there..." Her words totally paralyzed me, even though she still didn't know what I wanted to say to her... I wanted for once to tell her what I wanted and for her to understand my wishes or desire, but I gave in.*

By reconstructing the sequence of events in Joseph's narrative as a stage script we can try to identify the relational representations of other and self that are re-enacted between the son and his mother. Joseph comes home with the intention to ask his mother to agree that he go on a youth trip, and sleep away from home for a few nights. His wish is *to be given the freedom* to join his peers in a social activity to which they all were looking forward and to have fun. From previous experience he knows that this is not a simple request and that he will have to persuade his mother. He feels this time he has to convince her (son's wish/intention script). We get the feeling that he is determined at least to try and that as a starting point he vigorously sticks to his intention. We can try to imagine what goes on for Joseph from the moment he walks into the house and his actual interaction with mother begins. His mother greets him with what he calls her usual sentence: "*It's good thing you're home. I was already starting to worry about you.*" Hence, from the mother's reaction to his returning home the son gets a reminder of his mother's anxieties, her constant worry about his safe return home. One senses that the mother's response is automatic, ingrained in her parenting reactions (RO – mother's worry script). This leads him to bring up his desire to go on the trip by only mentioning that there was some talk about the *Sea of Galilee.* Now we feel that he is already walking on eggshells (RS – son's cautious script). Mother immediately reacts to the son's even mentioning this location, possibly guessing that Joseph is leading toward asking her permission to go on a trip to the *Sea of Galilee* (RO – mother's startle script). Joseph recalls mother looking at him and recollects her exact verbal reaction (even after almost 40 years): "*It's very far and it's very dangerous.*" In fact, this is not a far location and does not involve any extraordinary dangers. Mother's reaction, however, seems to confirm the son's fear, and his construal that mother cannot bear the thought of the dangers that she imagines or connects to such a trip. He refers to her words as *totally paralyzing* him (RS – son's paralyzed script). Most likely nonverbal cues, such as the look on mother's face and her tone of voice, also contributed to the sense of the mother's vulnerability that the son cannot face. In terms of Joseph's experience, once again he cannot make the next move. He feels he did not even have the chance to state out loud his desire (*for once I will tell her what I want)* and once again he "gives in." The narrative ends with Joseph's frustrated need to have mother understand and accept his desire.

This narrative brings to light many of the common core themes that we found in the relational world of the sons and daughter. In terms of the three CCRT components, "avoidance of conflict," as expressed in the narrative, can be viewed as a wish, or intention, on Joseph's part, as well as an RS that results from his perceiving his mother as vulnerable. In CCRT terms (see Chapter 2), the individual's RSs develop in response to earlier ROs, and Wishes sometimes become autonomous and turn into higher-level Wishes. We can assume from the way Joseph relates the encounter that he assumes from his mother's response to him that she would not be able to handle the worry that will arise in her if he were to take such a trip to the Sea of Galilee. This lack of freedom to express openly the child's needs in the face of the survivor parent's vulnerability is also associated with the feeling that one cannot even hope to be understood. Thus, the Wishes in this narrative include the granting of freedom to go away from home on a trip for a few days, to be understood, and at the same time to avoid conflict with mother (see box).

Wishes: to be given freedom, to be independent, and to assert myself; to be understood and to express myself openly; and to avoid conflict (with mother).

ROs: (mother's actual or fantasized response): is anxious, is vulnerable, and is controlling me almost without words.

RSs: paralyzed and silenced, gives in (submissive), avoids conflict, feels misunderstood, and helpless.

The experience of not being able to go away on youth trips that involved sleeping away from home is salient in one of the short stories in the collection *A Hat Glass* by Nava Semel (1985). Our analysis of Joseph's story prompted us to go revisit the literary expression of this dynamic in Semel's short story, titled "So What After All is a Trip?"

> "So in the end I didn't go on the trip . . . and even though it was only one trip, and everyone else has forgotten all about it long ago, it still disturbs me . . . and yet that trip still rolls around inside my head." In the story, three girls from her peer group invite her to stay with them in the same tent on this outdoor trip, which involves hiking. They ask her, "Will you come with us?" And she answers, "Yes, I will." . . . The date of the trip approaches and she still has not asked her father's permission to go. She packs the backpack. But when her father sees her, despite her insistent pleadings and her attempts to convince him to let her go on the trip, he declares: "I still have the power to protect. Here there won't be any trips." She cries aloud: "Dad, dad, nothing will happen to me. It is only a trip" (Semel, 1985; pp. 119–125; translated by the authors).

Nava Semel's story ends with the father locking the daughter in her room; there she sits on her bed for 3 days. The act of locking the daughter in the room appears to represent the experience of the lack of freedom in the face of the surviving parent. Semel captures this dynamic in which the daughter, who is named after her father's sister, who perished in the Holocaust, feels overpowered by her father:

> At night she dreams of how she rebels against him and during the day she shrouds herself in her disgrace (Semel, 1985; p. 123; authors' translation).

Going back to Joseph's story, which is much less dramatic, we see that even though he is not physically locked in his room, he too is bound and remains alone with his pain.

Father Waiting Anxiously at the Bus Stop

Zehava describes her father's anxiety about her safe return home and his overprotective behavior that was an integral part of her day-to-day routine.

> ZEHAVA: *One thing I do remember about my father, if I said I'd be back at a certain time, and I was late, he'd be waiting for me at the bus stop.*
>
> INTERVIEWER: When you were a child?
>
> ZEHAVA: *No. At all ages. It was a nightmare. There would be children waiting there, at the bus stop near our house. But they (her parents) didn't pay attention . . . For them this was the time the bus was supposed to arrive, so I must arrive on it. Do you know how shameful this was? Your father is waiting for you at the stop and everybody's walking in a bunch and your father's chewing your ear off in Hungarian.*
>
> INTERVIEWER: How did you take it?
>
> ZEHAVA: *I took it lightly.*

The interviewer, noticing the discrepancy between the use of the words "nightmare" and "shameful," as well as her tone of voice, still insists: "No. Really – how did you feel then?"

> ZEHAVA: *It was a disgrace, but I grew up from kindergarten with my peers.*

The interviewer inquires if Zehava ever told her father anything in response:

> INTERVIEWER: Did you ever once say anything to him?
>
> ZEHAVA: *Nothing. It was babbling from the bus stop to our house.*
>
> INTERVIEWER: But you said it was shameful in front of your peers.
>
> ZEHAVA: *Nothing, no anger or anything like that.*

In Zehava's RS there is an interesting mix of remembering the unease (nightmare, shameful) together with acceptance of the parents' behavior (taking it lightly). In fact, she seems not to have the option of asking her parents not to wait for her at the bus stop. Although she does not state explicitly in the narrative that her father was anxious for her safety, his anxiety was apparently the underlying motivation for his waiting for her there if she was late getting home. In Zehava's story, the social cost that she experienced as a consequence of her father's awaiting her on her return with her friends was lower (she can take it more easily) than in situations in which the child was obliged to forgo certain social activities entirely.

Commitment to the Parents

Parents' anxious waiting for the child to come home was a prevalent theme in the narratives of sons and daughters. The child's regular response to the parents' worrying was submission to their explicit and implicit pressure to be reassured of the child's safety. The expression of these core themes in the recalled interactions with the parents appeared in a wide range of variations. For example, in Shoshana's narrative (of when she was 19) she calls her mother on the phone "*to tell her that I had arrived, and everything was okay*" (this was before cell phones were available). The mother continues to insist that the daughter be in touch again, and call her in 2 hours' time. Shoshana complies with this, only to be told that she must come home at a certain hour from a party even though this meant leaving before the party even began:

> SHOSHANA: *She (mother) said, "Listen Shoshana, you're to be home at 8:00 P.M., I don't care how . . . " So like a good girl at 6:00 P.M., before the party even began and just as people started to arrive, at 6:00 I packed my stuff and went back home, and got home by 8:00 P.M. like a good girl.*

In Shoshana's story the description of the chain of events implies that mother's insistence that she be home by 8:00 P.M. was unreasonable (the party was at a place about a 2-hour journey from home).

Despite the distance Shoshana apparently has only one option in response to mother's demand, which is to return home "like a good girl" at the time set by her mother. Her response to her mother's *controlling response* is *to avoid conflict and confrontation.* She does not verbalize her frustration directly to her mother (see Chapter 5), and ends up totally surrendering to her mother's dictate. Shoshana tells the interviewer that this recalled encounter with mother from late adolescence was the first that came into her mind in response to the RAP instructions:

> SHOSHANA: *You see – this is the first thing I told you about. I've been carrying it with me for a long time... This commitment to my mother, not my father (who was not a Holocaust survivor).*

We do not know what Shoshana means by "*this commitment*" (the interviewer did not inquire on this point). The story setting suggests that part of the dynamics of this commitment of the daughter to her mother is feeling responsible for parents' feelings and well-being. An implicit message of the story is that the mother's wants (that her daughter be home early) or her fears take precedence over those of the daughter (to go to a party and enjoy it). The theme of commitment to parents as a core experience of the children appears to go hand in hand with their perception of their parents as vulnerable (RO), and consequently the children avoid confrontation (RS). In the following narratives we further explore these components of the CCRT.

TO PROTECT MOTHER IN RESPONSE TO HER OVERPROTECTION

The need to protect his mother in response to her overprotection of him was central to Moshe's relational script with his mother.

> MOSHE: *There was always this anxiousness to see the child with their own eyes. I would say she was overprotective and worried about two things: school or academic achievements and army service. I knew*

> *that if I told her the whole truth she would have sleepless nights and nerves, so it was always necessary to makes things look better, "to round out the corners." When I was in the army I felt obliged to be home as much as possible . . . I knew I had to do all the tricks I could to get home. It seemed like being selfish toward my buddies in the army unit, but it was more like a need to calm down my parents, mostly my mother.*

Moshe's account recalls Jacob Buchan's story that we began with. It is the child's responsibility to reassure the parents of his or her safety. Otherwise they won't be able to handle the anxiety.

Moshe explains that all three children live very close by to their mother. He refers to it as part of the strong family ties, but also as a need for proximity to her. He states that he never even considered the possibility of living farther away because it would have meant "breaking away." He also chose to study at a university close to home (not unusual in Israel as the country is small) so as to continue living at home with his parents during his studies (fairly unusual in that generation). Moshe expressed the need to minimize causing his mother any possible anxiety or upset as an imperative that he and his siblings obeyed. Here is his response to the interviewer's request for a specific RE:

> INTERVIEWER: I would like to ask you to focus on a specific episode that you recall from a more recent time, something that was meaningful for you, some interaction you had with her, that you can tell me – maybe something that she said to you and something that you said to her, and what happened in the end that was meaningful for you.
>
> MOSHE: *I can tell you (the interviewer), we've been so wary in the family all these years that I don't remember that we ever reached boiling point.*
>
> INTERVIEWER: It doesn't have to involve a conflict, just an exchange of words.
>
> MOSHE: *We try to enjoy ourselves but with as much caution as we can.*

From this response one gets the sense that the *cautious stance* is basic in Moshe's relational world. It seems to go hand in hand with the actual or perceived responses from mother, where giving her the slightest reason for worry would result in sleepless nights for her. Moshe's behavior toward his mother, as well as his personal decisions (where to study, where to live), involves making every effort to avoid any situation that potentially would entail conflict or confrontation with his mother.

COMMITMENT TO PARENTS IN ADULTHOOD

Orna describes her tendency to make herself available to fulfill any request, large or small, that her father made. She emphasizes that the possibility of not complying, which could potentially frustrate the father, was never an option, even when she herself had become a mother. "*Father would call me on the phone. At that instant, I drop everything. I have to take the bus... and I have a baby that I have to diaper and get dressed, and to take things for him before leaving the house. I cannot leave immediately when he calls me, I can't push a button and be there beside him.*" Father was perceived (RO) as needing her help, demanding and controlling, and Orna responded by fulfilling his expectation of compliance to his demands at once. Even when it was a hassle for her she went to great lengths not to keep father waiting. For example, if she missed the bus she wouldn't wait for the next one: She would push the baby in the buggy and actually run to get to her father's home. It was not nearby, and it was all uphill, but she felt she had to get there right on time: "*God forbid I should be late.*"

This kind of occurrence would usually end with Orna feeling that she was not doing a good enough job of taking care of her father. She always left his house in tears. In Orna's narrative the outcome is clearly negative. She felt compelled or obligated to respond this way and the encounter ended with her feeling upset. Note that this more recent episode is in the context of the father living alone as widower after the mother died. Still, one wonders if the commitment to the father in this case is amplified in the setting of his being a Holocaust survivor too.

PARENTS' SUFFERING AND VULNERABILITY

The perception of the parents as extremely vulnerable is related in the children's minds to the scars their parents carry that never heal: Indeed, they grow worse with the years. The sons and daughters grow up with the idea that their parents suffered immensely, and they struggle to comprehend their parents' incomprehensible traumatic past. At times the child's narrative echoed the parents' trauma directly, but often the echo could only be inferred (e.g., Joseph's story of the trip to the Sea of Galilee story, Shoshana's story of the party). A more direct reference to the parents' traumatic experiences appeared in Shmuel's account of the times his mother told him her story of how "she saw Mengele with her own eyes."

"All That They Went Through There"

Shmuel describes his experience in listening to his mother's stories. He emphasizes that for him it is not just listening to her and then it is over, but the sense that his mother relives these experiences. What is it like for him when she tells and retells him her stories? What is the experience for the son being on the receiving end?

> SHMUEL: *First of all it hurts me. It's my mother that was there – not a statistic, but she herself went through all those things . . . When my mother talks about what she went through, she feels it again, it is like a repeat broadcast of the suffering, the grief, all that they went through there. They lived under such unbearable conditions that sometimes I feel myself: how could I put myself in their place . . . To think here of such a small problem, it seems to me hard to cope with. But to think of what those people went through under those conditions . . . murder, and watching as the family are taken away to their death. So I try to*

put myself in the picture instead of her (mother). It's horrifying. To see the people and to think that they could go through this and stay human... It's something that... You know, I was in basic training in the army, I saw how people respond to stressful situations – nothing life threatening, and there were some people that lost it... So now as an adult I can understand what my mother went through, so even if she acts in a way that seems perplexing or strange to me, but to think that after all that she went through she is still functioning? We don't encourage her to talk about these things (her past). When she starts to get into this area, or rut, I try to move her thoughts to a different direction.

INTERVIEWER: How do you feel when she starts to talk about it?

SHMUEL: *Once she has seen some documentary, I can see that it gets her into a state... like a traumatic state, there are some external signs that I identify.*

INTERVIEWER: Like what?

SHMUEL: *Like a frozen look, her thoughts become erratic, she loses the fluency of speech... I immediately notice it.*

INTERVIEWER: How did you react when you saw these signs?

SHMUEL: *We (he and his siblings) tried to distract her; we may have turned off the TV. She doesn't object. She knows that we're simply trying to get her out of it, to avoid the possibility of her being harmed by it, won't be able to sleep, things like that.*

This son appears to be alert to his mother's condition and to the possibility and fears of what he refers to as "the scars of the trauma opening up." He has developed great sensitivity in reading his mother's verbal and nonverbal reactions: her look, her tone, the irregularity of her speech, and her incoherence.

Jacob Buchan (1998) in his novel of *Transparent Child*, provides us a portrayal of the child's perception of his suffering mother:

> Suddenly I understand. What affected me was her face. The face that was so tense... and the small eyes, the suffering watery eyes, and the quivering eyelids. A small and vulnerable bird (Buchan, 1998; p. 112, authors' translation).

Returning to Shmuel, the episode of the TV documentary had occurred 12–14 years before. In a more recent episode he recounted in the RAP interview, Shmuel still fears that his mother will be harmed by reliving her memories. He tells the interviewer that his mother recently visited a site at Atlit, near Haifa. In the closing years of the British Mandate in Israel/Palestine the site had been an internment camp used by the British authorities to incarcerate illegal Jewish immigrants from Europe who were apprehended. Now the place was dedicated to memorialize that period of illegal immigration. Shmuel's mother had been in the Auschwitz death camp, and then after immigrating to Israel she was sent to the "camp at Atlit." Shmuel was concerned that the visit to Atlit would awaken his mother's memories from the death camp. He says that had she asked him if she should go on the visit, he would have advised her absolutely *not* to go. Still, he adds that after the visit she felt fine. Even though his fears proved unwarranted, Shmuel retains the view that his mother might have been effected in a bad way.

This cautious attitude toward the surviving parents is particularly profound in respect to memories of the trauma. Yet this pattern appears to color the children–parents interactions in another way too. The picture of the parent as someone who both endured the impossible and at the same time is extremely vulnerable can be very confusing for the children.

Walking on Eggshells in Response to Mother's Vulnerability

Sarah's sense of her mother's vulnerability appears ever-present even in her simplest interactions with her mother.

> SARAH: *Because every time I think what a difficult life she had and how difficult it was for her and how much... how much she suffered and how much it really is a very unpleasant feeling, that if you don't do what she asks or what... if you hurt her in a certain thing, it's very hard for her after this. You feel... you feel that you are hurting*

the . . . I don't know how to explain it. She's very vulnerable, and it's difficult for me with this vulnerability.

INTERVIEWER: So you are like walking on eggshells.

SARAH: *Exactly. It's not always for the good, sometimes it's better to say things, and complete circles and draw some kind of ending mark and a line, and that's it. But it's always so difficult when you feel this.*

For many of our interviewees the price of avoiding any expression of protest against the parents was high and involved ambivalent feelings. This was particularly evident when sons' and daughters' avoidance of the implications of confrontation resulted in their forgoing their own desires to *save their parents.* Some children, particularly sons, expressed a certain idealization of their parents in light of their survival and felt they accepted and understood their parents no matter what. The following example from Nahum's interview depicts the avoidance of conflict in light of this absolute kind of acceptance.

Everything They Did Was Allowed

Nahum had great difficulty providing REs in the interview. He tried to tell specific situations, but every time the interviewer attempted to probe how Nahum responded to his parents at the time, or what his feelings were in these encounters, he gave very general and unemotional responses. Midway through the interview, when the interviewer asked him yet again if he could remember what he felt about his mother's behavior (e.g., mother pressuring his friends to eat more and to finish all the food on their plate), Nahum responded:

NAHUM: *For me, since I understood myself, since I understood myself, from a young age, that I had won the privilege of being alive. I mean through my parents. The situation here is that my parents survived the Holocaust, came here, I won a privilege, a great privilege, and I respected them for it. Everything they did was allowed; everything was accepted by me. You see, my mother could do anything, put me to*

> *shame, embarrass me . . . Also my father, he could do what he wanted. I never raised, I never raised my voice to them; I never got annoyed; I understood they are this way.*

Nahum goes on to tell the interviewer that his understanding for his parents was connected to feeling proud also of the way they treated his friends. He sounds fully content that the possibility of expressing any unease with his parents' behavior toward him or his friends was not an option. His RSs include not only *avoiding conflict* with his parents and being *self-controlled*; he also feels himself accepting of them and proud of them.

AVOIDANCE OF ASKING THE PARENT ABOUT THE HOLOCAUST

The cautious and avoidant stance toward the parents appeared to be particularly firm regarding the impermissibility of asking openly about the parents' Holocaust memories.

> DOV: *I remember they would sit with friends and tell all kinds of stories. My father never told his story; I would hear it from all kinds of other sources. That is, my father he never spoke about the Holocaust, what he went through, what he did, how he kept going, how he escaped. Nothing. Simply "a switch," and that's it. If I heard anything about my father it was from other friends, and he didn't deny it. If someone else told something, he didn't say, "No, it's not true." I also never asked him, or my mother either. I knew that somehow there was something and I didn't press them to talk or tell me about what they went through. My son, yes: he asked him in connection with some project he was doing at school.*
>
> INTERVIEWER: You were interested to know?
>
> DOV: *Did it interest me to know? It interested me to know; it interested me to know. But I didn't delve into it; I didn't want to push him to something he didn't want to tell me on his own initiative, that is – no. No, I didn't want to push him.*
>
> INTERVIEWER: Why not?

Dov tells the interviewer he doesn't remember why, but he assumes that perhaps he tried once or twice to get father to talk. Yet then he says: *"I don't remember, I don't want to say something unfounded, but maybe."* Then he again comes up with an option: *"But it's possible that I maybe tried once to talk to him and he silenced me. No... he didn't want to talk about it, I don't know why (he) did not want to talk about it... and no, no I don't know why, perhaps in some way he wanted to forget it."*

This account that Dov gives about not knowing father's story and not asking illustrates "the double wall" dynamic between the parents and the children. Bar-On (1995) called it "Parents do not tell and children do not ask." It is hard for Dov to decipher this cycle. He cannot put his finger on how it came to be that he did not ask his father directly. Clearly, he did not want to push, but was it father who did not initiate, or was it he who did not ask? He seems to hypothesize that he did once or twice initiate the subject, but he was silenced. The answers to these questions about this dynamic remain unclear to Dov: Who was responding to whose message? Was he responding to the message that father wanted to forget, to switch off the memories? There is a sense that this was an unspoken message. Dov cannot be sure that this was the case. What is clear is that his avoidance of the topic is very much present. Dov's conflict takes the form of wanting *to know*, but on the other hand of not taking any steps in this direction. His son (the survivor's grandchild) does take the initiative in this direction.

CLOSING COMMENTS

Taken together, the narratives presented in this chapter shed light on the experiences of survivors' sons and daughters, in which they often "walked on eggshells" in relation to what they perceived as their parents' extreme vulnerability and fragility (Bar-On, 1995; Wiseman, Barber, Raz, Yam, Foltz, & Livne-Snir, 2002). Specifically, the pattern that we refer to as "*mutual overprotection*" (Wiseman, Metzl, & Barber, 2006) appears to leave the children feeling they cannot even allow themselves to expect their parents to understand their needs (e.g., to take part in a social event away from home) if the needs conflict with the parents' anxieties (e.g., their fears about the child's safety). The children feel the need to protect their parents and to avoid hurting them ("*because if you hurt her . . . it is a terrible feeling*"); the parents are perceived as those who have suffered enough, and therefore cannot be confronted with the child's own needs ("*because I have long carried it with me . . . this commitment to my mother*"). This need to protect the parents hinders open communication and free expression of the sons' and daughters' desires, which as we showed is experienced with greater intensity during adolescence in face of the child's developmental needs for autonomy.

5

"Without Words": Themes of Interpersonal Communication

What was the experience like for the child who sensed in the air that there had been a horrifying experience that he or she had not been told about and that was not discussed between the adults and the children? Our participants grew up with parents who were faced with the almost unbearable possibility of telling their children about what they underwent during the Holocaust. Furthermore, they were raised in the 1950s, a time in Israel when survivors were not encouraged to discuss their experiences and the Holocaust was enveloped in silence by Israeli society at large (Bar-On, 1995; Segev, 1993; Shapira, 1997). Such silence was also described regarding the experience of survivors and their children in North America and in other countries, perhaps even more (Danieli, 1983, 1998; Krell, 1979; Rosenthal, 1998).

David Grossman in his novel *See under Love* (1986; translated 1989) appears to capture the experience of the child who has *the need to know* and wants to ask the adults what he feels *they dare not tell.* Grossman indicates to the reader that the story takes place in 1959. This was before the Eichmann trial was held in Israel (it began in April 1961), a landmark event in the process of breaking the silence (Segev, 1993).

The hero, called Momik, talks about his interaction with Bella, the owner of the grocery cafe in his neighborhood:

> Because don't forget that like all the grownups Momik knew Bella came from Over There, a place you weren't supposed to talk about too much, only think about in your heart and sigh with

> a drawn-out krechtz, oyyyy, the way they always do, but Bella is different from the others somehow and Momik heard some really important things from her about it, and even though she wasn't supposed to reveal any secrets, she did drop hints about her parents' home Over There, and it was from her that Momik first heard about the Nazi Beast.
>
> The truth is, in the beginning Momik thought Bella meant some imaginary monster or a huge dinosaur that once lived in the world which everyone was afraid of now. But he didn't dare ask anyone who or what. And then when the new grandfather showed up and Momik's mama and papa screamed and suffered at night worse than ever, and things were getting impossible, Momik decided to ask Bella again, and Bella snapped back that there are some things, thank God, a nine-year-old boy doesn't have to know yet... (Grossman, 1986/1989; p. 13).

This passage describes very vividly a child's need to know and to make sense of the adults' distressing behavior, such as parents screaming at night. The child, however, picks up the secretive tone around the parents' traumatic experiences, together with the unspoken message that they are not able to talk about their painful memories. Consequently, the child is afraid to elicit more pain and is afraid to ask, thus, remaining with the unknown and unbearable secret. The parents do not deliberately or consciously hide their Holocaust experiences from the child: In this sense, the phrase "conspiracy of silence" (Danieli, 1998) meaning the silence in the families of survivors should not be viewed as a "conspiracy" on the part of the survivor parents (Krell, 2000). The silence between the survivors and their children emanated from the parents' need to forget their traumatic experiences and to adjust to new social contexts (to move on with life), but also from their belief that withholding information about the horrors of the Holocaust was necessary for their children's normal development (Bar-On, Eland, Kleber, Krell, R., Moore, Sagi, Soriano, Suedfeld, van der Velden, & van IJzendoorn, 1998). As Bella asserts in her statement, there are certain things "a nine-year-old boy doesn't have to know yet."

The dynamics of the parents' need to protect the child, and the child's need to protect the vulnerable parents, which we termed *mutual overprotection* (see Chapter 4), takes on special meaning in relation to the themes of communication that emerged in the relational narratives. Going beyond the Core Conflictual Relationship Theme (CCRT) framework as a basis for identifying its three components [Wishes, responses from others (RO), and responses of self (RO)], we analyzed the narratives in a discovery-oriented manner. This analysis led us to the identification of a number of trauma-specific communication themes that characterize the way the second generation communicated with their parents. These themes entail what is said and at the same time not said between the children and their parents, what is communicated verbally with words and what is communicated in silence and without words, and what is known and not known.

WITHOUT WORDS

Reading the narratives over and over, we became aware of an interpersonal space "without words" that was somehow present in the encounters that the second generation told about meaningful interactions with parents. Sometimes this "wordless" presence was the major theme of the story, but mostly we detected it only when re-reading the stories in search of what was not, or could not, be put into words. The narrator appeared to consider this lack of words as a given in the story. Most likely it existed at a preconscious or even unconscious level. Let us return to the *Thirst Story* that was analyzed in Chapter 3 (Wishes for closeness and autonomy), this time paying special attention to what we can learn from it about the daughter–mother communication pattern manifested in this relationship episode.

I Did Like This with My Mouth

HANNA: *I remember once, I was a little girl, don't remember how old – 8, 9, 10, and I was very thirsty in the kitchen and my mother was busy with something, and she did not want to give me something to drink. And, I stood there and made all sorts of faces, with all the "poor me" in the world so that she would give me some water. I suppose that in the end she did, but I remember that I stood and I did this with my mouth [moves her lips to demonstrate to the interviewer] so that she'd realize that I was very thirsty. I guess that in the end she did give me (a drink of water), but it's interesting that I don't remember that, but instead I remember the bit about me standing there, asking for it, and I remember that she got mad at me; I don't remember the part where she brought me the glass of water.*

INTERVIEWER: Do you remember how you felt in this situation with mother?

HANNA: *I don't remember being hurt, or anything like that. I just simply really wanted to drink; maybe I even wanted more to annoy her just by standing there, and maybe I wanted to get a madder response from her. I don't... don't remember myself as pitiful. I remember I always wanted to stand on my own, and I never dared to do so with my mother. There was no such thing as saying NO or anything like that that kids do nowadays. But for me to say NO to my mother! That word never came out of my mouth, never once with my mother.*

Analyzing this recollected interaction between Hanna and her mother with the CCRT framework (see Chapter 3) we identified the wish for connection, which is frustrated by the mother ignoring Hanna, as well as themes of autonomy and power. What is most puzzling and idiosyncratic in this story is Hanna's way of asking her mother for a drink of water. Analyzing the communication aspects that are revealed in this relationship episode, we focused on the non-verbal component, which is so salient. In demonstrating to the interviewer the way she made faces at her mother, Hanna tells us that she expresses her thirst to her mother with her mouth, and with facial expressions. She wants mother to respond to her request, which is expressed *without words*, and she wants mother to understand her "sign language." Hanna further tells us through this narrative that she did not have a voice to express herself in relation to her mother. She cannot utter the word NO to her mother, and in talking about this barrier in their communication she returns to the mouth: "to say NO to my mother – that word never came out of my mouth, never with my mother." Hanna does not have the words to say what she needs and is unable to say NO to what does not suit her in relation to her mother.

In recalling this remembered encounter from childhood, Hanna, like many of our interviewees, did not mention the Holocaust explicitly in the narrative. Yet one can speculate about an association between this story of thirst and the terrible experiences of thirst, hunger, and other fundamental deprivations that Hanna's mother experienced in the concentration camp. Hanna might feel as thirsty as a person who, due to extreme thirst, cannot utter a word. Moreover, she seems to feel helpless, and without a voice or the ability to satisfy her most basic needs, like a person who is at the mercy of others. The way the "other" in this story, Hanna's mother, responds to her is not articulated in words. We do not know what mother said to Hanna, we only know that she remembers that her mother got mad at her. Hanna does not give a voice to her mother in this script either, and they both enact in a mother–daughter wordless interpersonal space.

The next narrative, told by Shoshana (recounted partly in Chapter 4), is again one in which the words are left unspoken and the story ends without a word being said.

I Did Not Utter a Word about It: The Party Story

After hearing the interviewer's instructions for the relationship interview, Shoshana began immediately by recounting the following relationship episode with her mother from late adolescence:

SHOSHANA: *Yes, I have a mother who is truly a Holocaust survivor, and there are many interactions because of it. In the distant past when I was 10 – no I was 19, in the army, and we were about to have a going away party for one of the officers that was part of our unit. I went to the army base in the morning and I remember that when I got there, about 2 hours later, I called my mother to tell her that I had arrived, and that everything was okay, and it was close to noon, when at that moment she announced to me: "You are coming back home now!" I told her, but mom, this is a going away party and all my friends are here, so she said okay, call me again in 2 hours. Then I called her again, she (mother) said, "Listen Shoshana, you're to be home at 8:00 P.M.; I don't care how . . . and the party was going to start at only 7:00 P.M.. I had just gone over early especially to help prepare the party because it was my day off and it wasn't even part of my army duties. So at 6:00 P.M. I called my boyfriend, who is now my husband, and told him that I had to go home because this was what my mother wanted and it was a fact. So like a good girl at 6:00 P.M., before the party even began and people were just starting to arrive, at 6:00 I packed my stuff and went back home, and got home at 8:00 P.M. like a good girl.*

INTERVIEWER: How did you feel? (Asking for the RS.)

SHOSHANA: *Awful, very bad, and I think it is very meaningful . . . you see this is the first thing I told you about, because I have been carrying it with me for a long time . . . This commitment to my mother, not my father (her father was not a Holocaust survivor).*

INTERVIEWER: What went through your head when you called and she said, come home immediately? (The interviewer is trying to encourage the interviewee to say more about her response to her mother's response.)

SHOSHANA: *I cried, I had tears in my eyes . . . it was the feeling that you weren't given the freedom, all the time you are fixated by the rigid family system.*

INTERVIEWER: What happened in the end?

SHOSHANA: *I came back home! Like a good girl at 8:00 (eight zero, zero), and I didn't utter a word about it.*

Shoshana acknowledges to the interviewer that this is the first memory of an encounter with her mother that comes to mind many years later, even now when she is married and has children of her own. At first she actually locates the story at the age of 10, which seems to suggest that it represents her encounters with her mother many years earlier still. Moreover, it could imply that even when at 19, and serving in the army, she felt in many ways like a 10-year-old girl in the extent to which she could stand up to her mother. She uses the term "good girl" twice in recounting the narrative. The themes of autonomy and avoidance of conflict that are apparent in this episode were explored in previous chapters (see Chapters 3 and 4) and the tendency of the second generation not to express anger toward the parents will be discussed further in Chapter 6. Focusing on the mother–daughter communication pattern in this narrative, the lack of communication or exchange between Shoshana and her mother is evident. The mother "announces" to the daughter that she has to be home at 8:00 P.M. She does not explain, and it is not open to discussion, but is stated absolutely, with no room for negotiation. As for the daughter, she does not really try to negotiate and experiences the situation as "a fact." One gets the sense that this "fact" is so to speak a "fact of life," such as the unspoken commitment to mother, which may be connected to mother's being "truly a Holocaust survivor." In the face of this fact, Shoshana goes home and does not say a word. She carries her hurt and frustration silently, and the story ends *without words.*

Things You Absorb . . . Things without Words

Chaim, a second-generation son, tells a relationship episode that he refers to as an emotional argument with his father over the plan that Chaim's daughter would go on a school trip to Poland. Israeli high schools arrange these tours (usually for students at age 17), which include visits to the sites of the Nazi concentration camps in Poland. The trip is optional and mostly paid for by the parents.

> CHAIM: *We considered the possibility that our oldest daughter would go on a trip to Poland. He (father) said to me, "No, I won't let her go to Poland; I am not prepared for her to go through this experience."*

Both of us, my wife and I (both second generation), were so angry. What does he mean, he won't agree? Even our younger daughters already know that when they are old enough to go on the school tours they will do so, unless, God forbid, we are penniless. No way! They'll go! I also promised myself that if I could I would go too. We swore that each of us would make an effort to make at least this journey. These are things we grew up with. It is obvious to us that we will go to see the concentration camp where my mother was and not because of things that we were told.

INTERVIEWER: Without talking much?

CHAIM: *I think it is, in my opinion, things that you absorb. These are things without words that you don't need to talk about to understand them, to feel them, and to live in their shadow. You don't need to give them titles. Now, no one told us that we need to go to Germany, or to Holland to see it, but it was obvious. When father said that "they should not go through the experience" what does that mean? We already went through the experience, if we like it or not, we are part of this experience. So what does he mean, we went through it; it is our history; we cannot detach or disconnect ourselves from it. These are our roots; we came from somewhere; we were not born out of space.*

This story about the interaction between Chaim and his father, regarding his daughter, the grandchild of the survivor parent, echoes the survivors' need to protect their own children, in this case a grandparent struggling to protect the third generation, a grandchild. The son does not accept this, and protests against his father's interference. The unspoken dialogue can be paraphrased this way.

FATHER/GRANDFATHER: *I went through hell and I will not let my granddaughter go through this hell.*

SON: *We already went through it; it is part of us, and you cannot disconnect us from your traumatic past. We absorbed it; we live in its shadow. You cannot pretend we were born out of space.*

Chaim uses the expression "without words," suggesting it is something in the atmosphere that you *absorb* and cannot disconnect from. The dialogue is very emotional but it does not appear to open the lines of the communication regarding the father's trauma. The visit to Poland seems to play the role of a "third party" through which the next generation can connect to their roots.

The question of what is absorbed and the feeling of "we went through it" is left unexplained in this narrative. Nevertheless, one gets the sense of it being a core part of the way this son of a survivor defines himself and his place in the world.

The use of the word "absorbed" suggests that it is something that the second generation feels is taken in and assimilated from birth. From his narrative it appears he seems to accept this part of his history and even sees it as part of his own children's history. The use of "absorb" reminded us of a clip from the movie *Because of That War* (Ben-Dor, 1988), which we made use of its title in Chapter 1. This clip, to be described below, also depicts the communication theme we called *knowing–not knowing*, which we suggest is a core theme in the interpersonal experience of offspring of parents who have experienced various excessive trauma.

KNOWING–NOT KNOWING

In the movie *Because of That War* Israeli singer Yehuda Poliker, the son of parents who survived Auschwitz, tells the scriptwriter Orna Ben-Dor (1988) how growing up in a family of Holocaust survivors impacted his music. We first approach the following text as if it was an account of a relationship episode (RE) that the son tells about a recurring interaction with his father:

> At home, Greek music was heard. Greek music that doesn't make one happy, doesn't make one feel great, only makes you gloomy and depressed. These are the songs they heard at home, songs about wars, about alien countries, about separations, about pain, about things like that, and it was terrible. It *absorbed* into me, and I now remember saying to my father, "Stop this song! It makes me cry. I can't listen to it! It makes me feel awful." And he would say to me, "It makes me feel awful too. It reminds me of my family,

> *if you knew what had happened*, and what I went through . . . you should hear it, *you have got to know.* I can't do without the music; I have got to listen to it (Yehuda Poliker in the movie *Because of That War*, Ben-Dor, 1988; authors' translation).

Although obviously we could not ask clarifying questions, as one could if this RE had been collected in a RAP interview, we can still attempt to identify the CCRT components (Wishes, ROs, and RSs) that can be recognized in this text.

WISHES: Poliker's primary wishes are to feel good, to be understood, to be seen, and to be heard. His secondary wish is to be in conflict with and oppose his father. RO: His father is vulnerable, in pain, and in control and at the same time out of control, and he hurts him. RS: He feels depressed, terrible, anxious, and not understood.

Following the application of the CCRT approach to the text, we now turn our attention to the echoes of trauma that are enacted in spoken and unspoken communication between father and son in this narrative. The father, who insists that the son listen to the music that is inseparable from his traumatic memories, tells the son that he "*cannot know*" what happened and at the same time insists "*you should know.*" The son is left feeling not only depressed and anxious but also with the conflict of being unable to shut out his father's painful past, and he absorbs his father's gloomy music. The father's impossible message is reminiscent of what Adelman (1995) referred to as a strong message from many survivors to their children: "Don't forget. Always remember." In the context of lack of open communication, however, to remember the unknown becomes a confusing and paradoxical injunction (Adelman, 1995; p. 361).

The conflict between wanting to know and not wanting or being allowed to know has been pointed out as a major family dynamic within the group of victims of war and persecution (Op Den Velde, 1998). For example, researchers examining these kinds of dynamics in Dutch war sailors and resistance veterans observed two opposite forms of communication. On the one hand, keeping silent, and on the other talking excessively about war experiences and traumas. The dynamics involved are much more complex, in that silence can be revealing and excessive talk can be obscuring (Bar-On, 1995). As Op Den Velde puts it: "We can state that communications about traumatic experiences – verbal or nonverbal – are always present in the family realm" (p. 152).

The following relational narrative from our study reveals the family dynamics involved in the unspoken overriding presence of the mother's Holocaust trauma as it was painfully experienced at the narrator's wedding. This episode also refers to music that is played, but in this case it is the mother (not the son) who cannot bear the music of the band (most likely cheerful) at her son's wedding.

We Did Not Know; She Did Not Tell

Going back to Zvi's wedding story (for the full narrative see Chapter 3), we now focus on the communication aspects in his story. Striking in our reexamination of Zvi's story was that after describing his mother's extreme detachment at the wedding (her taking tranquilizers and shouting at the band to lower the volume of the music) he spontaneously went on to tell the interviewer about his mother's diary:

> ZVI: *The minute she was on pills and all that, I knew that she wasn't with us at all... I didn't understand... I thought it would be an opening for some kind of togetherness with the whole family. But it didn't happen... We did not know anything about the Holocaust, we did not know about the whole connection... She wrote a diary and she didn't translate it into Hebrew. She left it in her mother tongue. Only when I was 18, at the request of my eldest niece (the oldest granddaughter), she translated it for the first time into Hebrew. Only*

> *then did we understand and learn what she'd been through. Until then we did not know anything, she did not tell us anything. We only knew that she had been in the Ghetto.*

Zvi's mother did not translate the diary into Hebrew until her granddaughter asked her to translate it. Until then his mother's story, which was written in her own language, remained unreadable and untold. This narrative demonstrates how in the context of "not knowing the whole connection" this second-generation son struggles to understand his mother's surprising and disturbing response. Like Zvi, we are left to guess whether the music at the wedding is related to the mother's traumatic Holocaust experiences. Could it be, for example, that she was in one of those camps where lively music had to be played while Jews were being "selected" and murdered? This in fact is the kind of question that the sons and daughters of parents who experienced severe trauma are afraid to ask. His mother's detachment during the wedding and her miscommunication with the band recalls the language barrier between the mother's language of the past and her son, who does not know her language and therefore does not know her story.

The family dynamics in which the survivor's story remains "unknown" to the sons and daughters, who in turn fear that questioning their parents may reopen old wounds, lead to a "double wall" of silence: "Parents do not tell, and children do not ask" (Bar-On, 1996; p. 168). As indicated in Zvi's story, it is often through the grandchildren, who feel more free to make the first move (upon her granddaughter's request the survivor grandmother translates the diary), that new opportunities arise for opening up lines of communication between the generations (Bar-On, 1995).

In our study based on self-report measures of communication and interpersonal patterns (Wiseman, Barber, Raz, Yam, Foltz, & Livne-Snir, 2002) we distinguished two subgroups of children of Holocaust survivors by the extent that "knowing–not knowing" pattern characterized their family communication pattern. The first subgroup, determined as possessing nonverbal knowing of the Holocaust (somehow always "knowing" about the parent's Holocaust experiences) despite the silence or the little and vague knowledge ("not knowing") about the parents' experiences, evinced the knowing–not knowing (Jucovy, 1985) pattern. The second subgroup, those whose parents were willing to share factual information about their Holocaust experiences and were characterized by lower reliance on nonverbal communication, displayed the "informative verbal communication" pattern. These two subgroups and a comparison group (adults born to parents who had immigrated to Israel before 1939 with their own parents) were compared. The knowing–not knowing subgroup of second-generation adults reported greater interpersonal distress and lower affiliation than did either their counterparts with informative verbal communication or the comparison group (see Wiseman et al., 2002). Moreover, the latter second-generation subgroup proved similar to the comparison group (with no Holocaust background) in their perceptions of their parents. This suggests that it is the lack of open communication in these second-generation adults characterized by the knowing–not knowing pattern that may be the key to their relatively greater interpersonal distress, rather than their being Holocaust survivors' descendents per se. The impact of open communication in close relationships is underscored by attachment theory and research.

COMMUNICATION AS PROCESS

The possible impact of open parent–child communication about the parents' traumatic Holocaust memories on the children's interpersonal patterns (Wiseman et al., 2002) can be understood in the context of working models of attachment (e.g., Bretherton, 1990; Grossmann, Grossmann, & Schwan, 1986; Kobak & Duemmler, 1994). Evidence from empirical studies of attachment at the representational level concurs with Bowlby's (1973) claim that open and coherent communication between parents and children from infancy to adolescence are associated with well-organized and revisable internal models of attachment relationships (Bretherton & Munholland, 1999; Kobak, 1999). When lines of communication are open, disruptive events can be discussed in the attachment relationship and threats to availability can be disconfirmed. Specifically in relation to intergenerational communication of the Holocaust trauma, Grossmann (1999) stated:

> Talking about traumatic threatening events in a realistic manner is, according to Bowlby (1988), essential for new internal working models to develop. Silence or false verbal information about potentially traumatic events connected to separation and loss particularly under the dehumanizing conditions of the concentration camp may prevent the development of adaptive new inner working models. As a consequence, the next generation is suffering from being excluded from the process of co-constructing new perspectives on life (p. 6).

In adulthood the communication patterns between second-generation sons and daughters and their survivor parents are not static. Although in childhood the "double wall" of silence seemed to prevail, in adulthood, with greater time passed since the trauma, a window to more direct lines of communication may open up. One interviewee, Ruth, described two REs, one from early childhood and one more recent, which centered on the communication theme.

It Was a Very Important Discovery

RUTH: *I remember something meaningful that she told me for the first time, when I was a little girl, about 3 years old. She told me that I should have had another grandfather and grandmother, and that they were murdered. I remember something to that effect. I remember that it was very meaningful for me and I ran to tell a friend . . . and it was really something, it was a kind of very big discovery.*

INTERVIEWER: How did you feel?

RUTH: *That it was very important, because I didn't know . . . and most of the people that I knew did not have grandparents. I had grandparents on my father's side, and I didn't even know that I was supposed to have another grandparent couple. I remember it being an important discovery and I remember I ran to tell my friend.*

This early memory contains a mix between what Ruth has and what she might have had but was lost (maternal grandparents). Still, the excitement that comes across appears to be related to the discovery, that she "is told" and that she runs "to tell" and share with a friend.

The second RE, describing a recent interaction with the mother in adulthood (Ruth is in her early 40s), underscores the process of communication over time.

This Time She Spoke More Freely

RUTH: *She (mother) was (visiting) the United States and she came back from over there. So she told us that her sister was at a convention of survivors in her community, and they videotaped it, and everyone who told their story received the videotape. So when she was at her sister's she saw the video and when she came back she told me about it. And then she talked about everything she went through in a more orderly way than usual, as we caught here and there words and events and we completed the pictures ourselves. This time she spoke more freely.*

INTERVIEWER: How did you react?

RUTH: *I became aware that a lot of things I did not know and a lot of things we added from our own imagination, and that she actually completed a certain picture that we had had previously in our minds.*

INTERVIEWER: Is it like you imagined?

RUTH: *Not entirely. Not everything.*

INTERVIEWER: How did you feel when she talked to you about it?

RUTH: *She cried, and of course I identified with her, so we both cried. It was very emotional, it was very moving.*

Unlike the detachment in Zvi's story, Ruth's story ends with a sense of closeness following the mother talking more freely with the daughter about her Holocaust experiences. Ruth appears to describe in her narrative the knowing–not knowing dynamic, in which only fragments of the story are known and much is left to the imagination (Bar-On et al., 1998). Yet when her mother just returns from a visit to her sister in the United States, which Ruth refers to in her narrative as the mother coming back from "over there" (interestingly she uses the term *Over There* that Grossman's [1986/1989] hero talks about), an opportunity opens for mother–daughter communication. This time the mother tells the story more fully, and the daughter experiences it as being told directly to her, rather than trying to catch a word or event here and there and having to complete the picture on her own. Ruth's narrative ends positively with the experience of being able to cry together. This kind of experience of mutuality seemed very rare in the narratives of the second generation, yet it underscores the healing power of opening lines of communication between the survivors and their children.

PART TWO

EMOTIONS IN THE NARRATIVES

This part of the book analyzes the interpersonal emotional schemas that appear in the relational narratives of the second generation. The emotions that are most discussed in the clinical literature on survivors of major traumas and their children are anger, guilt, shame, anxiety, helplessness, and loneliness. In addition to considering these negative emotions (Chapters 6–9) and their characteristics, we present narratives that refer to positive emotions (Chapter 10), such as feelings of joy and pride. Interviewees were not asked to recall an episode with a specific emotion; instead we identified the emotions that came up in the episodes as told by our interviewees. An exception to this nonspecific approach to studying emotions by means of asking for relational narratives (without specifying the emotion beforehand) was our additional request from narrators to tell relational episodes (REs) about loneliness (in Chapter 9).

The following chapters are organized according to the emotions that were identified in the relational narratives. We propose that the nature and quality of trauma-specific interpersonal communication between the survivor parents and their children (see Chapter 5) is key for understanding the emotional experiences that are depicted in these narratives.

The interplay between nonverbal presence of trauma and emotions is conveyed most powerfully in the passage from David

Grossman's book *"See Under Love"* in the part that is called Glossary: The Language of "Over There":

> **Wedding**
>
> *The celebration of marriage. Nuptials.*
>
> "When I married Ruthy, Aunt Idka showed up at our wedding with a Band-Aid on her arm. She had covered her number with a Band-Aid because she didn't want to cast a pall on the happy occasion. I felt crushed with grief and compassion for her, for what she must have endured to do a thing like that. All evening I couldn't tear my eyes away from her arm. I felt as if under that clean little Band-Aid lay a deep abyss that was sucking us all in: the hall, the guests, the happy occasion, me. I had to put that in here. Sorry" (Grossman, 1986/1989; pp. 356–7).

6

Anger

Anger is one of the most common and frequent emotions experienced by human beings (Canary, Spitzberg, & Semic, 1998). Anger may be felt outside social interactions but mostly it is the outcome of troubled interpersonal circumstances (Guerrero & Andersen, 2000). The origins of anger lie in self-protective instincts in the context of interpersonal aggression. People become angry when others insult, reject, criticize, or show aggression toward them, or when their relatives come under attack (Andersen & Guerrero, 1998). Even a person faced with an injustice may grow angry (Lazarus, 1991). In most situations, when someone feels anger he or she will try to deal with the injury by responding with anger against another person, which creates an uncomfortable climate for problem-solving and further hinders interpersonal communication (Kiesler, 1996). Being one of the strongest emotions in its impact, anger may cause damage and present interpersonal danger (Guerrero & Andersen, 2000). Anger may put a person at risk if he or she expresses it, and this may cause him or her to conceal it, consciously or unconsciously, or even direct it at a different person who constitutes no threat. Nevertheless, being able to express anger calmly, rather than inhibiting it or resorting to aggression, is an important relational skill (Guerrero, 1994).

Studies on sons and daughters of Holocaust survivors have documented the difficulties in the expression of anger and the regulation of aggression in this group. Clinical reports have suggested that survivors' children were overvalued and overprotected by their parents

(Jucovy, 1992). The survivors perceived their children as a source of new hope and meaning and expected them to be a form of restitution for the families, aspirations, and communities that were lost in the Holocaust (Nadler, Kav-Venaki, & Gleitman, 1985; Russell, 1980). The children's sensitivity to their parents' suffering led to a guilt-ridden protectiveness of the parents. This protectiveness, as we showed in the core Wish-Response of Other (RO)-Response of Self (RS) pattern (Chapter 4), may have led the child to feel it was dangerous to express anger. In other words, the risk that the child may have felt about expressing anger toward the parent was charged with the perception that it would put the vulnerable parent in danger, and consequently the child himself or herself.

An important study found that in a nonclinical sample of young adult Israeli Holocaust survivor offspring (HSO) they were less likely to externalize aggression than a non-HSO group (Nadler et al., 1985). Researchers have suggested that in children of survivors, acting out aggression toward the parents was problematic, as was any acknowledgment of aggression and conflict in general (Danieli, 1983; Wanderman, 1976).

Our approach to examining feelings of anger through sons' and daughters' narratives about recollected meaningful interpersonal interactions has the advantage over self-report, paper-and-pencil tests in its being indirect, like projective tests (i.e., the interviewee is not directed to report specifically about encounters that involved anger), and also in being reliable and valid (Wiseman, Metzl, & Barber, 2006). It is in keeping with the recent use of the autobiographical-narrative methodology in studies of emotions, particularly anger and guilt (Baumeister, Stillwell, & Heatherton, 1994, 1995). In our application of the Core Conflictual Relationship Theme (CCRT) framework to the narratives we first examined quantitatively the pattern of associations between the clinician-based CCRT standard category ratings of the RS of "I am angry" and the CCRT standard categories that according to the literature are the most relevant to the experience of anger in HSO. These relevant CCRT standard categories included three RO of the parents: 1) Other "is controlling"; 2) Other "is angry"; and 3) Other "is vulnerable; and two Wishes: 1) "to assert self"; and 2) "to be understood." In addition, given that the CCRT pattern of the HSO pointed to the RS of "avoiding confrontation," the association between this category and the RS of "anger" was also examined (Wiseman et al., 2006). The quantitative picture that emerged from examining the associations of the CCRT ratings of the REs on these categories yielded four major patterns:

(1) Perceiving the parents as "controlling" (RO) was significantly and positively associated ($r = .50$, $p < .001$) with "feeling angry" (RS).
(2) In contrast to the aforementioned, the correlation between an "angry" parent (RO) and an "angry" response of self (RS) was not significant ($r = .15$, ns), and there was no association between perceiving the parent as "vulnerable" (RO) and "feeling angry" ($r = .01$, ns).
(3) The wishes "to assert self" and "to be understood" both correlated significantly with the RS "feeling angry"" ($r = .42$, $p < .01$ and $r = .37$, $p < .01$, respectively).
(4) "Feeling angry"" (RS) correlated significantly with the RS "avoiding confrontation" ($r = .31$, $p < .05$).

After obtaining these findings, we engaged in an in-depth qualitative analysis of the recalled REs that involved feelings of anger. The themes that we identified are outlined below, together with the narratives that best demonstrate the specific complex interpersonal dynamics involved in the interpersonal emotional experiences of anger.

ANGER IN RESPONSE TO PARENTS' EXTREME OVERPROTECTIVE BEHAVIORS

The relatively strong associations that we found between perceiving the other as *controlling* (RO) and in response *feeling angry* (RS) can be clearly demonstrated in the following narratives. The parents' controlling behaviors often revolved around situations in daily life in which their extreme overprotective behaviors and fears for the child's safety became a burden on the child, and anger would build up.

Rachel describes her struggles with her mother's insistence on making her eat.

> RACHEL: *It was so important for her that I eat, and it was so important for me not to eat . . . I was mad at her . . . why is she making me eat? I was afraid she would catch me and make me eat . . . she simply chased after me through the street and I ran and hid.*

Rachel emphasizes to the interviewer that she knew that her mother meant well and that mother was acting out of her excessive worry, but she also states clearly that despite that knowledge it made her angry.

Benjamin describes a similar situation, but in his case he notes that the anger arose only later in life:

> BENJAMIN: *My mother used to dress me and feed me with a spoon until the age of 10. At the time I remember myself enjoying the extra care, but later in life I became angry about it as I became aware of the costs of such a relationship.*

The burden of the parents' worries is expressed, for example, by Sharon, who describes feeling angry when before every school trip, or going camping with the youth movement, her father told her: "*Every time you go on a trip I get more white hair.*" She adds: "*Today, as a mother, I try to hide my worries from my children and let them have their freedom.*" Although Sharon tells the interviewer that she felt angry, it is also clear in her description of the interaction with her father that she did not express her anger toward him directly.

The lack of expression of anger appears even more pronounced in the following narratives, in which the parent is openly aggressive toward the child, either physically or verbally in anger, but the child does not express his or her anger in response.

PARENTAL AGGRESSION OR ANGER AND THE CHILD'S LACK OF EXPRESSION OF ANGER

Given that anger is one of the strongest emotions in its impact, it may not be surprising that recalled encounters with an angry parent were memorable situations. What stands out in these recollections, however, is the lack of expression of anger on the part of the child. It takes on various forms in these narratives.

Fusion of Aggression and Caring: "You Forget Because She Spoils You as Well"

The use of physical aggression as a legitimate way to discipline children was not that unusual when our participants were being raised in the late 1950s and early 1960s. Danny described an episode in which his mother smacked him when he was 10 or 11 years old.

> DANNY: *One day my brother and I annoyed mother. We annoyed her very much and I ran to the bathroom and locked the door. She stood outside and said, "Danny I won't smack you, I won't hit you, I will do nothing to you, come out and finish eating." I came out and I got smacked so hard, I didn't believe it was my mom . . . I was used to getting hit by my dad, but I never was smacked so hard by mother . . . It was painful and I cried for hours on end in my room. I haven't forgotten this scene until this very day.*

Danny explains that he perceived his father as the one that hit and his mother was the soft one. He further tells the interviewer that he knows she was sorry because after that she went to her room and locked the door. "*I know it affected her, that she felt uncomfortable with what she had done . . . but except for that mother spoiled us all the time.*"

Although Danny ends by putting the focus on the way mother spoiled him, the interviewer tries to get back to the situation of the hitting.

> INTERVIEWER: Can you tell me how you felt when mother asked you to come out, and said she would not do anything, and then when you came out she hit you?
>
> DANNY: *I felt that she was a bit . . . that she betrayed me. Like I had this total trust in her, in mother . . . like every lamb that is close to its mother . . . and then I come out and get hit by her? But you forget it very fast because after that she's the doting mother . . . she doesn't leave you for a minute. You're in bed, so she brings you yogurt, you're going to school, so she brings you the bottle of juice to the school gate – God forbid you don't finish your soup. You know the usual things.*

The interviewer tried once more to take Danny back to the recalled situation and the point in the interaction when he came out and his mother hit him.

> INTERVIEWER: When you came out and she hit you, do you say to her, "How come you are doing this?" or "That hurts!"?
>
> DANNY: *I felt hatred, I felt some kind of, not to get into a struggle with mom, but I didn't understand her, I couldn't comprehend it.*

In this account Danny appears to be able to reflect on how he perceived his mother during this interaction and on the range of feelings that this encounter aroused in him. In his reply to the interviewer's repeated question on how he reacted to his mother hitting him (despite her promise) are condensed three separate, yet related, responses of self that appear to be part of the interpersonal dynamics of the angry feelings that the son experienced toward his mother. First, Danny is able to reflect on his strong emotional reaction to his mother's physical aggression toward him, namely he felt *hate*. Mother's behavior in the encounter perhaps elicited such a strong negative reaction also because of his being deeply offended by her betrayal (promising not to hit him and inviting him to finish his meal). This kind of acknowledgment in the interview of feelings of anger toward the parent was less common among the sons and daughters. Second, in his reply he tells us the story of *the avoidance of confrontation* with the parents, which is common in the children of Holocaust survivors. The son cannot express his anger openly to his mother and immediately indicates his intention not to get into a struggle with her. This can be seen also as self-protective as he probably cannot risk annoying mother even more. The breakdown of communication, or the closed channels between the mother and son, are apparent in our vision of Danny crying for hours in his room, and as he recalls mother locking herself in her room. The third response of self that Danny indicated in his reply involves the son feeling he *cannot understand* or make sense of mother's behavior. This sense that the parent's behavior is puzzling probably contributes to the avoidance, as the child cannot risk any further unpredictable response from the parent.

Finally, in this narrative Danny portrays his general perception of his mother's parenting style as utterly devoted to the children (*mother spoiled us all the time*). Unlike some of the other accounts that described this style of total dedication as a burden, Danny does not seem to express any dissatisfaction and accepts his mother's behavior such as waiting for him with a bottle of juice at the school gate or making sure he finished his soup. This inconsistency between the mother's extensive caring and her aggressive and unpredictable behavior might have been particularly confusing and hard to grasp. This kind of inconsistency was evident in other narratives, in which the parent's caring behavior was fused with rigid and controlling behavior.

My Father Had Nervous Attacks Sometimes . . . I Did Not Understand His Reaction

Another example of a relationship episode involving parental aggression, this time of an interaction between a son and his father, included an encounter in which the father is described as angry (RO), yet the natural response that can be expected, namely that the child will feel angry (RS) is lacking in the child's account of his response. Simon describes an episode that he recalls from adolescence (age 15–16) in which his father was extremely angry with him about something he did:

> SIMON: *He came home from work and was terribly angry with me... He took my radio and threw it on the floor and broke it to pieces that scattered all over. You see my father had nervous attacks sometimes... I don't really remember what I did that made him so angry, but I do remember that whatever I had done that upset him was not so extreme as to account for his action... I felt horrible... I was hurt. I didn't understand his reaction.*

In this example of a situation in which the father is aggressive toward his son, the son in response does not seem to have been angry with his father, or at least he does not say in this recalled account of the encounter that he felt angry toward father. He does state that he felt "hurt." Simon appears to perceive his father's reaction as not really connected to his own behavior and seems puzzled by his father's aggressive over-reaction to him. His own lack of reaction at the time is apparent in that he swallowed his hurt.

This is a case in point of how the father is "allowed" to be angry and to express his anger, whereas the son, who indicates that the father's aggressive reaction was unjust (which is expected to elicit anger in response), "allows" himself to feel mostly hurt. Feeling *hurt* is a less overt and threatening emotion than feeling anger toward the aggressing parent. This is in contrast to Danny's reflection on his first response of what seems like momentary *hate* in response to his mother's aggression (hitting him). Here, as in other narratives of the sons and daughters, the child seems to have perceived the parent as *losing control and as fragile.* This is in keeping with the quantitative CCRT finding in which there was a lack of association between the

RO category of perceiving the other as *vulnerable* and the RS category of *feeling angry* (Wiseman et al., 2006).

Difficulty Handling Parents' Anger

Other sons and daughters related episodes that described a general sense of having great difficulty in dealing with their parent's anger toward them. Liora's difficulty in dealing with anger is apparent in her recounting an interaction with her father when she was a university student. After living at home for the first 2 years at university (which was in the same city), Liora wanted to leave and rent an apartment to feel more independent. When she told her father her plan to live away from home he was extremely angry and disapproving. She recalls her father losing his self-control and shouting at her furiously in a very dramatic way.

LIORA: *I remember he yelled and yelled, and he was "like a lion in a cage." I didn't know how to respond to him.*

INTERVIEWER: With what kind of feeling did this leave you, in this specific interaction with father?

LIORA: *Terrible. I can't stand the feeling that someone is angry with me.*

INTERVIEWER: How did it end?

LIORA: *I felt helpless. I could NOT deal with him. Eventually my mother calmed things down and she absorbed the yelling and anger.*

Liora does not feel able to manage her father's anger, which actually involved opposing her wish to leave home. She further explained that she needed her mother to calm father down and negotiate with him on her behalf. Although she told the interviewer that in the end she did not yield, and went ahead with her plan, she appeared wholly unequipped to handle the anger directed at her by her father.

In Liora's case both mother and father were Holocaust survivors, yet she states that she had difficulty with her father's anger. In the following two examples the daughters underscore their cautious attitude to their mothers' anger and disapproval, in contrast to the more relaxed way they reacted to their fathers, who unlike the mothers were not Holocaust survivors.

Being Cautious around the Angry Parent

Pearl describes her difficulty in situations in which her mother was angry by contrasting it with her experience with her father's anger (he was not a Holocaust survivor).

> PEARL: *Whenever mother was angry she would hold on to it (the anger). She would not talk to us, and she kept it inside more and it was very present. With father we (Pearl and her brother) knew that even though he was angry he would calm down . . . he would get angry, but we knew it would pass and we could carry on as usual. With mother, if I was impudent with her she got angry and the anger would last for a long time. With her I was very careful not to hurt her, not to make her angry or annoy her, not to say anything out of place because in her case the anger was enormous and it lasted much longer . . . I guess father's anger wasn't that bad. He would get angry, but it would pass quickly.*

The sense that Pearl gives is that father's anger was bearable, whereas mother's anger was much less so. This led Pearl to try much harder not to reach the point of having to experience mother's anger. It sounded as if doing so would be exceedingly painful for both mother and Pearl herself.

Difficulty in Expressing Frustration Openly toward Survivor Parents

Sons' and daughters' difficulty voicing their frustration with their parents is closely related to the theme of "*commitment to parents*" (Chapter 4) and to the theme "*without words*" (Chapter 5). As you may recall, in Shoshana's narrative her mother phones her to be home early from a party, which Shoshana had actively helped to prepare: She was to leave even before the party began (Chapter 5). In her account of this event, in which Shoshana unquestioningly accepted her mother's demand that she leave the party so as to be home at a certain time, she referred to "*This commitment to my mother*, not my father" (*her* father was not a Holocaust survivor). Her lack of direct expression of her anger was apparent in her reply to the interviewer's attempts to get Shoshana to say more about her response to the mother's demand: "*I cried, I had tears in my eyes... it was the feeling that you weren't given freedom. All the time you're trapped by the rigid family system.*" Later, replying to more questions about "what happened in the end," she said, "*I went back home! Like a good girl at 8:00* P.M. *(eight zero, zero), and I didn't utter a word about it.*"

In this situation, which would be expected to elicit anger, the daughter did not even try to communicate her frustration to her mother; her anger and pain over "not being given freedom" was muted. This tendency not to express the anger in words, or even in action, seemed to characterize the reactions of HSO to their parents' behavior, especially when the behavior seemed puzzling or irrational. This "Party story" also depicts the frustration of the daughter's *wish to assert herself with her mother*, her *wish to be understood*, and the difficulty to negotiate openly with her mother about the time she had to be home, so that she would not have to leave the party even before it began. This kind of dynamic is in keeping with the quantitative CCRT findings indicated earlier that showed that each of the two Wishes – "to assert self" with parents and "to be understood" – correlated significantly with the RS of "feeling angry."

Parental Intrusiveness that Elicits the Child's Anger in Adulthood

Anger would arise in situations in which the parent's overinvolvement in the child's life carried well into young adulthood and adulthood.

The son or daughter would experience this as unwelcome intrusiveness on the part of the parent, which would stir anger.

Mother Pushing Son to Marry and Son Boiling with Anger: "Get Off My Case"

Asked to tell an episode about mother, Yoram refers to recurrent interactions with her in his twenties that involved his mother pressuring him constantly to get married as early as possible.

YORAM: *I guess like every mother she wanted me . . . she all the time only wanted me to get married as fast as possible. I did not feel any rush in this respect; I only got married when I was thirty (relatively late for his cohort). She would pressure me all the time like a steamroller.*

INTERVIEWER: What would she say to you? (trying to get a sense of the RO)

YORAM: *"So when are you going to find a nice girl already? When are you going to get married already? When am I going to have grandchildren from you already?" That kind of thing – just non-stop . . . In some ways I would stop paying attention to her. She just had to start going and I'd switch off, just not to hear it.*

INTERVIEWER: What do you mean? (trying to get a sense of the RS)

YORAM: *I would shut it out; I'd think of other things, only so that I wouldn't have to listen to what she was saying to me. Because listening to these things would drive me crazy.*

INTERVIEWER: It annoyed you?

YORAM: *I'd boil with anger. There were situations . . . that I would burst out at her – "Get off my case, leave me alone!" But at the end I did get married and she calmed down.*

It is interesting to note that only after the interviewer persists in trying to get a better sense of Yoram's response to his mother's pressure, by asking a clarification question, asking gently whether it annoyed him, only then does he spell out the extent of his anger and frustration.

Anger over Mother's Interference with Grandchild: "She's Still Trying to Manage My Life"

Another example of the parent's overinvolvement in adulthood being experienced by the child as intrusive is related in detail by Dina with regard to a relatively recent interaction with her mother that involved her own two-and-a-half-year-old daughter called Noa (the granddaughter).

> DINA: *My mother came over and happily showed me a dress she bought for Noa for Rosh Hashanah [the Jewish New Year and a High Holiday]. Now it is clear that it is not the gift for the holiday, but this is what Noa is going to wear for the holiday. So I told her: "Mom, you bought Noa a dress; I'm delighted, but this is not the dress she will wear for Rosh Hashanah." It was clear to me even before I had looked at the dress that even if it was beautiful I didn't want Noa to wear the dress that my mother got her. So she said to me, "Why not? Why shouldn't she dress up in something nice?" So I said, "Why shouldn't Noa wear something that I choose?" Mother said, "So she won't go out nicely dressed. She'll go to Synagogue looking a mess."*

At this point Dina tells the interviewer that she did not pursue the topic further, but continues telling how angry she felt.

> DINA: *I was annoyed about her managing my life. She bought a dress and she decided what my daughter would wear on Rosh Hashanah. This is in the same spirit of all the things she manages generally. Yes. [Laughs].*

Dina continues telling the interviewer that she told her husband and a woman friend about this encounter with mother:

> DINA: *You see, when I told them they laughed and they didn't understand why I got so upset. That I got so mad that my mother does this. This reminded me of another incident where my mother also called Noa's clothes a mess. I dressed her in a simple T-shirt and I saw out of the corner of my eye that my mother was going to change it. I didn't go into the room so as not to get mad. Instead I heard from outside*

> *the room Noa asking her, "Why are you changing my top?" She's only two and a half, so my mother explained to her that it was hanging off her ("It's your older brother's shirt"). When Noa came into my room I asked her, "Noa, why are you wearing a different top?" so she quoted what my mother had said (it was hanging off her). So I asked my mother, "Why did you change her shirt?" She said, "Noa asked me to."*

A conflict of wills is evident from the way Dina relates the interaction. She perceives her mother (the grandmother) as pretending that it was the granddaughter's wish to change the T-shirt. One suspects that this "battle" or fight over dressing the granddaughter according to her grandmother's taste instead of Dina's is a variation on the theme of control. It is as if this second-generation daughter is "the little girl" fighting for autonomy, who wants to choose her own dress, even if mother does not think it suits her, or is the right one for the specific occasion. When the interviewer asked her more specifically about her response to mother ("How did you feel when mother brought over the dress?") she replied:

> DINA: *First of all, I'm used to it. I've had a lot of practice at it. It's the same with food. I say I've got enough; I don't need you to bring me anything, but all the time they bring me stuff. Whenever they bring me things I get annoyed anew. Like with the dress, I just want her to get out of my way with the dress.*

In this narrative the mother's attempts to give are not accepted as gestures, but as impositions of her wishes that elicit anger in the daughter. Dina explains to the interviewer that this incident that angered her is part of the larger picture of what she refers to as the "*Culture of Worry.*" This is ever-present in the way she feels her parents treat her in their controlling attitude and intrusiveness. We can also view Yoram's narrative about his mother's constant pressure on him to marry as overinvolvement and intrusiveness, which go hand in hand with the parent's worry.

ANGER EPISODES IN OTHER CLOSE RELATIONSHIPS: EXPRESSION VERSUS LACK OF EXPRESSION

The difficulty in communicating negative emotions openly with their parents was referred to by some sons and daughters as a pattern of avoiding confrontation. They seem to encounter similar difficulties in other close relationships. Some, however, referred to their spouse as a welcome relief from these difficulties in open expression of anger.

Feeling Comfortable Expressing Anger with a Spouse: "I Argue Only with Him: With Him Alone Am I Safe"

Tamar contrasts her lack of confrontation with her mother with the way she argues openly with her husband.

> TAMAR: *I don't like arguing at all, and in fact... I argue only with him [the spouse] because only with him do I feel comfortable... With my mother I don't feel comfortable (confronting her), I don't want to do her wrong... only with him am I not threatened... With him alone am I safe.*

Big Fight with Husband

Liora describes herself as always being "very nice" and "very quiet," and never says no – "at least not outwardly." The episode that she recalls in relation to her spouse is a big fight with him in which she felt he was not paying attention to her distress at that time. She was angry and shouted and yelled very loudly. She said things without thinking. She was trembling and weeping. The husband responded with great anger, but she says that he did so without bursting out or yelling like she did. "As if it doesn't touch him." He expressed himself rationally and this infuriated her and made matters worse. When the interviewer asked how this encounter ended, Liora replied, "I don't think it ended." She went on to say that she believed that it did not get resolved. It somehow receded or calmed down and was swept under the rug. "And then you move on."

Liora's narrative is an example of an unresolved conflict. She seems to remember it as an outstanding event because this time she did express her anger. The husband's response is experienced as cold and the conflict is not resolved.

Angry at the Wife

Barry describes a situation in which he had a very bitter argument with his wife about what he perceived as her parents' overinvolvement in their life. He was angry at her for engaging them in things in which he thought they were not supposed to be involved. He was annoyed that they "get under her skin and make decisions for her." It was completely unacceptable to him. He did not think it was right that she consulted her parents about everything and that she even shared with them things he felt were for them alone as a couple. The outcome of this argument was that his wife was furious and stormed out of the house. Barry waited a few hours and then called her at her parents' house, went there, and took her out to a restaurant to talk. His wife told him that he was too hard on her parents: They only wanted to help and he did not understand her.

He said that it was he who had made the move and gone to fetch her. On the one hand he indicated that he felt he had to compromise and that he could see also the positive side to her parents' help. On the other hand, he spoke about this conflict in a way that did not sound very emotional. Barry asserted that from the very moment his wife left the house in great anger he felt certain she would get over it. Apparently, he could not really deal with his wife's anger directly, and he described the whole situation by downplaying his emotional reaction (deactivating the attachment system). Instead, he focused on the outcome of this conflict: His wife came home and he learned to accept her parents' practical help. Although Barry presented this as a resolved conflict, one does not get the sense that the way he handled it led to greater closeness and mutual understanding in the couple's relationship. We do not know if Barry's wife is also a child of survivors, but if she is, this would perhaps be an example of marital implications through the parents' overinvolvement impinging on the children's lives.

Anger at a Friend

Difficulties in dealing with feelings of frustration and anger in some of the interviewees were expressed more directly regarding friends than family members. Difficulties in regulating feelings of aggression are apparent in the REs that Bill describes concerning a memorable interaction with a close friend who had also been his fellow worker for many years.

BILL: *This is an event that happened about 20 years ago with a friend that I had known through work for many years. We worked on a joint project and we had a deadline and worked until late every night. Suddenly, after he worked on it for a few days, he turned to me and said, "Listen, I don't understand what I am supposed to do here." At that moment I got up and I took all my stuff and I walked out. Only after about a week and a half did I go in again . . . I was terribly angry at him, some kind of abnormally intense anger.*

INTERVIEWER: How did your friend react?

BILL: *He was completely in shock . . . He was shocked, and I was also shocked by what I had done, but I had been extremely angry.*

INTERVIEWER: Did you expect a certain reaction from him, or weren't you thinking at that moment? (The interviewer is trying to see what Bill's intention was, or whether this was an impulsive reaction.)

BILL: *No, I wasn't thinking at that moment. I simply got furious at him and left.*

Bill explains that this kind of incident that involved extreme anger and walking away has happened to him on different occasions, mostly in connection with work issues. He reports that he and this particular friend have remained friends to this day. Some time after the event they laughed about it.

LACK OF EXPRESSION OF ANGER IN CONTRAST TO SPOUSE'S EXPRESSION OF ANGER TOWARD ONE'S PARENTS AND CHILDREN

Interestingly some interviewees contrasted their own lack of expression of anger to their spouse's ease of expression of anger, especially toward their own parents (the spouse's parents-in-law) or their children. In this respect, perceiving the spouse as more comfortable with feelings of anger was experienced as underscoring their own constriction of anger and its expression in the family.

Wife's Anger at Parents-in-Law

Some men described their wives as the ones who externalized the anger that they themselves did not seem to feel in reaction to their own parents. For example, Ron depicted his wife's anger toward his parents (her parents-in-law) in response to situations in which he did not express any anger to them. It sounded as if he was asking himself if he should feel angry at them too. He recounted a specific occasion when he was at home recuperating from an operation, and he recalls that he was in quite a lot of pain. He was already married with young children, but his mother showed no special concern as to how they were managing. His mother did not come to visit him to see how he was doing. He says he had not really paid any attention to his mother's behavior until his wife voiced her anger under those circumstances.

> RON: *My wife was angry with my mother. She said to me, "She doesn't care, she doesn't come to visit you, she didn't ask about you, or come to help prepare meals or help with the children."*

Ron explains that he was more disturbed by his wife's anger at his mother than by any complaints he had toward her. He said that he knew his mother cared; although after his wife told him how annoyed she was with his mother "*at least five times*" he began to harbor some doubts. Maybe his wife's anger was justified: Should he feel angry too? He was still struggling with this issue:

> RON: *You see it's not true she doesn't care, but it is a fact that she did not come to help; she did not come to see what is happening; she did not try to make it easier for my wife and children. I wasn't thinking about it so much with regard to myself.*

So it is not he who is angry with his mother. He also further stated – "in his mother's defense" – that they did not ask her directly for help; yet his wife apparently thought it was obvious that his mother should help, without being asked directly. Ron does not appear to possess the anger, and one wonders if his wife was voicing also his anger. Or was it perhaps more her own anger and Ron did not expect greater involvement on his mother's part in this situation?

Spouse's Anger toward the Couple's Child

Pearl's difficulties in expressing anger (see her previous relationship episode in relation to mother) were also apparent in her relationship with her adolescent daughter. When the daughter gets annoyed with her and tells Pearl to get out of her way or is rude to her, Pearl does not respond at all. She distances herself from her angry daughter: "*I don't want to get into fights with her. If I see that she's very irritable I leave her alone, and it passes.*"

In narrating the episode with her daughter, Pearl contrasts her reaction with the way her husband reacts to the daughter. Although she cannot deal with the daughter's anger and does not react in anger, she sees her husband (the daughter's father) as having no difficulty in reacting in anger and setting limits: "*She knows (the daughter) that he (her husband) is much more forceful with her, so she gets angrier.*" From this statement, it is unclear whether Pearl's daughter gets angrier with her or with her husband. From the episode it appears that Pearl appreciates this kind of division of parental roles, with her husband, unlike herself, being able to confront the daughter. It is, however, also consistent with her description of her *fear of her mother's anger.* Describing an episode with her spouse, she recalls a positive experience in which he was very relaxed on a family vacation with the children. *"He wasn't hard on them; I was harder and he was at ease."* The interviewer asked how she felt about his being relaxed and cheerful. She replied: *"I was happy that he could laugh with the children and not be as strict as he usually was with them at home, and it was pleasant to see it can be this way."*

Hence, in Pearl's stories the significant other is often described as angry in an extreme way (mother, daughter, and husband). She rarely responds in anger, but instead waits for it to pass and tries to avoid situations that may ignite the other's anger.

CLOSING COMMENTS

Previous studies have suggested that HSO did not externalize anger so as to protect their traumatized parents from further pain and hurt (Nadler et al., 1985). The categories that emerged from the narrative analysis enable a deeper understanding of these dynamics in relation to two related themes: parents' overprotective behaviors and the sons' and daughters' sensitivity about open expression of anger toward their parents.

As we have illustrated, the narratives that concerned anger toward the parents often centered on their overprotective behaviors. Such behaviors were perceived as stemming from a good, caring intention on the parents' part, in response to which the HSO appeared to feel obligated to them for their special care, even when it became a burden. Nevertheless, the parents' overprotection (e.g., feeding the son with a spoon until the age of 10, worrying about the daughter going on a trip, insisting that the daughter return home early from a party that had not even begun) appeared to lead to frustration, which in many cases was not expressed openly (e.g., not saying a word, being careful not to hurt the angry parent). Not expressing the frustration may have been due to the wish to protect the parents, to feelings of guilt about the parents having suffered enough, or to the realization that the parents had good intentions, and how can one be angry with people who have good intentions. The narratives on encounters in adulthood refer more directly to the burden of the parents' "worry culture." In addition, from the adult's retrospective standpoint, in relating these encounters that involved their parents' overprotection, which at time was fused with aggression and anger, the sons and daughters are focusing on their difficulties in regulating and negotiating feelings of anger openly.

The literature on the psychology of emotions suggests that in contrast to aggression, the experience and expression of anger can have positive interpersonal consequences (Izard, 1991). If the anger episode includes appropriate expression of anger, this may even provide an opportunity to strengthen the relationship between the angry person and the target of the anger. In the context of the dynamics of *mutual overprotection* and the difficulty in confronting the parents, the narratives portray the sensitivity of the sons and daughters to the experience and open expression of anger, especially in their interpersonal relations with their parents. There was little if any evidence that the expression of anger was seen as helpful by the HSO, perhaps because of their tendency to inhibit these overt responses.

7

Guilt, Shame, and Embarrassment

The narratives in this chapter focus on the echoes of trauma as reflected in the dynamics of interpersonal guilt in relation to the survivor parents and in the emotional experiences of shame and embarrassment. The literature groups social emotions into four broad interpersonal clusters: affectionate, self-conscious, melancholic, and hostile. It has been suggested that these four clusters are embedded within social contexts and help shape and define the nature of close relationships (Guerrero & Andersen, 2000). The "self-conscious" emotions of guilt, shame, embarrassment, and pride are deemed particularly social in nature because they tend to occur in interpersonal or public contexts. The first three emotions are discussed in this chapter; pride is considered in the chapter on positive emotions. Here we delineate certain narratives according to the predominant self-conscious emotion in them (guilt or shame and embarrassment), although some of the recounted experiences clearly involved more than one.

GUILT

In contrast to traditional theories that depict guilt as an intrapersonal phenomenon based on self-judgment, contemporary researchers on emotions (e.g., Baumeister, Stillwell, & Heatherton, 1995; Jones, Kugler, & Adams, 1995) view guilt as an interpersonal phenomenon found in close relationships. According to this view, people may indeed experience guilt when they are alone, but the actual source of this unpleasant emotion is primarily interpersonal worries and problems (Baumeister, Reis, & Delespal, 1995) or interpersonal situations and relationships (Tangney, 1992). Generally, people tend to feel guilty when they gain something in an inappropriate or erroneous manner, or when they cause damage, loss, distress, or disappointment to a significant other or fail to help such an individual (Vangelisti & Sprague, 1998). Guilt evinces at least two phenomena. First is the empathic distress experienced as a result of the suffering of a loved one or victim (Hoffman, 1982). Second, one experiences anticipatory separation or exclusion anxiety due to the possibility of loss or damage to the relationship as a result of the guilty transgression (Baumeister, Stillwell, & Heatherton, 1994; Bowlby, 1973). Guilt, therefore, also serves as an interpersonal protector by maintaining and strengthening relationships.

A special case relevant to the present study is the guilt felt by a person bearing no responsibility for any transgression. For example, children may take responsibility for aggression or hostility between their parents. Sexually abused children may feel guilty even though they are clearly not the transgressor but the victim (e.g., Lamb, 1986). In the case of Holocaust survivors, the phenomenon termed "survivor guilt" (Lifton, 1967) was described as feelings of guilt for outliving loved ones, even though the survivors themselves were also victims of the same atrocities (but somehow managed to survive). It has been suggested that children of survivors are prone to feelings of guilt on two accounts: The parents' guilt feelings may have been transmitted in some fashion to their children, and the children may feel guilt for their parents' suffering even though the children clearly lack any responsibility. Higher levels of guilt may go hand in hand with the inhibition of the expression of aggression and anger (Nadler, Kav-Venaki, & Gleitman, 1985), and greater difficulty in anger resolution (Solomon, 1998). In her review of the studies on North American offspring of Holocaust survivors, Felsen (1998) indicates that greater feelings of guilt are part of the characteristic picture of these offspring.

The quantitative picture that emerged from examining the associations between the ratings of the different Core Conflictual Relationship Theme (CCRT) components reflected in the relationship episodes (REs) revealed two major patterns with regard to guilt (Wiseman, Metzl, & Barber, 2006):

(1) Perceiving the parents as "vulnerable" [response of other (RO)] was associated significantly ($r = .27$, $p < .05$) with "feelings of guilt" [response of self (RS)].
(2) There was a positive association between the two RS categories of "avoiding conflict" with the parents and '"feelings of guilt " ($r = .27$, $p < .05$).

The in-depth qualitative analysis of the recalled relational encounters that involved feelings of guilt enabled us to shed more light on the experiences of interpersonal guilt in the narratives of these children.

Guilt over Causing the Parents Worry and Pain

Stories that described the parent as vulnerable and resulted in the narrator feeling guilty appeared to involve a dynamic in which the sons or daughters felt that they caused the parents undue worry and pain. This was usually described in reference to the events that elicited painful reactions from their parents, particularly when they realized that they did not anticipate the impact that pursuing their own wishes would have on their vulnerable parents. In these cases, as the following story shows, feeling guilty was often an outcome of not being sufficiently "vigilant" regarding the parents' anxieties and sensitivities.

Mom Thought, "The Child Has Been Murdered"... I Felt, "What Have I Done?"

One woman described a memorable event in her late adolescence when she borrowed her father's car for the night. After meeting some friends she decided to return the car and then continued on with her friends (in their car) for a late outing in the city without notifying her already sleeping parents. She describes the encounter with her parents after she returned home:

> NIRIT: *My friends dropped me off at home... the time was close to four in the morning... from the distance I see the lights on in the house... I go in. My mother is crying... she woke up and saw I hadn't come back yet... She saw the car in the parking lot and thought that something had happened. She started calling around to my friends' homes, saying "the child has been murdered," but none of them knew where I was. It was very painful. In retrospect I understood her.*
>
> INTERVIEWER: When you got home and she was crying, what was the interaction between you like, what happened, how did you respond?
>
> NIRIT: *There was a lot of anger, definitely lots of anger toward me and blaming me. They did not say: "Thank God you're back." I also felt shame toward my friends because my parents called and woke up everybody in the middle of the night. It wasn't pleasant. But on top of it all I felt – what have I done?! I knew that there was a lot, a lot of worry. My mother always worried. It was something that was internalized in me, that they live for us, for our sake. You always had to report where you were going and what you were doing. Even until this very day I feel obliged to report to them.*

The interviewer inquired further whether Nirit could remember how she responded, as well as how she felt in response to her mother's anger and blame.

> NIRIT: *I realized what I had done; there was tension; there was a lot of anger and accusations... I remember feeling troubled for a number of days until they (her parents) got over it. But there was this enormous burden... I felt I had worried them and that I had inflicted pain.*

Nirit continues by divulging other aspects of her response. She reports feeling "very sad and distressed" upon realizing how she had worried her parents by not telling them where she was, considering this was not the norm at their home. She describes a sense of "*suffocation and feeling that I am being embraced too tightly,*" especially during what she considers as the usual adolescent rebellion period. In spite of this, she still emphasizes her absolute understanding (in retrospect) of the undue pain her parents experienced as a result of her actions.

> NIRIT: *I understood. I understood. I think after that I never did those things again. Although somewhere I did want my independence, but I understood; I completely understood.*

In Nirit's story we identify the themes of the wish for independence and the parents' lack of ability to grant autonomy due to their anxieties. The recalled episode is about a time when Nirit's usual commitment "to report to the parents" and to assure her parents of her safety were not at the forefront of her mind. The "transparent child" (Chapter 4), who was painfully aware of his parents' extreme vulnerability, ran home as fast as he could to reassure his parents that he was not hurt in the disastrous Purim event in the city. In Nirit's story she chose, probably unlike other times, to go along with a spontaneous plan with her friends without thinking of a possible scenario that would cause her parents alarm. One might speculate that she did not inform her parents that she had parked the car back at home and was going off again with her friends because she did not want to wake them up, but perhaps also because she did not want to risk the possibility that they would forbid her to continue on with her friends so late at night. She did not anticipate that they would wake up to check that she was back and would become concerned on seeing the car parked outside and herself absent from the house. For them she was a missing child. Given her parents' tendency to assume the worst (the child was murdered), Nirit felt responsible – "*What have I done?!*"

Although Nirit felt ashamed that her parents' calls awoke her friends' parents, she also expressed an understanding that, given the worry she stirred up in them, they felt compelled to find out if "their child was alive" even though the timing of the calls was inappropriate. In her response to this event she emphasizes understanding her parents and having a guilt-driven resolve not to cause them future pain (*I think after that I never did those things again*). This kind of guilt seems tied to empathic distress (Hoffman, 1982) about the parents' suffering.

Guilt for Inadvertently Arousing the Parents' Trauma-specific Memories

The children often tried to comport themselves so as to prevent situations that could be hurtful to their parents. Such states are at times inevitable because situations that might potentially touch on parents' traumas cannot always be anticipated. This is particularly relevant when the parents' traumatic experiences are not openly talked about but are enveloped in a veil of silence.

She Did Not Tell Me Why the Noise Drives Her Crazy . . . I Insisted

Feelings of guilt are implicitly expressed in the story about the son who wanted his mother to buy him an electric hand drill (Chapter 3). As you may recall, Shaul's mother did not want to buy him an electric drill because "*the noise drives her crazy.*" He insisted: "*At the time I didn't notice it so much, I insisted . . . I usually got everything I wanted.*" To his surprise, so did she: "*I do not want a drill in the house; I do not want this noise in the house.*" Initially, his mother did not tell him *why the noise drove her crazy*. Only much later ("*about 2 years later*") did his mother explain to him, "*during the Holocaust, she did forced labor . . . Her job was to drill all day long in the tins. This noise, she said, I can NOT hear.*"

Upon telling his story, Shaul seems to feel guilty for insisting on having his own way and unknowingly arousing his mother's traumatic Holocaust memories. He describes to the interviewer the tension between his mother's refusal and his insistence as a child ("*But I . . . I want a drill, I need it for my working tools*"), which stemmed from his lack of understanding of the personal meaning of the noise of the drill in light of his mother's traumatic Holocaust experiences. As he states, "*I didn't consider it at the time . . . I only later understood; I didn't really pay attention at that time; I would have done it much more calmly, but as a kid . . .*"

In this story the son's guilt arose from his inattention to his mother's need to avoid cues associated with her traumatic past, seeming to suggest that he should have known the reason for mother's reaction (why the noise drives her crazy), without ever even being told.

The Army Official's Surprise Visit

Samuel's relational narrative provides another example of not guarding against parents' sensitivities, and being caught by surprise in a situation that triggered their traumatic past. He describes an episode that occurred when he was age 18 and was about to begin his mandatory military service. As part of the regular screening process before being drafted, he filled out some questionnaires in which he was asked to provide personal details about his parents. Soon after, an army official came to their home without any advance notice to interview the parents:

> SAMUEL: *The fact that suddenly soldiers in uniform came to the house – it aroused all kinds of associations and it frightened her. She went into a panic and hysteria . . . She burst out crying and started shouting.*

His mother's reaction elicited guilt in Samuel because he unknowingly put her in what turned out to be a stressful situation, "*as she always connects the army with killings and war.*" He regretted having provided direct and detailed information about his parents in the questionnaire and that this information had prompted the home visit. He felt that he should have thought of the possibility of soldiers coming to their home to inquire further. As in Shaul's case, Samuel's guilt stems from inadvertently activating his mother's traumatic memories.

In addition to feeling guilty for not foreseeing this chain of events, Samuel reveals to the interviewer that he felt shame and embarrassment over his mother's uncontrollable behavior: "*I wanted to bury myself, to vanish.*"

I Am Not Guilty for What Happened to Her, It Is Not My Fault

The experiences of guilt in the above narratives seem linked solely to specific situations in which the son or daughter felt responsible for the parent's distress in a specific situation. In the next narrative (*The Guilt Story*), however, the daughter expresses general feelings of guilt for her mother's suffering during the Holocaust. Sarah, a woman in her early forties, is married with three children. In her relational narrative she describes a recurrent situation in which her mother first criticizes her for not keeping her house nice and neat. Before she even has a chance to try to tidy up herself, her mother will begin cleaning the house. Sara's idiosyncratic response to this recurrent interaction with her mother is guilt:

> SARAH: *Everything I do I feel some kind of feeling of guilt toward my mother. Maybe I didn't do enough for her; maybe I hurt her. I try to overcome it, because I cannot live all the time with this kind of feeling, of guilt. I am not guilty for what happened to her; it is not my fault. It took me really a lot of time to get free of it; I am not sure that I am free of it totally, that is the truth.*

Here Sarah conveys her struggle with ongoing feelings of guilt. Although trying to free herself from its grip, she also recognizes the guilt's power over her. Her many attempts to convince herself that it was not her "fault" suggest that she is still not fully free of her guilt but does rationally realize that she is not to blame. Her experience is "split."

Sarah finds her mother's behavior confusing. She demands that Sarah tidy things up but then does the work herself. In trying to make sense of her experience, Sarah connects her mother's behavior to one of the few stories that her mother told her about her experiences during the Holocaust:

> SARAH: *It turned out that she once got from the Germans, she got an additional portion of food near her bed, there in the* [concentration] *camp; she found another... she found some kind – I don't know, some sort of a piece of cloth and put it on some piece of wood – there they had some box instead of a table, and she put it like a tablecloth and she also found a flower and put it there... And for this she got from the Germans a reward, another portion of food. Maybe, I always thought to myself, maybe this imprinted on her that this issue of being organized and clean is so very important for her.*

The unique quality of guilt among the sons and daughters appears to go hand in hand with the knowing–not knowing pattern of intergenerational communication (Chapter 5). In Sarah's relational narrative the "knowing–not knowing" about her mother's experiences in the concentration camp is depicted by the rare fragment from the mother's Holocaust story. The "piece of cloth" may be viewed as a piece of information that covers the mother's traumatic past. Sarah's story, as is often the case with trauma, is expressed rather incoherently and contains elements that appear removed from the harsh reality of the concentration camp (a flower, a reward). Her mother's rare discussion of her traumatic experiences, with much remaining "undiscussable" (Bar-On, 1999), left room for Sarah to fantasize about her mother's experiences and the mark they left. The parents' unknown past and the resulting fantasies contribute to feelings of guilt in the child who bears no responsibility for the atrocity.

SHAME AND EMBARRASSMENT

Shame is a negative emotion that arises when individuals perceive themselves as inferior to others, as having committed relational transgressions or omissions, or as having lost face (Andersen & Guerrero, 1998; Ferguson & Stegge, 1995). In shame the focus is on the opinions of others in reference to the self. This is accompanied by a sense of being exposed and observed. Although shame can induce interpersonal aggression, people who feel shame usually try to hide themselves and avoid communicating with others. This avoidance exists because actively communicating might illuminate the pain, which is generally convoluted in feelings of shame. Such behavior disrupts the preservation of interpersonal connection (Tangey, 1995). Research on shame has shown that the presence of others exacerbates the negative feelings that the person experiences, leading to avoidance behaviors such as face hiding, gaze aversion, burying the face in one's hands, body slouching, head lowering, and fleeing from social contact (reviewed in Andersen & Guerrero, 1998). Despite the wish to avoid social contact, most people who feel shame share their feelings with important others in an interpersonal meeting that follows the shameful experience (Rime', Mesquita, Philippot, & Boca, 1991).

Embarrassment is defined as a form of social anxiety that occurs when unwanted attention is focused on a person. The unwanted attention can stem from presenting oneself unfavorably before others such as peers or strangers (Bradford & Petronio, 1998) or from receiving excessive praise (Miller & Leary, 1992). Like guilt, embarrassment is related to specific interpersonal events, and like shame there is a strong focus on being observed by others. Shame is, however, a more global and enduring emotional state than embarrassment, which is typically more specific and fleeting.

From our analysis of the narratives it appeared that our interviewees seemed to refer to shame more often than to embarrassment. The phrases "shame," "I felt ashamed," or "he/she caused me shame" are perhaps more commonly used in colloquial conversation (at least in Hebrew). "Embarrassment" or "I felt embarrassed" may simply be utilized less frequently. The narrators also generally used shame and embarrassment interchangeably. Therefore, we consider shame and embarrassment together in these narratives.

Losing Face in Light of Parents' Overprotective or Intrusive Behaviors

In our attempt to understand the dynamics of anger among the children of survivors we earlier described their mixed feelings about their parents' overprotective behaviors. This pattern of parental overbearing care was also described as leading to feelings of shame, especially when the parent's behavior was evident in the presence of others.

The first two narratives exemplify interactions revolving around the mother's attitudes and behaviors concerning food.

Come Eat Your Banana

Avi relates what he defines as a recurrent episode from his childhood. He recalls his mother running after him in the streets shouting, "*Come eat your banana.*" He remembers the neighbors peeping out at them: "*It didn't make me laugh . . . All the children were playing 'catch' and my mother is running after me . . . The children were playing 'hide and seek' and she hides behind me and feeds me the banana . . . I felt they started laughing at me.*"

Avi's mother's behavior appears embarrassing because he was observed by others in the street, presenting them both in an unfavorable light.

Why Is He Leaving Food on His Plate?

Doron recounts an episode from his childhood that showcased his mother's behavior about food as she served him and a friend.

> DORON: *At elementary school, I remember I had a friend and we used to spend a lot of time in each other's home. One time during a meal,*

it was supper and he left some food on his plate. My mother sort of attacked him. I remember I felt very uncomfortable. She turned to me and asked me, "Why is he leaving food on the plate?" She didn't communicate directly with him (the friend), but instead she asked me: "Tell me, why he is leaving food on his plate, why doesn't he finish eating?"

INTERVIEWER: Did she ask this aloud?

DORON: *Yes, out loud and he also heard it and I felt uncomfortable.*

INTERVIEWER: What did you feel?

DORON: *I felt embarrassed for my friend . . . I thought it was insulting to the friend. But I think he understood. Not that he said anything, but I think he understood.*

INTERVIEWER: Do you remember if you said anything about it to her at the time or later?

DORON: *No. By the way, she did not mention the Holocaust. On the contrary, she tried to repress it, these things.*

Doron perceives his mother's questions about the leftover food as insulting to his friend. His mother does not address the friend directly and finds fault in his friend's eating behavior. Consequently, Doron feels embarrassed in front of his friend. He may also feel embarrassed about mother's rigid rule that one must finish all the food on one's plate. Another possibility is that he felt shame over having his mother cause his friend embarrassment.

Doron's conclusion of his narrative suggests that he believes his mother's awkward behavior was related to her experiences during the Holocaust. He further indicates in the interview that his mother's traumatic experiences at Auschwitz caused her to react so violently to the idea of wasting or throwing away food. Although it was his friend's behavior that upset his mother, she turns to Doron as if he were responsible for his friend's not eating everything and forcing her to throw food away. Interestingly, Doron does not disclose his embarrassment to his friend or mother. Although he feels that his friend understood without words, he senses he cannot express his feelings to his mother for fear of touching on the Holocaust experiences he thinks his mother is trying to repress.

Haim Maor, an Israeli artist and a child of Holocaust survivors, showed a work of art entitled "*Forbidden words*" in his 1994 exhibition called "The forbidden library." The first word listed is "FOOD." Other words common to both Maor's list of forbidden words and Doron's narrative are: "MOTHER," "SURVIVE," "CAMP," "SILENCE," "MEMORIES," "FORGET" (Maor, 1994).

I Did Not Like Being Different . . . It Is a Lousy Feeling of Shame

Not appearing different from other children is typical of adolescents' need to belong to their peer group. Survivors' children are especially sensitive to situations in which their parents' behavior deviates from expected norms. This was commonly evident in the stories like the aforementioned involving food, as well as in those about the parents' difficulties accepting their children overnight trips away from home. In Chapter 3 we presented narratives describing the parent's difficulty in granting autonomy and the interviewees' frustration over the wish for autonomy. These situations also elicited an array of responses including avoidance of confrontation (Chapter 4) and anger (Chapter 6). Furthermore, there was in some cases a sense of shame and/or embarrassment in consequence of the parents' overprotective behaviors in front of the peer group.

In recounting how his parents did not allow him to go on overnight trips as an adolescent, the interviewee reported frustration with the situation but also the feeling that he did not want his peers to know that his mother forbade him to go. "*My mother absolutely did not agree that I sleep away from home for a few days. Often I would have to make up excuses to my peers about why I wasn't going on these trips because I was ashamed of it. Everyone would go on these trips and I'd have to make up a story.*"

In another case the father allowed the daughter to sleep away from home but only if he acted as chaperone. This caused her great embarrassment. Reminiscing over her first time camping out with her scout troop, Sharon described how, much to her dismay, her father insisted on joining her as an accompanying parent. She remembers that her father got very angry with the camp leaders and berated them for what he perceived as their lack of organization. This made her very uncomfortable because at the time she saw the leaders "as God" and looked up to them. He also clashed with them because it was raining and he would not let her sleep in a tent like everybody else. Instead, he insisted that she sleep in his car. She expresses her feelings of shame.

> SHARON: *I was ashamed of it . . . very unpleasant all of this. I wanted to bury myself. I didn't like being different. I didn't like the overprotectiveness . . . it's a lousy feeling of shame.*

In sum, the sons and daughters often feel the need to hide on account of their parents' display of intense worries about food and general health hazards. The extent to which these worries are characteristic of parents in the population as a whole is quite difficult to determine from our data. Our impression is that they are more commonly found among our interviewees.

Another type of "shame narrative" refers to a specific or outstanding event in which the child is suddenly faced with a parent's specific trauma-related sensitivity.

Unwanted Attention in the Context of Parents' Panic

The guilt-eliciting situations described previously in which the child is suddenly faced with a fragment of the parent's traumatic past (e.g., the noise of the electric drill or the fear of people in army uniform) also appeared in a situation that triggered the child's embarrassment. The story that Gidon told involved his mother's extreme reaction to a dog that they encountered while riding in an elevator.

You Do Not Expect Your Parent to Embarrass You

> GIDON: My *mother and I got into an elevator and then some dog came in and she reacted with total panic. She immediately jumped out of*

> *the elevator and made some strange sounds. I had never seen her like that. She then told me the story about the time she was 5 years old, when they crossed the border and dogs were chasing them. Since then, she has had this trauma about dogs.*

When asked how he felt in this situation, Gidon responds that he felt embarrassed.

> GIDON: *There were people there, and I didn't understand why she got so scared because of a dog. The dog didn't even look threatening. You don't expect your parent to embarrass you . . . all of a sudden she jumps and shouts.*

Experiencing surprise at a parent's reaction is similar to the guilt-provoking situations described earlier in which the child is suddenly faced with a fragment of the parent's traumatic past (i.e., the noise of the electric drill, or the fear of people in army uniform). Facing these reactions in the presence of an audience, be it familiar people (neighbors and peers) or complete strangers, strengthens the feeling of shame. Gidon's reaction to the unwanted attention he felt his mother caused by her panicky reaction to the dog in public is probably more fleeting than the reaction described in the narratives that involved the presence of peers. Hence, it can probably be considered more akin to feelings of embarrassment than shame.

Going back to the list of Haim Maor's forbidden words, we find the word "DANGER" followed by the word "DOGS." These are played out as part of the drama in Gidon's story.

In general, when considering the idea of "forbidden words" we found that the depicted experiences of guilt and shame and embarrassment often involved encounters with parents that echoed these seemingly innocent or neutral words (e.g., food, dog). They carried diverse personal meanings when viewed within the context of parents' personal memories of threats to their own and others' lives.

8

Anxiety and Helplessness

The themes of anxiety and helplessness in the relational narratives of children of survivors manifest themselves not only through the parents' actual or perceived responses to situations [Responses of Others (RO)] but also through the narrators' own reactions [Responses of Self (RS)]. We have already described the children's perceptions of the parents' vulnerability and suffering that led to the sons' and daughters' need to protect their parents as part of the central relational dynamics of mutual overprotection (Chapter 4). In this chapter, we focus on the narratives that we identify as exemplifying how the parents' anxiety and/or feelings of helplessness are etched in the narrators' emotional memories of their parents and of themselves.

ANXIETY/FEAR

Fear is considered to be a primary emotional experience that is innate and evolutionarily adaptive. Experiencing fear (or any emotion, for that matter) is an extremely complicated process consisting of perception, neurobiological responses, expressive behaviors, and cognitive appraisals. Although most people experience fear relatively infrequently, it is thought to be the emotion that many people dread the most (Izard, 1991). The felt or perceived threat to the individual's security or safety motivates efforts to alleviate the threat and escape from harm. An intense experience of fear is usually vividly remembered for a long time, including the scene associated with the fear experience (Izard, 1991). Furthermore, some theorists believe that emotional structures are stored at a broadly contextual level and that activation of emotional responses is most likely to occur when one is presented with the feared object, the appropriate context, and primed meanings (e.g., see Barlow, 2004).

Fear is manifested immediately in uncontrollable facial expressions and verbal utterances (Andersen & Guerrero, 1998). Most of the time, feelings of fear are shared with friends, partners, and acquaintances through discussions of the specifics of the fear and the description of the frightening stimulus. Fear is expressed automatically, but its expression might negatively impact a person's image in particular interpersonal contexts because revealing fear might be considered by some to be indicative of weakness, cowardice, or incapability. Therefore, people try to control fear and avoid fear-eliciting situations, and yet they may find it difficult to conceal their fear. The expression of fear, despite the attempts to hide it, shows how important it is as an interpersonal phenomenon (Andersen & Guerrero, 1998).

In studies that rely on self-reports, fear is typically measured by having respondents rate the degree to which they feel frightened, tense, nervous, anxious, uncomfortable, and nauseated in response to particular objects or situations. Physiological manifestations of fear, such as elevated heart rates and respirations, tension in the muscles, trembling, cortical arousal, and greater skin conductance are associated with the respondents' self-reports of fear. Although physiological arousal assessment may fluctuate substantially, it has been suggested that self-reports of fear represent the overall emotional state (Mewborn & Rogers, 1979; Witte, 1998). Thus, we will refer to the narrator's self-accounts of recalled events that have aroused fear and anxiety.

According to Izard (1991), anxiety needs to be defined as distinct from fear. He indicates that it is a combination or pattern of emotions that includes fear as the key emotion but it also includes other emotions, such as sadness, shame, and guilt. Anxiety is also always anticipatory, as it involves future events and possible future events (Borkovec, Robinson, Pruzinsky, & DePree, 1983). It has also been more broadly defined as man's fundamental ontological state (e.g., May, 1983), and the experience one has when confronting the possibility of nonbeing (death and any form of loss or fundamental change). Thus, anxiety is self-reflective and potentially interpersonal and relational in nature.

From interpersonal and attachment theory perspectives, anxiety over relationships often reflects concern about abandonment and the reciprocation of love, which is characteristic of anxious-ambivalent attachment (Feeny & Noller, 1996; Shaver & Mikulincer, 2002). According to Bowlby (1973), major events that lead to insecure attachment and proneness to fear are threats of being abandoned and the possibility of losing a parent. The presence of a trusted caregiver that is both accessible and responsive is a strong deterrent to fear (Izard, 1991).

Focusing on anxiety experiences of children of survivors, we find both the possibility of direct and indirect transmission (Felsen, 1998; Schwartz, Dohrenwend, & Levav, 1994) of anxiety to be relevant. Certainly, there are precedents in the trauma literature for such transmissions, and therapists themselves are not immune from hearing their patients' traumatic experiences (e.g., McCann & Pearlman, 1990). In the case of our sample, both direct and specific transmissions of anxiety are allegedly caused by the parents' anxiety reactions that comprise part of the "survivor syndrome" (Niederland, 1968). The indirect and perhaps more general transmission of anxiety is attributed to the strong feeling of impending disaster that characterizes some families of survivors which, in turn, contributes to a more intense level of free-floating anxiety (Nadler, Kav-Venaki, & Gleitman, 1985). In the relational narratives we describe, however, the experiences of anxiety that we identified appeared to be most striking in those cases when sons and daughters appeared especially vulnerable to the parents' spoken and unspoken messages of anxiety and impending catastrophe. In the broader clinical literature this sense of impending disaster has been described as follows: "The world is a potentially dangerous place, I might not be able to cope with whatever comes down the road, therefore I need to anticipate all possible dangers in order to avoid catastrophes" (Borkovec & Sharpless, 2004; p. 212).

Parent–Child Shared States of Anxiety

From a young age, children are sensitive to their parents' nonverbal and verbal emotional states. In parent–child interaction, through state-sharing (Stern, 1983), the child shares the parents' positive reactions and emotions, such as pleasure and contentedness, or negative ones, such as irritation and anxiety. In the narratives that depicted states of anxiety, the explicit or implicit signals of the parents' anxiety are picked up by the child, leading to his or her own state of anxiety.

Fear of Abandonment: "These Worries She Passed on to Me"

When he was young, Giora recalls how he and his mother would wait every night for his father to come home from work: "*I remember waiting . . . sometimes a long wait . . . me and my mother used to sit at the window, in the dark, waiting for father to come back home.*" He speaks about the concerns involved in this kind of lengthy anticipation: "*There were always worries . . . maybe something happened. Why didn't he arrive?*" His mother *would never talk* about her concerns, but he could tell how worried she was because of her gestures and "*the white color of her face.*" He adds: "*These worries she passed to me.*"

This story draws a picture of the state-sharing anxiety of Giora and his mother, sitting in the dark every evening as part of his routine life as a child. We speculate that perhaps due to mother's traumatic memories of loved ones that abruptly were torn away, not returning home, and never to be seen again, she is anxious to see Giora's father return home safely. His mother's sense of impending doom and feeling of anxiety sinks in and merges with his own anxiety. His mother does not share her fears verbally and openly with him, perhaps because she does not want him to worry. Giora nevertheless picks up her implicit fears (via her gestures and pale face) and is sensitive to her unspoken messages. He experiences these in all of their intensity. It remains possible that the mother being a chronic worrier is a personality feature that is not attributed solely to her Holocaust past (Brown, Barlow, & Liebowitzs, 1994).

The long-term effects of the survivors' traumatic separations were manifested in their ways of dealing with the brief separations that are a routine part of daily life. In the movie *Because of That War* (Ben-Dor, 1988), this ongoing fear is described vividly by the father, who is a survivor of Auschwitz:

> Every day when I came home from work, I would go to search for my children, really every time . . . I would go look for one, then go look for Yehuda . . . he would be playing in the school yard with the kids . . . he would call out: "Dad, I am here." Because he knew that I was searching for him. The other son – I would go looking . . . because, I felt like the way my first family vanished suddenly, and I was left with no one, I would always live with the thought that it can happen.

Later in the movie, the father's rigid routine is echoed in the account of the son himself. He tells the scriptwriter that every day when he was playing outdoors, he would pay attention to when his father came back from work because he knew his father was checking to find his children. He would preemptively call out loud to him: "Dad, I am here."

Shared Panic of Mother and Daughter: "We Were Like Two Shaking Fish"

The sense that the parents' anxiety was handed down to the child is expressed in Ronit's narrative. The story she tells is about a memorable interaction with her mother in adulthood, when Ronit is already herself a wife and a mother. She begins the narrative by describing her respect for her mother. She states that her mother is "a very special woman, very emotional, very, very smart." Then Ronit continues to express what she feels her mother passed down to her and indicates to the interviewer that this may be related to what we are studying.

RONIT: *You see, she passed on to me the good things and the things that are less good. This I think may be actually related to your research. It is the issue of the nervousness, the panic . . . all these things that I got from her big time.*

After this general introduction of her perception of her mother and herself in relation to her mother, Ronit now turns to relate a specific relationship episode (RE) with her mother that demonstrates her identification with her mother's anxiety and the similarity in the way in which they reacted with panic to a frightening noise.

RONIT: *I was at my mother's house on Saturday afternoon when we suddenly heard a very serious sound of an explosion. You know, it was during that period [in Israel] when buses exploded due terrorist attacks. You see the thing is that we all heard the noise (her husband and children who were all visiting at her mother's house). Now what happened to me and to my mother did not happen to any of the others that were there and heard the same noise. I picked up my little one (her own daughter), and I and my mother started screaming and running together in the same direction, without even looking . . . Everyone else continued to talk as if nothing happened, my husband and the other children stayed where they were on the porch . . . It turned out that it was only the sun powered water heater on the roof of the next-door neighbor, which exploded and caused this noise.*

It should be noted that such exaggerated startle responses are common in people who have experienced trauma (American Psychiatric Association, 1994). Ronit continues to depict the contrast between the others' indifference to the noise of explosion and the way she and her mother were alarmed by the noise and their dramatic reactions.

RONIT: *It was only me and my mother that continued to run with my little girl . . . even though we saw that it was nothing, we both reacted*

> *this way, and afterwards for another 10 minutes the two of us were still shaking like two fish. You should have seen the others, no one came out, no one even looked to see what happened, but the two of us were like two shaking fish, with my little girl half naked on my arms and we were really ready to escape, I don't know where to. I think my eyes came out of their place . . . my husband said that I am abnormal, it is the first time that he said that to me. He is very different, he is optimistic, much calmer, and I don't know what I would have done without him. I don't know how I myself looked then and there, but I saw her (mother) and I'm sure that I did not look much better than her.*

In this recounted relational narrative, Ronit not only identifies with her mother, but she also indicates to the interviewer that she views her own anxiety and panic as a direct transmission of her mother's experiences: "*I think it is very strong in me and I think I really got it from her.*" It is intriguing that she describes their anxious reaction by using an idiosyncratic image of "*two shaking fish.*" Perhaps, like fish out of water, they feel unable to properly breathe, or this may represent their unspoken fears, like the silence of fish.

Trying to get a more differentiated view of Ronit's perception of her mother's actual or anticipated behavior or reactions (the RO), the interviewer asks Ronit to speak specifically about her perception of her mother. She replies by referring to her mother's Holocaust background and its intergenerational effects.

> RONIT: *I always yield to her, because I always say – she came from there; it is not her fault . . . and she had problems with being able to give birth . . . we are only two children. She had difficulty getting pregnant and then keeping the fetus because she was too weak after being malnourished for years . . . during the pregnancy she had to stay in bed for 9 months. So with regard to my mother I know she went through a lot, so I say she is allowed. But why did I get to be this way? This is what I ask myself . . . that she is this way is obvious, but why am I like that? It hurts me because it is something that passes on. It hurts me very much to see that my children are like that*

> *already... when you will conduct a study on the third generation you will also find that it passes on, or at least in our family. I have children that are like my husband (anxiety-free), but I see that my 10-year-old daughter that she will be like me, and it hurts me to see that. As much as I try to help her, I cannot. In this area, I am not a good role model for her.*

Ronit makes the direct connection between her mother's traumatic experiences to her own oversensitivity and general anxiety. She also insinuates that she is continuing this pattern by transmitting anxiety to the third generation, perhaps only partially (as she sees the effects in only one of her daughters). She attributes the lack of effects on the other children to her husband's more secure attitude and behavior. Ronit is puzzled why she reacts like her mother who "came from there," even though she was born after the war in Israel. The use of the term "*came from there*" reminds us of Momik the child in David Grossman's story, whose parents came from *Over There* (see Chapter 5 on communication). It is interesting that in another relationship episode, Ronit mentions that her mother talked very openly with her, with one exception – the Holocaust. She indicates in this respect that she knows almost nothing about her mother's experiences, such as how long she was in the concentration camp, or even the year she came to Israel. "*When we were children all we knew was that she went through the Holocaust and therefore you need to strengthen your belief (in God), but we never knew any details.*"

The pattern of Holocaust-related communication that we called "knowing–not knowing" appears to characterize Ronit's intergenerational communication about her mother's traumatic past (see Chapter 5). Her report is consistent with our finding that children of survivors who were characterized by the knowing–not knowing pattern are also the ones reporting higher interpersonal anxiety when compared with their counterparts who either experienced informative verbal communication or who had no Holocaust background (Wiseman, Barber, Raz, Yam, Foltz, & Livne-Snir, 2002).

They Had Marks of the Holocaust . . . All Kinds of Fears

The fears of her surviving parents are perceived by Irit as part of what she calls "*the marks of the Holocaust*" that were evident on her parents. She first talks about her father who died 3 years before the time of the interview. Her father died at the age of 72 from complications during a heart bypass operation. Irit shows the interviewer a picture of her father and tells him that her father was "*not at all old in spirit,*" and he even looked younger than his age. She qualifies this by saying that all his life, "*you could see on him the marks of Holocaust.*" She continues to portray both of her survivor parents in contrast to herself, as she was born into a different reality remote from their traumatic experiences.

> IRIT: *All his life, my father, and also my mother, it is as if they stayed in the remains, they had these marks that we the Sabras [Israeli-born] did not have. They had all kinds of fears and worries. They always had a cupboard in the house with tons of food in it, that God forbid there will not be enough. Maybe there will be a depression-like era, or people will walk hungry in the country, who knows when that can happen; therefore, one should ensure that there is food in the house. They always used to tell me that I should have 1 kg. sugar and I should have a few jars of coffee, and they always buy me more and more, because the house has to be full, so that there should not be shortage. Potatoes, even though now they are the only two people in the house, she always buys much more than is needed so that there should be enough food, just in case . . . If she comes over to my house and sees I have only five potatoes, she starts screaming, "Why do you have so few?" These are remains (residues) of the Holocaust; I think it is a consequence of the shortage they had then.*

Irit sees her parents as living anxiously in their traumatic past, especially with regard to their fears around shortage of food, which seem to her like "remains" (leftovers) from the extreme shortage of food they suffered. Her choice of the word "remains," is interesting, as it also means those who remained/survived, and it also means "ruins." Her image of her parents is of living anxiously in the aftermath of the massive losses they endured, and not able to really live in the present. Taking a metaphor from archeology, we can speculate that these "ruins" are a testimony to the struggle to survive in a different place and time.

The More That Is Hidden from the Child, the Greater the Anxiety

Despite the clear distinction that Irit makes regarding her lack of concern over shortage of food (being a Sabra) and her parents' fears and worries, in another narrative she talks about her sharing her parents' fears facing their health problems. Although one may consider that concerns about her parents' health problems are natural, the lack of open communication about health issues exacerbates her anxieties rather than relieving her of them.

IRIT: *My mother never wanted us to get worried, not before and not after (a medical operation), she would always hide her pain. She never talked about what was bothering her; she was very introverted. She did not want us to worry about her.*

INTERVIEWER: How did you feel about mother not letting you worry?

IRIT: *I actually think it is NOT so good. After I married I lived far from my parents and every time she had some health problem or my father was hospitalized they would hide it from me. Would not tell or inform me about it. But the more is hidden the greater the worry. The hidden (or concealed) is greater than the manifest. Every time I used to call home and they would not answer the telephone, I would begin to worry: "Where are they? Why are they not home? What happened?" I would start anxiously calling around relatives. Maybe they know where they are . . . and I would start calling and looking for them in hospitals. It is not right to conceal. To this very day, many times she does not want to tell me the truth. But today, I know already how to pull out more from her.*

The combination of the parents wanting to protect their child, in this case the parents hiding health concerns, and the child's commitment to the parents as well as the attempt to deal with the unspoken anxiety of the parents, appear to set a unique context for these sensitivities.

Parents' Anxiety as a Burden: I Did Not Have the Strength While I Was Giving Birth

The close involvement of the parents with their children in adulthood often revolved around reassuring the parents' anxieties. This often meant that the parents continued to expect an ongoing knowledge of the son's or daughter's whereabouts. The parents' desire to take part in the adult child's life was especially experienced as an extra burden under circumstances in which the children themselves had to deal with natural stressful life events.

Miriam's narrative of a more current relationship episode with her mother focused on the day she gave birth to her third child. She says she remembers this episode from 5 years ago very clearly and that every time she remembers it she laughs. In the morning when the water broke, she dropped off her children at the kindergarten and school and drove to the hospital with her husband. She did not let her mother know that she was going to the hospital. Her mother had the habit of calling her every morning; she always called her to say, "Good morning, what's doing and how are things?" That morning, however, Miriam was already on her way to the hospital when her mother called anxiously again and again, with no answer. Miriam continues to relate mother's attempts to find out what is happening, making it clear that she did not want her mother to know that she went to the hospital to deliver the baby.

> MIRIAM: *Around 1:00 in the afternoon, the children were returned home and I was still in the hospital and I announced to my older one very clearly that grandmother is not allowed to know where mother is because she was so sensitive and took everything to heart. When my mother called at 1:00 and was told that I went shopping, so okay, she*

accepted it. But when she called again at 2:00 and was told that I had not yet returned from shopping, she said it cannot be and that I went to give birth in the hospital. They told her no way. But she got dressed [laughs], she wanted to be in the delivery room, and she came over to me. When I saw her I looked at her and I was shocked. Here I am in the delivery room and my mother is by my side [laughs].

INTERVIEWER: Can you tell me about the interaction between you and her when she arrived at the delivery room?

MIRIAM: *The first thing she said (in Yiddish) was "Why didn't you tell me?" and I answered, "For what do you need to know? In order to worry? Isn't it easier that I call and say everything is fine and it is already after the delivery is over?" She said, "But you know that I worry! You should have told me!" You see I cannot say she was angry. She was standing near by my side and her anxiety and concern were above and beyond.*

The interviewer then turns to ask Miriam how she felt when her mother arrived (focusing on RS). Miriam answers that it bothered her and then attempts to explain her reasoning.

MIRIAM: *It bothered me because I was afraid that SHE would be stressed. She is a very sensitive woman, very sick all these years. I was afraid that she would take it to heart. I wanted to be sure that nothing should happen to her from the tension that we were naturally in during the process of giving birth to the baby. On purpose, I did NOT want her to know that I am in the hospital, because I know she is a real worrier. I didn't have the strength while giving birth to also need to worry about her. I wanted someone that I knew could attend to me, not to have to take care of her, to help her with her anxiety and to calm her down from her worry.*

The burden on the children of the parents' anxieties and worries was also described with regard to the pattern of mutual overprotection (Chapter 4). In this context, we see the extra burden involved in this dynamic when the sons or daughters were under stress themselves. While under stress or experiencing anxiety, such as during the natural stress of giving birth, they did not feel that they could carry the additional burden of their parents' stress because they felt it was up to them at all times to attend to their parents and take care of them; however, what we see is that different individuals reacted differently to the parents' anxiety. One became very anxious (Ronit) and another less so (Miriam). In most cases, we see a dedicated attempt to be considerate of the parents, perhaps out of guilt (see Chapter 7).

HELPLESSNESS

When we examined narratives describing extreme feelings of fear intertwined with anxiety, we found that the narrators were also experiencing helplessness. Helplessness is not only characteristic of depressive states but also found in relation to anxiety, loneliness, health problems, and even death (Peterson & Bossio, 1989). Helplessness includes cognitive, emotional, and motivational components, which are created from a lack of contingency between the organism's actions and their outcomes. When exposed to an uncontrollable situation, the organism learns that the actions do not impact the trauma, and therefore generalizes this helplessness to other situations (Seligman, 1975).

Mikulincer and Caspy (1986) identified a number of categories that characterize situations of helplessness, including events with aversive consequences (such as sickness, death of a beloved person, and failures in exams and in interpersonal relationships), events with uncontrollable consequences, and events with negative consequences that could not be anticipated in advance. Emotionally, helplessness includes several primary emotions, such that the person feeling helpless may experience emotions of guilt and anger directed to the self (when one feels responsible for the outcomes) or anger addressed to an external object, which is more likely when someone or something else is perceived as responsible for the helplessness (Mikulincer, 1994).

Research has documented a relationship between a history of traumatic events and helplessness (Gibb, 2002) and between the severity of posttraumatic stress disorder (PTSD) and feelings of helplessness (e.g., Casella & Motta, 1990; Reynolds & Brewin, 1999; McKeever, McWhirter, & Huff, 2006). Accordingly, in treating trauma victims, it has been suggested that the process of working through the reality of past helplessness is important to minimize its force in driving current behavior (Roth & Newman, 1992).

In considering helplessness experiences in children of survivors, it can be speculated that the fear of facing uncontrollable life-threatening circumstances, like those that their parents faced, may appear in the narratives that included extreme fear. In addition, the impossible task of saving their parents, who suffered immensely before their births, may lead them to adopt life missions such as "never again" allowing themselves to risk helplessness. Upon further examination of the narratives that were characterized by the theme of helplessness, one can also see the narrator expresses a strong degree of death anxiety that involves feelings of despair, sadness, and passivity.

Death Anxiety and Helplessness

Few events can elicit feelings of helplessness more than the inevitability of one's mortality. The subject has preoccupied philosophers for millennia (e.g., Malpas & Solomon, 1998). Thus, given the intensity of experiences in both the parents and some of the children of survivors, it is not unexpected that death anxiety plays a prominent role.

Similar to Ronit, who viewed herself as overanxious and tending to react with panic, Rina described herself as an overly anxious person who finds it difficult to regulate her anxiety. Rina, who like Ronit also contrasted herself with her husband, expressed death anxiety in the two recalled interactions concerning memorable interpersonal events that involved her husband and herself. In the first narrative, she relates a traumatic memory of a near-death situation while swimming in the sea with her husband.

The Whirlpool Story

Rina explains that the event occurred when she her husband went to the beach about 2 weeks after their wedding. The two of them went into the water to swim and, even though it was not at all far from the shore and the water was very shallow, they were suddenly sucked into a whirlpool. She recounts her thoughts at the moment of the whirlpool and tells what happened next.

> RINA: *What do you do in such a situation? What? What, I ask you (refers to the interviewer), what do you do? That is it; we are finished. I am going to die together with him. We are finished; we are going to die.*
>
> INTERVIEWER: and what happened, how . . . ?
>
> RINA: *I lost my senses; I was terribly stressed. I really got into a panic; I became hysterical and he dived and pulled me out, and simply threw me to the shore. After that he came out, as if nothing happened. We were worn out; it was so frightening, really frightening.*

After the interviewer asks what Rina and her husband said to each other after the incident, she recalls that she expressed her disbelief that a whirlpool can occur so close to the shore (in such shallow water). Then he explained to her that the worst way to react is to become hysterical and that is the reason people drown. What is important is not to panic, and what you need to do is to dive and come out on the other side. You need to go with the flow and slowly, slowly come out of it. When the interviewer asked how she felt after her husband's explanation, she replied:

> RINA: *I was in total hysteria. His explanation seems very logically easy, but it is difficult to apply it. You see he proved that it could be done because he did it, but me. . . .*
>
> INTERVIEWER: How did you feel with him proving that it is possible?
>
> RINA: *That I can rely on him that in fire and water he is with me. I think that this is the best example that I can really depend on him. But you see, I was unable to do it because I panicked; I just did not know what to do with myself!*

We can see that in response to the interviewer's focus on the husband's competent (or life-saving) reaction, Rina does express an appreciation of being able to depend on her spouse in this kind of life-threatening situation. In telling her dramatic story about how they almost drowned as newlyweds, however, she ends the narrative by focusing on her panic reaction and helplessness ("I was unable to do it"). She seems to convey self-depreciation, as well as desperation about her helpless reaction and inability to trust herself (since then she almost never goes into the sea).

The second story that Rina tells also involves her reacting in what she calls "hysteria in reaction to fear." This was a more recent event that happened when her husband went for 45 days of reserve army duty in the North, at a time of tension in that area. The day he finished his duty and returned home, he came back covered with dust and they were supposed to go to a social event. He turned to her and said, "Okay, I will go in to take a shower; I will get dressed and then we can go." She says the minute he came out of the shower, Rina felt like she was gasping for air and felt she was choking; she thought she was dying. She told her husband to take her to the hospital and there they diagnosed it as hyperventilation. "*I was hysterical from the fear. I didn't understand what was happening to me... I thought my lungs stopped functioning... either they connect me to a lung machine or I am finished.*" The doctor examining her noticed her husband was unusually tan for this time of year and asked him, "How come you are so tanned?" When her husband answered that he had just come back from reserve duty in the North, then the doctor said "Oh," like he already understood everything, and he continued by saying "there are many cases like this."

In this last story, the symptoms (which are termed response of self (RS) in the Core Conflictual Relationship Theme method) that Rina describes are consistent with a panic attack, such as sensations of shortness of breath, feeling of choking, and fear of dying (*Diagnostic and Statistical Manual of Mental Disorders*-IV-TR; APA, 2000). It can be speculated that while her husband was away on reserve duty she was anxious for his safety; however, she held herself together and functioned as needed, including taking care of their children. Once he is safely back, the tension that she felt during the 45 days that he had been away on army reserve suddenly overwhelms her.

The helplessness illustrated in this woman's narrative was relatively atypical for our sample. In the cases that it did appear, it seems that the subjective experience of the narrator (in most cases, women) is of vulnerability and difficulty coping effectively. In the meta-analytic study (see Chapter 1) by van IJzendoorn, Bakermans-Kranenburg, and Sagi-Schwartz (2003) they drew a distinction between nonclinical samples of children of survivors and clinical samples, such as survivors' children who themselves were Israeli combat veterans suffering from PTSD after the 1982 Lebanon war (Solomon, Kotler, & Mikulincer, 1988), or breast cancer patients (Baider, Peretz, Ever Hadani, Perry, Avramov, & Kaplan De-Nour, 2000). They concluded that only among offspring who had experienced other serious stressors (e.g., combat exposure or breast cancer) was there evidence for the influence of the parents' traumatic Holocaust experiences on the children's adjustment (i.e., more severe PTSD symptoms).

Helplessness with the Newborn Baby During the 1991 Gulf War

One of the male participants, when requested to relate an interaction with one of his children, chose to speak about a memory that involved the youngest child, who was a 2-month-old baby during the unusual situation in Israel around the first Gulf War in the winter of 1991. At that time, the entire country was under attacks by Iraqis Scud Missiles that could land anywhere in Israel.

> RAMI: *Our youngest daughter was 2 months old during the Gulf War. When there was an attack alert, we had to go through this procedure that involved putting babies younger than 6 month in a sealed crib kit that was designed to provide protection (against chemical warfare) for them. That was a very stressful situation for us, as putting our*

> *baby daughter in the crib without the ability to hold her under these circumstances caused the baby to cry . . . a terrible and most dreadful crying. I clearly recall how, not once, but on a number of occasions, the baby girl cried almost to the point of suffocation. I and my wife got into a conflict over how to handle this under these circumstances – what is preferable, that she will suffocate from crying in this sealed crib or to take her out of it which meant taking the risk that she would suffocate from the gas attack?*

To the interviewer's question about his memories and feelings from that time, Rami refers first to the extreme fear he felt and then indicates feeling helpless.

> RAMI: *What I remember is fear, an enormous fear. I never knew what fear was until I was forced to go through such a thing with my daughters (another girl was a few years older), the most precious thing to a person. With the baby it was a feeling of utter helplessness, because in our area, at least the first few times that there were attacks and shells fell, they sounded very close to us, and the uncertainty of whether the missiles were carrying gas (chemical attack) or not.*

Rami ended this story by expressing that this was his most traumatic memory related to this daughter. He emphasized the helplessness in the context of feeling responsible to protect your child: "*It is the thought of going through this with your children which is the worst dreadful experience that anyone could have.*" According to theory, the helplessness in this unusual situation stemmed from the uncontrollable circumstances that the citizens were faced with and the realistic incapability to change the situation at hand.

The reason we bring up Rami's story is that it may be related to his earlier experience as a child of a Holocaust survivor in that he recalled childhood memories of abandonment and helplessness. In preschool, he moved with his family to a different city, and he remembers that the transition was exceptionally difficult for him. He recalls that his mother would bring him to the preschool, and he would escape because he did not agree to stay on his own. In the beginning, his mother would stay with him. When she had to start leaving him there, however, he did not adjust, and he indicated that he feels now that this transition was traumatic for him.

When the interviewer asked Rami, "What kind of feelings arose in you toward your mother?"

> RAMI: *I think that a feeling of detachment, abandonment, as a child, every child experiences this; these are the kinds of things I remember. Maybe I felt helplessness; yes I think I felt helpless.*

Although one would likely agree that children, while growing up, are faced with circumstances that are not under their own control, in Rami's relational narratives the most prevalent themes included anxiety and helplessness. These appeared either in response to situations that were beyond his control or that he feels responsible for not being able to provide safety for significant others. In the narrative about the baby, the concrete, practical fear of the baby's suffocation can also be viewed as a metaphor for the helplessness that Rami may feel in the most fundamental sense, as he reacts to other events that are perceived as beyond his control.

Overbearing Helplessness in Seeing the Aging Parents' Suffering from Illness

Finally, in many of the narratives about more recent episodes with their parents, the participants related interactions and feelings around illnesses and death of their now elderly Holocaust survivor parents. A higher percentage of fathers, compared with mothers, died prior to the time of the interview, possibly due to a tendency for the fathers to be older than the mothers and to the fact that men die earlier than women. It also appears that there was a higher percentage of fathers who died at a relatively young age (especially from cardiac problems and cancer), although there were also mothers who died as well. In some narratives, the interviewee expressed painful helplessness at not being able to help their ill parents. They appeared to attribute a unique meaning to seeing their parents' suffering from illness, particularly in light of the trauma and suffering that they had already endured at a younger age. This was described as an overbearing experience of helplessness, powerlessness, and sadness.

Ron, for example, describes feeling "sadness and helplessness" upon seeing his mother sick with cancer in the hospital.

> RON: *All of a sudden your mother has cancer . . . I remember she told me: "I overcame the Nazis and at the end came the cancer and it overcame me?" It is sad to see how a woman, who managed to survive so much, is beaten by the cancer.*

Until now, we have described our participants' helplessness, but there were also accounts in which they described the helplessness of the Holocaust survivors.

They Couldn't Resist, but We Can

As victims of Nazi persecution, the extent of the survivors' helplessness in the horrible reality (or unreality) of the Holocaust is difficult to grasp. One of the men, Amos, refers in his account to a conversation with his father about the possibilities of escape and active resistance during the Holocaust. He recalls that as a child of about 12 or 13 years old his father would tell him how one day the Nazis came to their home; they took everybody and organized the whole family and made them march. In response Amos would raise the question to his father, "*Why didn't you do anything? Why didn't you fight back? Why didn't you resist?*" His father answered him by trying to describe the impossible situation with which they were faced. "*It's not so easy to resist when you are with a family; you are with children, with the grandfather and grandmother; you are worn out, without food . . . when there is a hope, if only a percentage of hope that there is a chance to survive, so how can you try and throw them away?*"

When the interviewer asked Amos how he felt with his father's response, Amos replies that he has some difficulty recalling his exact feelings, but he can recall the feelings surrounding this issue, his hatred toward the Germans. He remembers as a child he would fantasize that "we would have a border with Germany that I could serve in the army, and somehow fight against the Germans . . . to take revenge . . . and express my feelings of revenge." He then adds that "they couldn't resist, but we (in Israel) we have an army and our own guns and we can protect ourselves . . . they couldn't resist, but we can." In this narrative, we can see how Amos is troubled by what he perceives as the father's helplessness and passivity. This is translated in childhood into wishes for revenge toward those that victimized his father and family.

9

Loneliness

Loneliness is an affective and cognitive reaction to a threat to social bonds, hence, a universal experience inherent in the human condition (Rotenberg, 1999). Every person may experience loneliness at some time in life, at least transiently, but severe and persistent feelings of loneliness can have dire consequences for mental health and well-being (Heinrich & Gullone, 2006; McWhirter, 1990). Much research on loneliness has centered on individual differences associated with loneliness in adults (Ernst & Cacioppo, 1999), and more recently in childhood and adolescence (Perlman & Landolt, 1999). The salience of acute feelings of loneliness in survivors of trauma, both in the midst of the traumatic experiences and in the aftermath of trauma, is well documented in the clinical literature (Dasberg, 1976; Herman, 1997). In this chapter we present our analysis of the echoes of the parental trauma in the recollected subjective loneliness experiences of the sons and daughters as expressed in their narratives.

Research on parental antecedents of loneliness has suggested that parents may "hand down" their loneliness to their offspring (Lobdell & Perlman, 1986). More broadly, Rotenberg (1999) referred to the parental antecedents of loneliness as "parents' affective states and behavior that affect their children's loneliness" (p. 176). Rotenberg tested the relationships between various parenting variables and loneliness in children and adolescents in a cross-sectional study. He concluded that multiple factors may account for parental antecedents of loneliness in children, including quality of attachment

(Cassidy & Berlin, 1999), parenting styles of warmth and involvement, and parents' promotion of peer relationships. Of course only longitudinal designs can adequately test the causal paths between these parental factors and the loneliness of the offspring. In many cases, however, such as our case of adult children of Holocaust survivors, such designs cannot be applied. Instead we need to rely on these children's retrospective recollections of loneliness experienced during childhood and adolescence. We assumed that the characteristics of survivors' parenting, be it through attachment or through parenting style, and the possibility that the parents themselves suffered from loneliness, making them incapable of promoting peer relationships, played a role in the offspring's loneliness.

Given that loneliness is a subjective experience, researchers and clinicians cannot observe it directly. Loneliness research has relied almost entirely on self-report measures such as the Asher Loneliness scale (Asher, Hymel, & Renshaw, 1984) for children and the Revised UCLA Loneliness scale (Russell, Peplau, & Cutrona, 1980) for adults. It has been contended that a more phenomenological approach, based on narrative analysis of descriptive personal accounts of loneliness experiences, is needed for understanding the subjective meanings of loneliness for different people in various contexts (Stokes, 1987; Wiseman, 1995). A phenomenological–structural method was applied by Mikulincer and Segal (1990) to the analysis of laypersons' (university students) free descriptions of particular loneliness episodes that they had experienced. An analysis of the causes, feelings, and responses related to these loneliness episodes led to a differentiation of different subtypes of loneliness feelings: social estrangement, paranoid, depressive, and self-focused. Hymel, Tarulli, Hayden Thomson, & Terrell-Deutsch (1999) conducted a qualitative analysis of children's own personal narratives and accounts about situations in their lives that give rise to loneliness. Based on children's own voices about their experiences of loneliness they found that they associated loneliness with a variety of interpersonal contexts or causes such as loss, dislocation, temporary absence, conflict, rejection, broken loyalties, exclusion, and being ignored. They also expressed loneliness on affective and cognitive dimensions (Hymel et al., 1999).

STUDYING LONELINESS EPISODES IN THE RELATIONSHIP ANECDOTES PARADIGM INTERVIEWS

In studying experiences of loneliness in children of survivors the need to rely on narrative methodology that would be able to capture their subjective relational experiences is accentuated further (see Chapter 1). Research on adult offspring of Holocaust survivors has suggested that survivors' children experienced greater psychological distress while living at home with their parents than they experienced in adulthood (Schwartz, Dohrenwend, & Levav, 1994). Accordingly we asked our interviewees to narrate loneliness episodes that they recollected from childhood and adolescence while living at home with their survivor parents. The recollected loneliness accounts were obtained as part of the Relationship Anecdotes Paradigm interview (see Chapter 2). In addition to the ten stories that interviewees were asked to tell we asked them to tell us an eleventh story (M. Mikulincer, personal communication, October 1996). The instructions for this eleventh story were as follows: "Now I will ask you for an eleventh story in which I would like you to recount an episode of loneliness during childhood/adolescence in the context of the family."

These loneliness accounts (the eleventh story) were analyzed together with the other relational narratives that our interviewees told about meaningful interactions with their mothers and fathers that our judges identified as including loneliness feelings (Wiseman, 2007). All these identified loneliness stories were read by our judges who made independent notes on the kind of situations that aroused loneliness in childhood and adolescence. We then searched for the specific loneliness themes that emerged in these accounts and considered the subjective meanings of these experiences for the sons and daughters of the survivors. The process of the narrative analysis was similar to the one applied in our analysis of the other emotions in the interpersonal stories (see Appendix).

The core themes of loneliness that we identified pointed to a distinction between loneliness experiences in light of direct versus indirect manifestations of the trauma in the parents' behaviors and responses to the child. Direct manifestations are related to the parents' responses resembling specific posttraumatic stress disorder symptoms, such as intrusive traumatic memories, or numbing and detachment, whereas the indirect manifestations include the perceived parental caregiving style as depicted in the loneliness accounts. Finally, the theme of loneliness as a result of not having grandparents and extended family, as they had perished in the Holocaust, was also voiced in the narratives (Wiseman, 2007). The core themes are described together with the narratives that represent each of these loneliness themes.

ECHOES OF PARENTAL INTRUSIVE TRAUMATIC MEMORIES

One of the *Diagnostic and Statistical Manual of Mental Disorders' IV-TR* (American Psychiatric Association, 2000) criteria for posttraumatic stress disorder is "intense psychological distress at exposure to internal or external cues that symbolize or resemble an aspect of the traumatic event" (p. 468). These intrusive memories tend to appear both in dreams and in waking life. Most commonly, in waking life certain cues appear to evoke the painful memories. These cues may take the form of different actual images and sensory images (smells, auditory cues, etc.), which were connected to the trauma and appear to intrude into the survivors' consciousness. We found that some recalled episodes included the child facing the parent's intrusive memories that in turn aroused acute feelings of loneliness on the part of the sons and daughters. These experiences in which the parents' intrusive traumatic memories suddenly became salient appeared to leave the child feeling he or she did not understand the other and was left alone to deal with the impossible – to make sense of the *indescribable and the "undiscussable"* (Bar-On, 1999) Holocaust trauma of the parents.

In the first example, Hanna appears to associate between her mother's general recurring startle responses and her own overriding chronic feelings of loneliness during childhood.

Mother's Startle Responses

In response to the interviewer's request to tell the eleventh story about an episode of loneliness during childhood/adolescence in the context of the family, Hanna states:

> HANNA: *There are so many incidents that it is hard to choose. Yes, I felt lonely for many years. I could not bring friends home freely. My home was so serious and we didn't lack anything materially. It was not difficult from that point of view . . . it was simply the kind of home that was not happy. There were years we really felt this load with mother, the burden she carries. We really grew up with it. I was aware of it, though I did not really understand it, but I was aware. These fears and jumpiness she has, until today she has these fears. Yes, definitely lonely. I think I felt lonely most of the time.*

In this narrative Hanna depicts an overriding feeling of loneliness as she was growing up under the impression of her mother's traumatic past. One gets the sense that mother's burden is ever present in the serious and unhappy home where there is no room to bring friends. Hanna is left alone to try to make sense of "the load" and then turns to mention in a somewhat incoherent way mother's fears and jumpiness. Perhaps it is these startle responses, which most likely are incomprehensible to the child, which left her puzzled by her mother's reactions. After mentioning the mother's jumpiness Hanna suddenly exclaims: "*Yes, definitely lonely.*" At this point in the account, it seems unclear who she is talking about, who is definitely lonely? Is it her mother who felt lonely, or is it she? Then Hanna states: "*I think I felt lonely most of the time.*"

The incoherent style of the narrative seems to echo the daughter's experience of her mother's jumpiness and being faced alone with the attempt to organize these disorganizing experiences with mother (Scharf & Mayseless, 2006). Moreover, the daughter most likely also feels her mother's loneliness at times in which the mother is perceived as suffering from intrusive memories of the traumatic past. Such echoes of the mother's loneliness as experienced in the daughter's feelings of loneliness were also evident in other narratives.

In contrast to the aforementioned account that seemed to be more diffused, in another account of loneliness in the face of the parents' intrusive memories, Rachel referred to specific cues that evoked her mother's intrusive memories.

Images of Fire

> RACHEL: *As a child I did not know any details about what and where she was during the Holocaust, only that she went through the Holocaust, but one thing she did disclose and it was engraved in me, that she very much disliked "Lag BaOmer" [a Jewish holiday on which bonfires are lit] because it reminded her of the (concentration) camps. On Lag BaOmer she had to go out with us children to celebrate around the fire, like all the parents do on this evening, and she could not go out of the house. My father would always go with us on that day.*

In response to the interviewer's request that Rachel describe more specifically what as a child she felt in that situation, she responded:

> RACHEL: *Her misery, gloom, why does she have to suffer until this very day; why does she have to carry it . . . why can't she break away from it . . . I really felt sorry for her about the Holocaust; the loneliness . . . she lost everything in the Holocaust, literally everything, all her family. As a child I felt pity for her; I never judged her and I justified her. You see I tied everything to this concept of loneliness and loss.*

Rachel's account emits a strong sense of loneliness as connected to her mother's immense losses. She expresses a strong wish that her mother could detach herself from her traumatic past, but indicates how this is impossible. She appears to alternate between her mother's loneliness and her own. In its form, Rachel's narrative is fragmented, as if she is unable to put these feelings into words or find a way to describe them. This more indistinct sense of loneliness may be related to the traumatic aspects that color the experience, in a way that makes it impossible to differentiate between the "figure" and "ground." This *blurred feeling* regarding *loneliness and trauma* arises spontaneously in Rachel's narrative when she later mentions in this context a more recent experience of impending disaster in connection with the first Gulf War in 1991. There was fear in Israel of gas attacks from Iraq (they did not materialize, although there were missiles attacks). Rachel refers to that time, when her mother experienced nightmares: "*She kept seeing the gas chambers and the fires in the concentration camps . . . it hurt me to see her so helpless. It was also very difficult for me; I could not help her.*"

In light of her mother's traumatic memories, Rachel expresses strong feelings of helplessness (see Chapter 8), as she is unable to help her mother escape the recurrent and distressing intrusive memories and distressing dreams, both features of posttraumatic stress disorder.

ECHOES OF NUMBING RESPONSIVENESS AND DETACHMENT

Another direct manifestation of the parental trauma was depicted in relation to experiencing the parents as lacking in responsiveness and showing detachment. Feeling that their parents could not share their moments of happiness or pride due to their general numbing of feelings and sense of impending disaster stood out in the more painful loneliness descriptions.

Parents' Mourning-like Reaction and Detachment

JACOB: *Loneliness in relation to the family? Yes, the moment we decided we were getting married. Of course, her parents welcomed the news with joy; my parents' reaction was like mourning. They accepted it in the end, but I don't know why it was this way. Later on, when we announced that my wife was pregnant; their response was very cold and unenthusiastic. Their message was, don't get too excited, don't count on it, and don't get a room ready for the baby. And after the baby was born prematurely and was hospitalized they said, don't get attached to her.*

Jacob describes further his parents' recurrent lack of responsiveness and empathy. He states that at first he felt some bitterness over not being understood, but then he became indifferent and he decided *to detach from them*. He feels he cannot blame them because of what they went through. "*It is a trauma of inconceivable magnitude.*"

When asked about his feelings Jacob describes his reserved stance and his lack of open expression of feelings; however, an exception to this is his attachment to his wife, with whom he does share his feelings. Holocaust survivors live their present remembering their past, reminding themselves and their loved ones how fragile one's reality is; trying to save Jacob from possible disappointment, his parents' restricted reactions seem to leave him alone and hurt. In response the son has learned not to share his experiences with his parents and portrays a distrustful stance toward others (Wiseman, 2007).

PERCEIVED PARENTS' CAREGIVING STYLE IN THE LONELINESS EXPERIENCES

Indirect manifestations of parental trauma were often expressed in the recalled loneliness accounts in relation to the child's perception of the parenting style they experienced while growing up. Some accounts included recalled general depictions of their day-to-day or recurrent child–parent interactions, whereas others described specific memorable encounters that aroused feelings of loneliness in childhood.

Parent's Inability to Provide Physical and Emotional Care

In his narrative David expressed a general sense that his mother was incapable of taking care of him, in terms of basic physical as well as emotional needs. A recurrent childhood experience was his mother's yearly departure, leaving him with the ultimate experience of abandonment.

> DAVID: *I don't know a lot of places where... once a year, mother disappears on you for a whole month because she goes away for a whole month. My mother used to leave us in order to receive treatment that she was entitled to as a Holocaust survivor.*
>
> INTERVIEWER: What type of treatment?
>
> DAVID: *My mother had both physical wounds and emotional wounds. Only later I learned the reason for her absence. At the time (age 6) I did not know why she disappeared... here you are a child and your mother is not there for a whole month, and there is no explanation for it. It is not something you can receive an explanation for at the age of 6 and understand it. So you are angry, hurt, you feel neglected; it is natural.*

In this painful narrative, David relates his experience of abandonment, his mother's need to be taken care of "to treat her wounds." She cannot take care of her children even though he clearly states: "*She wanted so much to give, but was incapable.*"

Being Left Alone Prematurely to Manage on One's Own

In contrast to the previous relatively rare account of feeling abandoned, recollections of being left on one's own that led to situational loneliness feelings were rather common. These situations were usually described as a blend of fear and loneliness. Mostly the parents would go out for a few hours in the evening and leave the child without a babysitter or any other caregiver. The experience often meant not only having to deal with one's own fears but also taking care of a sibling. For example, Eliezer described a memory from age 10 or 11 of a specific time his parents went out dancing and left him and his twin sister alone on a stormy night.

> ELIEZER: *That night it was raining very heavily, with thunder and terrible lightning. She (the twin sister) heard the rain, saw the lightning, and then heard the thunder and she really panicked and started to throw up. I didn't know what to do... There was no one to turn to... An hour passed and then another, and I was anxious. I managed to calm down the child, but what'll happen if she gets another panic attack? I felt more lonely than afraid.*

Eliezer turns to the interviewer to impress on him that he had to deal with his twin sister's distress not as an older brother, but as a child of the same age. He says: "*You see, think about it, here I was with her and we are both the same age. It felt lonely in needing to deal on my own with my twin sister's panic.*"

In such situations as these, children are faced with the parent's expectation that they can handle being on their own and assume the role of a parent (parentification). This may be colored also with the common experience that the parents are going to have fun, leaving the child behind. Yet there is a sense that the child feels the parents are not aware of the distress this may cause under these circumstances.

The child's feeling that he is expected prematurely to perform basic caring tasks such as preparing food for himself was most striking in Nathan's narrative.

The Raw Meat Story

> NATHAN: *At age 8 or 9... I used to return home from school and was expected to prepare alone the food for lunch and to cook it for myself [in Israel elementary school children return home around 1:00 P.M.*

> *and the big meal is usually eaten at lunch]. My mother usually came back from work later. One day I cooked for myself food; it was liver, but even though it was still raw I started eating it. My mother arrived that day after 5–10 minutes, and she saw that I was eating rare liver (because it looked as if it was cooked, I fried it lightly on both sides and that was it)... since then she understood that she must not leave us alone, and that she has to take care of us.*

In response to the interviewer asking Nathan to recall the moment his mother arrived and her response in this episode, he recounted his mother's shock: *"She was shocked, for a few seconds, she was scared, she said 'Oh my goodness, you are eating uncooked meat,' and then she said: 'I must not let you prepare lunch on your own, I need to prepare your lunch.'"* Regarding this recalled episode he seemed to express some conviction that maybe it taught his mother a lesson. His perception was that mother hurt him unknowingly; as she did not know that he could not take on preparing the food for himself. He both felt lonely and abandoned, as well as somewhat pleased that mother got scared (that she felt guilty) and this led to her taking on the responsibility to prepare lunch and to care of him.

The feeling of the child having to cope prematurely on his/her own that led to situations that aroused feelings of loneliness centered on basic needs for safety and protection. It is possible that these situations stand out as failures to provide such safety. As Nathan's narrative illustrates, however, these failures seemed to be a consequence of the parent's misperception regarding the age-appropriate tasks that, as a parent, you can expect your child to perform on his or her own.

Role Reversal and the Wish to Be Understood

A central interpersonal parent–child dynamic involved the sons and daughters difficulty in asserting their independence in light of their parents' anxieties and worries (Chapter 4). Responding to the parents' overprotective behaviors the child felt obliged to attend to them and to their vulnerabilities at the expense of his or her own desires, which often accompanied feelings of loneliness. This dynamic in the parent–child interpersonal processes was depicted in Joseph's story of the *Trip to the Sea of Galilee* (presented fully in Chapter 4). The point we stress here in the context of loneliness is Joseph's wish that he could express his desire to mother and that she would understand him. In this recalled encounter with his mother Joseph (at age 13) wanted to ask for her permission to go on a youth trip to the Sea of Galilee. Briefly stated, the sequence of events was such that upon entering the house Joseph encountered his mother's "worry script" and "startle script"; in response he remained completely unable to voice his original determination to persuade his mother to let him go on the trip: "*her words completely paralyzed me.*" Faced with the surviving parent's vulnerability, Joseph is left feeling there is no place for his own desires, and his resolution to have his voice heard and understood collapses: "*that for once I will tell her what I want and that she will understand my will . . . but I gave in.*"

Accounts like those of Joseph that depicted the child's difficulty to rebel against the survivor parents' overprotection and the pattern of role reversal in the parent–child relationship (Scharf & Mayseless, 2006; Shafet, 1994) usually arouse feelings of loneliness. These feelings were not only felt in relation to the parents, but also in relation to the peer group, as the child was unable to join in social activities that stirred the parents' anxieties. Research has shown that the parents' overprotective parenting style (Wiseman, Mayseless, & Sharabany, 2006) and nonpromotion of peer relationships (Rotenberg, 1999) contribute to loneliness. In the context of the echoes of trauma the lack of open communication between children and their parents usually centered on a conflict between the child's desire (usually for independence) and the parent's overprotective responses that did not leave any room for negotiation (see Chapter 4). Under these circumstances, the parent's fear of pending disaster stands as a barrier to the child's wish to be understood and to express his or her needs openly.

Frustrated Need for Open Communication

The parents were perceived in the narratives as mostly emphasizing attention to the child's physical needs; however, the feeling that the parents were lacking in the ability to provide emotional support was more prevalent in the loneliness accounts.

The Balls on the Duvet Story

The feeling of wanting to be listened to and the frustrated need to share openly thoughts and feelings with her mother is portrayed in a unique way in Zilla's story.

> ZILLA: *I never came home and found the house closed; I was not a latchkey child. But my mother never asked me, "How was your day in school?" or "How was it at the youth movement?" She always asked me if I needed money. I didn't lack any clothes, but I lacked a sympathetic ear. I had a duvet with a pattern of balls in all kinds of colors and I always told these balls everything that I went through . . . I used to say to myself: "It doesn't matter that my mother won't listen to me, but these balls will always listen to me." I always fought with my mother not to change the duvet, because then I wouldn't have the balls.*

Regarding the general lack of sharing of emotional experiences with parents, research has shown that individuals who perceive their parents as responsive and high in warmth and involvement report less loneliness in adolescence and adulthood (Hazan & Shaver, 1987; Rotenberg, 1999). In the loneliness accounts of children of survivors, the emphasis on the lack of open communication may be further amplified by the lack of open intergenerational communication about the Holocaust trauma (Chapter 5). Zilla's story about talking to the colored ball pattern on her duvet may not be unique to being raised by survivor parents, but the lack of sharing and openness may well be related to a more general atmosphere of silence in families of survivors of various traumas.

SOCIAL COMPARISON WITH OTHER FAMILIES

Loneliness recollection that included a general sense that their homes were different from other children's homes (of nonsurvivor families) was expressed by many narrators. This social comparison aspect of loneliness stood out specifically in relation to the size of family kin in nonsurvivor families.

I Did Not Have Grandparents, Aunts, and Uncles: Something Is Missing

Leah describes how when she was growing up she thought that all families were the same: mother, father, a boy, and a girl. When she went to school she found out that there were children with really big families, with uncles and aunts, grandfathers, and grandmothers, a discovery that made her feel lonely.

> LEAH: *Suddenly I felt something was really missing in my life. It started in the summer break of first grade, when kids said that they are going to their grandfather and grandmother for the vacation . . . I felt different. I didn't understand the meaning of the concept of grandparents, I didn't know there was such a thing, and then I felt I had lost something. There were those that had at least one grandmother or grandfather; they got pocket money and a Hanukkah gift, and these old people sometimes came to school events. It made me feel a sense of loneliness. I really liked to go to other homes; there were always many people around and it was full of life.*

The lack of extended family, especially grandparents, which is augmented by social comparison, may be found in other family constellations (e.g., being an only child). In children of survivors, however, it is most likely profoundly felt in the context of growing up with parents whose family of origin had perished. Relating to the parents' massive familial losses was echoed in some narratives as a burden on the parents that is also felt by the child who absorbs the parents' loneliness. This was expressed in some narratives as undifferentiated from the child's feelings of loneliness. In these cases, such as in Rachel's Images of Fire story, survivor parents' may apparently "hand down" their loneliness to their offspring.

LONELINESS AS FAILED INTERSUBJECTIVITY

We assumed that growing up with parents who had endured massive trauma would be manifested in the offspring's recalled loneliness experiences in the context of the survivor family. The themes that emerged appear to represent varying tones and salience of the echoes of the parental trauma as expressed in our narrators' loneliness accounts. Theories of loneliness have included psychodynamic, social, cognitive, and more recently attachment theory (reviewed in Heinrich & Gullone, 2006; Perlman, 1988; Perlman & Landolt, 1999). The proposition that "loneliness is the individual experience of failed intersubjectivity" (Wood, 1986, p. 188) is suggested as the most suitable conceptualization to capture the essence of recollected loneliness experiences in survivors' offspring (Wiseman, 2007). According to Wood, failed intersubjectivity involves the experience of *not being understood by others*, *not understanding others*, and the *absence of shared understanding*. The distinctive features of childhood and adolescent loneliness that emerged from our narrative analysis elucidate and demonstrate this conceptualization of the subjective meaning of loneliness. The children of survivors had loneliness experiences in which they experienced the parent as not understanding them, they did not understand the parent, and they lacked shared understanding.

The painful experience of failed intersubjectivity appeared especially profound in situations that stimulated parents' fears and anxieties, when shared understanding became impossible. Situations in which the parents' traumatic memories were salient appeared to leave the child feeling he or she did not understand the other and was left alone to deal with the impossible – to make sense of the "indescribable and the 'undiscussable'" (Bar-On, 1999) Holocaust trauma of the parents. Survivor parents found it difficult to communicate openly with their children about their traumatic memories so the trauma remained unarticulated, leaving the child puzzled by the parents' behavior and reactions ("not understanding the parent"). Moreover, feeling the burden of the parents' losses and worries, which takes part in the role reversal pattern of parent–child relationship (Scharf & Mayseless, 2006), exacerbates the child's sense of not being understood by the parent ("*that for once she will understand my desire*"). Under these circumstances, the children lack opportunities for open interactions with their parents and for negotiations that are often a requisite to reach a sense of shared understanding.

The absence of shared understanding that was at the heart of some of the narratives can be further understood through the other side of the coin of loneliness, namely, experiences of shared meaning and mutuality between the child and the surviving parent. Recently, with the growing recognition of survivors' need to tell and descendents' need to deal with their parents' traumatic past (Chaitin, 2002, 2003), new lines of communication have opened between them. Such experiences of open communication were rare in the narratives from childhood through early adulthood that we collected, but their healing power is becoming more evident for both survivors and descendents. In treating patients that grew up in families that had experienced extensive trauma, clinicians need to be sensitive to the possibility of their patients' vulnerability to experiences of failure in intersubjectivity in their past and current relationships. Opportunities for open dialogue and interpersonal negotiation can be provided in different forms of psychotherapy, as well as in experiences of mutuality in the person's current close relationships (see Chapter 12). Such corrective emotional experiences of shared meaning and understanding are especially important for those who grew up with a sense of loneliness in the context of the echoes of the parental trauma.

10

Joy and Pride

Within the Core Conflictual Relationship Theme (CCRT) framework it is a common observation that the relationship episodes (REs) that are told spontaneously in the course of psychotherapy sessions, or upon request in Relationship Anecdotes Paradigm (RAP) interviews, have a higher frequency of mainly negative rather than mainly positive CCRTs (Luborsky & Crits-Christoph, 1998; see also Chapter 2). A positive CCRT means the narrator has described an interpersonal event in which there was no interference (or no expectation of interference) with the satisfaction of his or her wishes, or a sense of mastery of being able to deal with one's wishes. For example, the wish to be loved is satisfied by another person who is affectionate [positive response of other (P-RO)] and the self feels accepted and happy [positive response of self (P-RS)]. In contrast, a negative CCRT means that the narrator describes an interpersonal event in which there was interference with the satisfaction of his or her wishes (or this is expected to occur). For example, the wish to be loved is unsatisfied by the response from an other that is rejecting [negative response of other (N-RO)] and the self feels frustrated and angry [negative response of self (N-RS)].

In our study, the instructions of the RAP interview that we used asked the interviewee to tell a relational narrative "about a specific event that was personally important or a problem to you in some way" (Luborsky, 1998a; p. 110). Although a "personally important event" may involve positive aspects or may result eventually in a positive outcome (i.e., "happy ending"), the relational narratives that we collected more often involved stories of emotional-laden events that overall had a negative rather than a positive quality. Indeed, individuals tend to recall negative interpersonal events that are "unfinished business." In this regard Luborsky (1998b) contended that "possibly the high frequency of negative responses in narratives derives from the need to remember and talk about negative or traumatic events or the need to master negative or traumatic events" (p. 320). The negative valence of the emotions that we identified and described in the previous chapters (i.e., anger, guilt, shame, embarrassment, anxiety, and helplessness, and loneliness) is consistent with this observation. Nevertheless, the positive valence of the emotions of joy and pride is also evident in the narratives, even if less frequently. Given that there has been a tendency in the literature on the intergenerational effects of the Holocaust to emphasize negative effects and vulnerability, it seemed important to present the narratives that involved positive feelings to portray the relational world of the sons and daughter in its diversity and richness.

JOY

Joy is a feeling of intense happiness that is often elicited by interpersonal interactions in which the individual is being the object of love, liking, affection, and acceptance or by receiving praise or admiration from others (Guerrero & Andersen, 2000). Schwartz and Shaver (1987) showed that 40 percent of the participants in their study who reported experiencing joy did so in the context of close relationships. With regard to the communication of joy, because it is one of the most positive emotions, individuals almost always express their feelings of joy to other people. Joy and happiness are communicated through positive facial displays, particularly smiling. The telling or sharing of happy feelings with others is usually a rewarding and pleasant experience for most people. Even positive achievements have a strong interpersonal context, in that they are most likely to generate happiness if they are observed by, told to, shared with, or praised by others (Andersen & Guerrero, 1998).

The Joy of Feeling Loved and Supported

The narratives that included components of joy and of feeling loved and supported were told in regard to parental support and spouse support. We will describe them in turn.

Feeling the Parents' Support

A few narratives introduced the feeling of being supported by a parent, interestingly many of these stories, but not all, involve the same-sex parent.

The Ice Cream Story

The first story that Dorit recalled is from approximately age 4 or 5. She remembers her mother one afternoon promised her she would go with her to buy ice cream if she would do something she asked her to do. Dorit says she cannot recall now what it was, but she remembers being good and doing what mother asked and she was supposed to get the ice cream as a prize. She further relates the unfolding of this episode.

> DORIT: *Mother was busy, so she told my sister, who was 6 years older, to go with me instead of my mother in order to buy me the ice cream. But then I got angry and told my mother, "You think I need the ice cream, all the fun is to go out with you to get it." I remember I said something like that, and that she really went with me. She understood what stood behind it and she went with me.*

The interviewer asks Dorit about the appeasing of her initial anger that mother wanted to send her to get ice cream with her older sister. To this Dorit responds with no hesitation:

> DORIT: *You see at first she didn't understand that the point was not the ice cream. But once she did, then she went with me. It truly gave me*

> *the feeling that she really responds to me. She really supports me – and that is a good feeling.*

Dorit's narrative about the fun of going with mother to buy ice cream is a story of a wish fulfilled. She is clear that this is a story not about wanting ice cream and getting it. Instead of the ice cream being the target of her desire, what she wanted is the fun of going with mother to buy the ice cream. Mother understanding her and "going with her" symbolizes the mother's understanding of her daughter and her acceptance and responsiveness.

This ice cream story stands in sharp contrast to the *Thirst Story* (see Chapter 3), in which Hanna's wish for connection is frustrated by her mother not understanding her, which leads Hanna to feel that she is not being responded to by her mother. As you may remember, Hanna does not articulate verbally her wish for a glass of water, but instead she "signs" to her mother with her mouth, and with facial expressions (without words). In contrast, Dorit articulates what she wants from mother. To paraphrase the expression "I scream for ice cream," Dorit "*screams it is not about the ice cream*" and mother understands that Dorit wants her company. From an attachment framework we can see in this story the dynamics of parent–child relationships that are characterized by secure attachment (Bowlby, 1980). Secure individuals are characterized by the combination of a positive representation of others and a positive representation of self. In Dorit's story we can see how mother is portrayed positively as understanding and responsive and Dorit feels positive about herself – loved and worthy. Thus, in CCRT terms both the RO and the RS are positive and the outcome is positive (her wish for fun with mother is satisfied).

One can wonder if this story is remembered because it is consistent with the relational patterns of Dorit, beyond the ice cream incident. The nature of the other stories that this woman told in the RAP interview suggest that it is consistent with her positive models of both self and others. Moreover, we can speculate that most likely Dorit's memory of her being able at a young age to communicate her needs so clearly to her mother is indicative of a secure relationship characterized by open communication. As we illustrate in the *Ice Cream Story*, such open communication in the context of supportive parents provides a secure base for the child that enables her to discover and correct misunderstandings in parent–child interactions (Bowlby, 1988; Bretherton & Munholland, 1999). This is the flip side of the coin that we illustrated in the *Thirst Story* in which open communication is lacking, and there is no opportunity for the mother and daughter (Hanna) to correct or repair their misunderstandings.

Fun with Father – "Doing" Together

A few of the interviewees described the quality time they had with their father. One woman says her father was a person who was fun to be with and she enjoyed it when he took her to all kinds of places and widened her knowledge. Another man whose father died at the relatively young age of 57, recalls his father as "a fun dad." The fun interactions with him were around "doing things together" rather than around conversation. Micha describes their relational "doing" as follows.

> MICHA: *I felt really good with my dad. I did not have conversations with him because he was a very introverted person, and he had difficulty communicating verbally. He was not an Israeli; he was not a "Sabra"; he was what you would call the generation of the Holocaust. So the relationship involved him really spoiling me, buying me things and doing things for me and with me. When I was already a university student (in his early twenties) and began to be more independent and lived away from home he would come meet me, usually on Thursdays and would take me and we would go out for a movie and then he would take me out to a really good restaurant. I would wait for these Thursdays to meet with him and to have fun together. Also as a child I remember we would go to the movies together; these were really fun occasions for me to go out with him... he would initiate going to the movies and I loved joining him and having fun together.*

Father's Backing: He Stopped and Focused His Attention on Helping Me Out

Amnon recalls, as a young child, a time of difficulty after he was seriously injured in an accident when father was supportive. The accident happened when he walked to school and while crossing the street a car hit him. He was injured and was hospitalized with a concussion for about 2 months. After returning to school he had difficulties catching up and his grades went down. Amnon remembers his father's unusual involvement and efforts to help him readjust to school at this critical point.

> AMNON: *My father was focused on his work and his career. I would not see him that much, as he would get up at 7 in the morning to go to work and return in the evening. But when I had these difficulties he went and spoke to my teacher so that they would show consideration and he would encourage me. I remember this, because he went a few times to speak to the teacher and kept in touch with her and he really took an interest. And things really slowly got back on track, it was difficult, but it was good as after that things really got completely back on track.*
>
> INTERVIEWER: Can you recall what you felt?
>
> AMNON: *I felt really good that he was helping me and supporting me. The moment he was involved, I felt he also took responsibility, and it was not only up to me. Suppose if I fail an exam, there is someone looking out for me, and is helping me. I felt that he took such a big interest; he stopped and focused his attention on helping me out.*

In considering the narratives that were told about interactions with the fathers, in general, the fathers were portrayed as the providers for the family. They were hard working and away for long hours from early in the morning to the evening. This was the common picture of the division of labor in Israeli families during the late 1950s through the late 1970s when our interviewees grew up, regardless of their specific Holocaust background. In his narrative Amnon expresses the special meaning of his father's involvement in that he interrupted his work schedule and met with the teacher a few times. Because this narrative was told as a relationship episode with father, we do not know how mother was involved in this situation; she is not mentioned at all in the narrative, and in fact the narratives that Amnon related about mother did not include this event. It may appear that the father's involvement was due to the importance of school. Unlike some of the other children (for example the pressure to study in Aharon's narrative in Chapter 3), Amnon experienced his father's involvement as an expression of welcomed support in coping with the school difficulties that arose as a consequence of his hospitalization and his adjustment difficulties after the accident. We get the sense that the support was not experienced only as instrumental but a feeling that father's support felt good also in an emotional sense.

Financial Support that Gives Joy to Both Father and Son

Like other sons, such as we saw in Micha's narrative about doing things with his father, Avi also described his father as an introverted and closed person. In his depiction of his father, Avi emphasizes his father's extreme introverted personality in the following way: *"He was an introverted person in a frightening or awful way . . . everything he absorbed inside, everything he absorbed inside."* In a way this description can be viewed as the background to the specific encounter that Avi relates about the time his father supported him financially toward a mortgage on a new home. Avi recalls that he asked his father for some financial support and that he was pleasantly surprised by the large amount of money his father gave him, which was way beyond his expectations. He remembers he jumped with joy and kissed and hugged his father. Avi says he was extremely grateful for this help and felt his father's pleasure in giving it to him. He ends the story by telling about how afterward when his father would come visit him in his new home he would sit down comfortably and say to Avi: "It is so pleasant for me to come visit you here." Father's expression of his happiness about Avi's new home that father helped him to pay for also warmed Avi's heart and he would take great pleasure in these visits.

It is of interest to note that in all three cases that we presented here in relation to the father, both parents were Holocaust survivors (not only the mother of the narrator), and all three are males.

Good Feelings in a Dream about a Deceased Father

Feeling good about being supported by father was expressed in a relatively unusual way in the narrative that Alisa told about a dream she had that involved an encounter with her father. The dream occurred about 12 years after her father passed away.

> ALISA: *In the dream I remember that I and he (father) are sitting side by side and we were sitting and talking, and this was after I haven't seen him for many years. I asked him if he knows what happened with me and the amazing thing was that he said he knows. I remember also that he stroked me tenderly. The incredible thing for me was his answer that he knew, and then I understood that he actually knows about me even though he is not with me. Then I had this image that the two of us reach a mountain and behind this mountain it was like the Garden of Eden... it was a wonderful feeling that he is somewhere and he accompanies me in all kind of things that happen in my life, even though rationally I don't quite believe it... But the dream was so strong that when I woke up although I knew it was a dream, for a minute I was not sure if it was for real or a dream.*

This story that Alisa tells about her dream about her deceased father most likely represents some idealization of her father who is depicted as "knowing." We can speculate that the fantasy of the Garden of Eden represents father's goodness as well as him "knowing" about Alisa's life in a soothing way. In any case, the dream does portray Alisa's positive inner representation of her deceased father as expressing tender care and loving toward her.

Feeling Spouse's Love and Support

The Surprise Birthday Party

Before she begins to recount specific relationship episodes, Michal talks about her feeling of compatibility with her husband (they have been together for more than 20 years). She describes herself in relation to him using an idiosyncratic metaphor: *"I am like the bonfire and maybe he is the water."* She further explains, *"He is calm . . . he does the balancing around things that happen with the children, like when the children were younger and they would get hurt, break things, wounded . . . he calms things down; he is the spokesman; he is the security . . . and it is thanks to him that I keep my sanity."*

Asked to focus on a specific encounter, Michal recalls the surprise birthday party that her husband organized for her 2 years ago. She was taken totally by surprise as it was all organized so well. Her husband managed to carry out the surprise in such a sophisticated manner that she did not clue in at all, and even the children kept it all secretive.

MICHAL: *It was kept so hush that I truly did not see any of it coming [laughs]. No one, including the children, gave away any clues. I did not discover the preparations and was so surprised. All this organizing is something that a woman expects less from a man. I felt a spark of admiration toward him. Here suddenly I who am used to giving to others, suddenly I am in the receiving end; it is so much and so great. It was fun to be the center of the celebration, the "birthday girl," without doing any of the work at all. It was so pleasant. It is a good feeling.*

PRIDE

The feeling of pride has been considered among the self-conscious emotions together with guilt, shame, and embarrassment, which are emotions that are both intensely self-focused and interpersonally focused (Guerrero & Andersen, 2000). Unlike the negative valence of the emotions of guilt, shame, and embarrassment (Chapter 7), pride is a positive and uplifting emotion that is personally gratifying. Pride as an emotion has been classified by emotion researchers as subordinate to joy, with the latter being considered a more basic emotion (Shaver, Schwartz, Kirson, & O'Connor, 1987). Pride is typically generated by appraisals that one is responsible for socially valued outcomes or that one is a socially valued person (Mascolo & Fischer, 1995). Usually pride is dependent on a social audience, and a person's success is usually a source of pride when it is recognized by relationally significant others (Andersen & Guerrero, 1998; Greenwood, 1994). Under certain interpersonal circumstances, however, too much pride can create resentment, rivalry, or envy.

With regard to interpersonal communication, pride may be shared with others by nonverbal displays, such a broad smile or celebratory gestures of triumph. Children seek especially to share their pride over accomplishments through eye contact with significant others (Leary & Meadows, 1991). Pride is also usually shared verbally with significant others as a way of interactively receiving recognition for one's accomplishments.

In terms of the CCRT standard category system (Barber, Crits-Christoph, & Luborsky, 1998), among the responses of self, feeling proud is a subcategory of the category named "feel self-confident" together with "am or feel successful" and "feel self-assured." In our narratives the expression of pride was embedded in the narrator's experience of the others in their close relationships, especially feeling proud in relation to their parents and their children.

Pride in Personal Achievements and Their Children's Achievements

A few of the interviewees, especially sons, expressed moments of pride and triumph around personal achievements. The successful achievement of completing university studies carried special meaning in relation to the parents' background. Survivors' schooling was interrupted abruptly due to the war and it was impossible in many cases to resume their studies after the war ended. Their children were often told that they had the opportunity to study and progress academically with the message that it cannot be taken lightly. Shlomo states his pride in this context of fulfilling father's aspirations. "*My father always wanted me to study at university and this was very important for him. When I completed my university studies I was very excited and proud. I felt that I was fulfilling my father's dream."*

Another man tells about the retirement party that was held for his father at the father's work place. During this party his father introduces the son to his fellow workers while referring to the son's successful accomplishments. He says: "*They each came over and shook hands with me while complimenting me over what they heard about my success. I felt very proud by the honor they gave me in the presence of my father. I was a bit embarrassed by the attention, but I also felt excited and touched.*"

Accounts of pride in the narratives, as can be expected, were more often expressed in relation to the achievements of the children of the narrators. These achievements included outstanding performance in school (e.g., excelling in school) or in sports (e.g., son wins a soccer cup or a medal in a swimming competition). For example, Alon told about the time his daughter (in grade school) wrote an essay that was to be submitted without the name of the writer, and every class chose the best essay. His daughter's essay was voted the best. Then all the best essays were presented during a special event in front of a large audience of parents and children and other guests.

> ALON: *My daughter went up on stage and read her essay. There was even a photographer that took pictures of the event for the local newspaper. I felt so excited and proud. I don't think I could have read in front of so many people. I saw the other children there who got confused and did not read their essay in a steady pace. But she got up there and without stuttering she read her essay in front of so many people. I felt like telling everybody: "In case you don't know, so this is my daughter."*

Pride and Admiration of Parents

Not only the Holocaust survivors demonstrated pride in their children, but also the children, the participants in our study, were proud of their surviving parents.

Admiring the Parents for Surviving and Rebuilding Their Lives – "I Would Probably Have Died on the First Hour"

Some of the interviewees expressed their general outlook on their parents as survivors. Anat says to the interviewer that when she thinks of her parents, the word she comes up with is *admiration*. She then tries to explain this as follows.

> ANAT: *It is admiration on the very fact that they survived and that they succeeded to also stay normal, that they even were able to build a family together.*

Anat explains that now that she is older than were her parents during the war, she realizes in retrospect that "*they were really strong people.*" She then tells the interviewer how she would imagine herself in their place and what would have happened to her.

> ANAT: *Many times I would play with pretending what would happen to me if I were their age and in their place when a war broke out. Today I can say that I for sure would have died during the first hour. I used to play with what might have happened to me if I could . . . I would join the Partisans to fight against the Nazis, but today I know in retrospect that they were very strong people.*

Interestingly, we can speculate that only as an adult is she able to perceive how much strength was required by her parents to survive. It sounds that while growing up Anat would imagine herself as someone who would fight against the Nazis. Her childhood fantasy of fighting back is similar to the active resistance that Amos talked about in his narrative about asking his father about "why didn't you fight back" (Chapter 8). Now from the vantage point of an adult, Anat does not condemn her parents for not fighting but rather appreciates her parents' survival as a triumph in its own right. Her changing view of her parents may parallel the more recent change in the perception of the survivors in the Israeli sociocultural context from an overemphasis on those who fought like the partisans and disdain for the Diaspora

Jews that did not fight back toward more respectful attitudes for their survival.

Mother Was Never Tired . . . I Don't Understand How She Did It

Although some of the daughters were critical of their mothers, there were those who expressed deep appreciation and admiration for their mothers, who despite their traumatic past, were able to mother them in an exemplary and commendable manner. This kind of admiration was especially evident when daughters talked about their deceased mothers.

Iris describes her mother with much admiration and love. The mother who died 6 years before the interview is described as a warm and beautiful woman. Iris says that even though her mother worked outside the home she was always there when you needed her as a mother and wife. When asked for a specific episode, she recounts the memorable occasion when she and her husband returned as newly weds from their honeymoon.

> IRIS: *We went on our honeymoon and when we arrived back to our home it was sparkling; the fridge was packed with food; everything was all prepared and ready; just put down the suitcase and live happily together for ever and ever. You see that's my mother; we always knew that if she is needed she will be there. She doesn't come out with slogans or play games; she just does for you even though all her life she worked hard outside the home. I admire her for it. I was always a latchkey child, but never in any way did I feel that way. I myself am not able to succeed as she did; I really don't understand how she did it. I would come home and the house would be sparkling clean; the food waited for me, then she would come home around 3 in the afternoon and she was never tired. She always had time for me. I really cannot explain how she did it. Even after I gave birth she would come and help. I would value her help so much that I never took advantage of her willingness to help out.*

Iris admires her mother and she sounds in awe of her mother's resourcefulness and endless devotion. Unlike some of the other stories we heard in which the mother is not attentive, or is perceived as not helping, or as overly intrusive (Chapter 4), Iris talks about her mother's involvement with enormous respect and gratitude.

This kind of admiration toward the parents was expressed in particular with respect to the parents' ability to focus on the child, while putting the parents' pain aside. Eleanor recalls the mix of joy and pain when she announces to her dying mother that she is pregnant. In light of the pain of the mother's terminal illness, she is touched by her mother's joyful response. She admires her mother for pretending that all will be fine in that she will live to see the baby born. "*Even though it is clear to everyone that she will not live to see the baby, I really admired her for her strength and her ability to be happy with me. I felt she really was able, despite all the pain, to share with me in that moment the joy of my announcing my pregnancy to her.*"

Wanting the Parents to Enjoy Their Grandchildren

The importance of the continuation of the family by having grandchildren was present in many of the narratives. The sons and daughters referred to their lacking the experience of having grandparents (see Chapter 9). They wanted their children to enjoy the experience of having grandparents, as one woman put it: "*I wanted to marry young and have children while my parents were still alive to be sure that my children would have grandparents.*" They also attributed importance to providing their parents the pride that comes from having grandchildren and from enjoying them.

The Granddaughter's Injection of Health Visit in the Hospital

Beth chose to tell about the time she came to visit her father in the hospital and brought her 7-year-old daughter with her. She tells with great pride how this visit was so special for her father who takes great pleasure in the granddaughter's visit.

> BETH: *My father was in the hospital and he felt so helpless there. I decided to bring my daughter with me to visit him, even though she was only 7 years old. I know it is not such a pleasant place for a little*

> *girl . . . to see her grandfather in the hospital, but she was so great during the visit . . . so mature and cooperative; she even helped me to feed him. I felt like for him seeing his granddaughter brought him to life. Her visit was an "injection of health" for my father. I felt so proud of her and I was so happy that I brought her with me as she made him happy.*

In her account Beth is mainly focused on her father's response to the granddaughter's visit. Although she did mention the possibility that this kind of hospital visit may cause some distress for the little girl (her daughter), it is considered minimal in comparison to its so-to-speak curative effects on her father.

Pride of the Children of Holocaust Survivors about Their Relationships with Their Children

In the narratives about their children, daughters particularly expressed a sense of accomplishment and pride in succeeding to form what they considered to be caring and open relationships with their children.

Aliza feels proud about her ability to help her oldest daughter, who was 9 years old at the time of the interview. Her daughter was distressed about problems she encountered with her teacher at school. In her narrative, Aliza describes how she put everything aside and spoke to her daughter about what she was going through. She speaks with pride about her special ability to see the situation.

> ALIZA: *I think I have special sensitivities that I can really get outside of myself and look inside other people and see things through their eyes. As a child I would practice this ability during classes in the way I looked at my teachers. Also now I can really see how people work and it helps me understand things and to catch all kinds of things that people don't necessarily want to show. I used this ability in the advice I gave my daughter on how to resolve the situation with her teacher. At first she opposed my advice, but then she went according to it, and everything worked out for the better. I was very pleased to see that the problem was solved and I think my daughter was very grateful.*

It appears that that Aliza expresses self-confidence in her ability to help her daughter, even to the point of some omnipotence. It is clear that she really enjoys the feeling of being a competent and helpful parent to her daughter.

Another interviewee tells a narrative about an interaction with her daughter in which she felt proud about the way she was able to have an open discussion with her daughter about "leaving school before the day ends" or skipping classes. She says that she was pleased that following their conversation on this issue her daughter accepted her point of view. *"I felt that she trusts me, that she knows I will support her. That even if I say 'no,' that she will able to show me her point of view. Still I know that my opinion is very important to her. She is open with me, and tells me about her personal experiences in school and also socially. It is a great feeling for me."*

In such narratives about interactions with their children, feelings of pride emerged as related to the narrator's experience of being able to stand up for their children and to keep an open mind to their needs. This theme may be particularly salient given the fact that their parents, probably not only due to their past but also due to their immigrant background, were less able to act as their advocates. The changes in the social context of course need to be considered, because in the early 1960s parents did not interfere with teachers' attitudes and saw the teacher as the authority in school matters, and parental involvement was less frequent than nowadays.

Another aspect of the relationship that emerged as a source of pride was the experience of the child confiding in the parent even with respect to dating. For example, Miriam takes pride in her son's close and open relationship with her. In her narrative about an interaction with her son she tells about a recent conversation with him in which he consulted with her about a girl he met and was not sure if he should continue seeing her.

> MIRIAM: *He went out with this girl for a few days and he came and said to me, "Mom you see, I don't feel there is a click, what do you say, should I carry on?" I told him, "If you see that it is not working*

out and you don't feel a special relationship with her then there is no point in continuing it; it wouldn't be good for her either." So he thought for a minute and then he said, "You know what? You are really right it really looks like it isn't working out." So he stopped the relationship with her due to consulting with me.

INTERVIEWER: How did you feel with him sharing his hesitation with you?

MIRIAM: *Really happy and pleased. I bring up my children to be open with me. I am relatively young in age and in spirit, and I tell them that not long ago I experienced what they did and I know what it is like; I haven't forgotten how it is. I really put an effort to be friends with my children. I think I brought them up the right way. Not to lie to their parents, to always come and tell me. Even if things aren't going well in school that they would know that I know what is going on with them. If they don't feel like going to school, I accept it and don't throw them out of the house. So that he doesn't run away and not arrive in school and then they will call me from school to say your son did not arrive today. That I would know and then I can protect him. I like to feel that I solve problems that come up with my children. I feel proud of the way I bring them up, that they are successful and doing well; it brings me a lot of happiness.*

These examples are presented here specifically in relation to the mothers feeling proud of the way they handle the parenting role and their feeling good about the relationship that they succeeded in forming with their children. The experience of parenting their own children, especially when the children reach adolescence elicits a whole range of experiences. In the next chapter we elaborate on the current experience of both women and men of parenting their children, while considering the parenting that they themselves experienced while growing up in survivor families.

PART THREE

HEALING TRAUMA IN THE CHAIN OF THE GENERATIONS

This part of the book examines the echoes of the survivors' trauma as it transforms down the generations from survivors' children to their own children and from the survivors themselves to these grandchildren. We focus on processes of healing in the chain of the generations as the "*music of knowing–not knowing*" goes through a process of "working-through" in families of survivors within a wider changing sociocultural context. In Chapter 11 we present our analyses of narratives of sons and daughters of survivors regarding their relationship with their parents during adolescence in comparison to the narratives they tell depicting their own current relationship with their adolescent children. We examine the latter relationship through their eyes, as well as through the eyes of their adolescent children (the survivors' grandchildren). In light of the parenting our interviewees received from their survivor parents, they appear to aspire to develop a different parent–adolescent relationship with their own children. As we will show, the *quest for corrective parenting* centered especially around the themes of granting autonomy and keeping open lines of familial communication.

Processes of working-through in the lives of the adult children of survivors may involve corrective experiences that they undergo in their relational world or through various forms of psychotherapy. In Chapter 12 we conclude by considering the clinical implications of our insights into the echoes of trauma in relation to knowing–not knowing processes for working with patients raised in families that experienced extensive trauma.

One of the most striking changes in the familial-social-cultural context of the music of knowing–not knowing is the greater freedom of the third generation to be in a position to listen to their grandparents' story and to have the liberty to ask questions. The dynamics of the questions that were not asked out loud between the second generation and the survivors is exemplified in the following excerpt from an interview that one of HW's students, whose grandmother is an Auschwitz survivor, conducted with her mother as part of her university course in spring 2006 (cited with permission from the student and her mother).

> *In 1956 I played with children that were immigrants from North Africa and I came home with lice in my hair. When my mother saw the lice... the whole ordeal of her attempts to get rid of the lice became very traumatic in this respect. From that time on (from age 8) until I went to the army (at age 18) she did not allow me to grow my hair below the neckline. The minute it grew I had to have it cut.*

This woman's daughter (the grandchild) asks her mother: "*Did you ask her why? Did you try to resist?*" Her answer tells us the story of the lack of the child's freedom to ask in the face of traumatized parents.

> *You do not ask questions. These are things that you do not decide about. There was no teenage rebellion like today. She said I could get lice and I was also already afraid of this possibility because it meant going through the terrible treatment with kerosene. When I was young I didn't understand where her trauma with the lice came from... she didn't explain... We knew she couldn't sleep at night... we didn't know why – no one told us. We knew we were not supposed to ask her questions about the Holocaust.*

The survivor's granddaughter asks her mother: "*But I wonder how as children you knew not to ask?*" The second-generation daughter answers: "*Through an innate sense, I think.*" In Chapter 12 we reflect further on these powerful knowing–not knowing processes and discuss some clinical implications for processes of healing trauma in the chain of the generations.

11

The Second Generation's Experience of Parenting Their Adolescent Children

The relational themes that we portrayed based on the narratives that the sons and daughters told about their recollected experiences seemed to have a distinctive emotional intensity, especially in relation to interactions with their parents during the stage of adolescence. Previous research has found that the developmental tasks of adolescence, namely separation-individuation, autonomy from parents, and achieving intimacy while avoiding loneliness (Blatt & Blass, 1992; Erikson, 1968; Josselson, 1980, 1988), constitute special issues and challenges for the second generation (e.g., Bar-On, Eland, Kleber, Krell, Moore, Sagi, Soriano, Suedfeld, van der Velden, & van IJzendoorn, 1998; Brom, Kfir, & Dasberg, 2001; Freyberg, 1980; Mazor & Tal, 1996; Shafet, 1994; Wardi, 1992). The distinct Core Conflictual Relationship Theme patterns that we identified in our study (see Chapter 4) were played out during adolescence in the tensions that the sons and daughters experienced between striving for autonomy and the need to protect their vulnerable parents, who had suffered enough, leading them to avoid confrontations with their parents. Consequently, the parent–child pattern of "mutual overprotection," whereby the child despite the parents' controlling behavior is careful not to inflict further pain on them, was translated during adolescence into a relative absence of rebellious behavior on the part of the sons and daughters.

Now that the second generation have children who have reached adolescence, we were interested in exploring how the unique characteristics of the parent–adolescent relationship they experienced while growing up may play out in their current relationship with their adolescent children. How do they experience parenting their adolescent children, and what meanings do these experiences have for them? We studied these questions through the eyes of the parents (the second generation) and of their adolescent children (the third generation).

In contrast to the large body of theoretical writings and research on the developmental challenges faced by adolescents, the challenges of parents dealing with children at this stage of life have received significantly less attention (Steinberg & Steinberg, 1994; Steinberg & Silk, 2002). Parents are required to change their perceptions of their child and to adapt to the changes that the adolescent undergoes during this period, which are physical, pubertal, cognitive, and social (Collins, 1995; Scharf & Shulman, 2006). The processes of separation and individuation during adolescence (Blos, 1962) may involve the defiance of parental authority, rebelliousness, de-idealization of the parents, and increased emotional separation. The parent may have difficulty coping with these changes, which may lead to increased strain in the parent–adolescent relationship. The complementarity of issues raised by the challenges of parenthood as their children reach adolescence and their own mid-life issues at this phase might intensify the strains in the parent–adolescent relationship (Steinberg & Silk, 2002). As Scharf and Shulman (2006) put it:

> In sum, adolescence entails major changes for adolescents and their parents, which make this period especially challenging. For adolescents, the peer group, and in particular close friends, serves as a support system in this transition. Parents who are engulfed with additional dilemmas of life-span issues have to find their own resources, redefine their parenthood, and adapt it to the needs of their adolescent child (p. 321).

In setting out to study parent–adolescent relationships we focused on the possibility that the parenting experienced by the second generation from their survivor parents may have impacted their own parenting style (Fonagy, 1999). Developmental psychology defines intergenerational transmission of parenting as "the process through which purposively or unintendedly an earlier generation psychologically influences parenting attitudes and behavior of the next generation" (van IJzendoorn, 1992; p. 76). Among the mechanisms at work in intergenerational transmission of parenting appear to be the way parents interpret their children's behavior, as well as the way they interpret their own parents' behavior in retrospect, parents' expectations from relationships, and parents' meta-cognitive functioning. The growing literature on the internal representations of parenting (e.g., Bretherton & Munholland, 1999; Slade, Grienenberger, Bernbach, Levy, & Locker, 2001; Mayseless, 2006; Scharf & Shulman, 2006) was relevant to our study on parent–adolescent relational experiences, including the interplay between the recollections of the relationship with one's parents and the current relationship with ones children.

Based on interviews that he conducted with second-generation adults, Hass (1990) reported that they often try to promise themselves not to repeat their parents' behaviors that had adversely affected their own development. They try to give their own children more freedom and avoid overprotecting them. Paradoxically, this attempt to provide their children with the kind of parenting that their survivor parents could not provide them may lead to the other extreme, namely lack of control and the absence of appropriate boundaries and limit-setting. Alternatively, given that this attempt involves reprocessing and resolving the parenting that one experienced from one's own parents (Scharf & Shulman, 2006), it could lead to adaptive parenting and positive outcomes. In examining the parenting experiences of the second generation we explored these alternatives by considering themes of continuity and change in parent–adolescent relationships.

CHANGE AND CONTINUITY THROUGH THE GENERATIONS

The themes of change and continuity in the parenting style of the second-generation parents that we present here are based on an in-depth narrative analysis of interviews with parents and their adolescent children from an Israeli high school–based sample (Wiseman, 2005; Wiseman, Goldberg, Remez, & Ben Shmuel-Zetelny, 2005). This separate sample (collected in 2002–2004) consisted of mother-father-adolescent triads; the adolescents were school-based boys and girls. Mothers' ages ranged from 37 to 58 years, and fathers' ages from 41 to 59 years. Adolescents' ranged in age from 15.5 to 18.5 (mean 16.95 years); all were from intact families. The adolescent was defined as a grandchild of survivors (third generation) according to the criterion of having at least a mother who was the daughter of a parent who survived the Holocaust (n = 33). Of these, in more than half of the triads (n = 19) both mother and father were children of survivor parents. For more demographic details and information on this sample see the Appendix.

In this separate study, the adolescents' mothers and fathers had independent personal interviews, including a Relationship Anecdotes Paradigm (RAP) interview (see Chapter 2), that assessed themes of parent–adolescent relationships in recalled interactions with their survivor parents and current interactions with their adolescent child. Adolescents underwent a RAP interview that assessed themes in their relational narratives with their father, mother, and peers (the peer data are not discussed here). The semistructured interview with the parents also included questions adapted from other methods of assessing relationship narratives and obtaining parental recollections (Mayseless, 2006; Putallaz, Costanzo, & Smith, 1991; Scharf & Shulman, 1998, 2006; Slade et al., 2001). These questions were designed to assess parenting intentions and reflections on similarities and differences between the parents' experiences with their parents in adolescence and their view of their children's experiences with them (for examples of questions from the Parenting Adolescence Experiences Interview, see Appendix).

To shed light on change and continuity in parenting through the generations we analyzed and compared the themes that emerged in each family on two levels: 1) the stories that the parents told of their recollected interactions during adolescence with their parents (the adolescent's grandparents) in comparison to the stories that the parents told about their current interactions with their adolescent child; 2) parents' stories about current interactions with the adolescent in comparison to the adolescent's stories about their current interactions with their parents. We also include the parents' own thoughts and reflections about their recollections of the parenting that they received during adolescence and the way they currently parented their adolescent child.

Herein we demonstrate different degrees and variations of change and continuity in the parent–adolescent experiences of parents who are sons and daughters of survivors.

A MOTHER'S QUEST FOR CORRECTIVE EXPERIENCE THROUGH PARENTING HER ADOLESCENT DAUGHTER

Chaya's parents were both Holocaust survivors; her mother survived the war in hiding and her father was a survivor of a labor camp. She and her husband, who is not a son of survivors, have three children. We interviewed their adolescent daughter Inbal, who at the time of the interview was in twelfth grade (age 18). Inbal is the second child in the family and has an older brother and a younger brother. We first focus on the themes that emerged in Chaya's interview in relation to her experience of parenting in light of the parenting she experienced while growing up with survivor parents.

Parent–Daughter Relationship through Mother's Eyes: Chaya

Chaya seemed to have been motivated to provide her daughter Inbal with a different parent–child relationship experience from her experience with her parents. An in-depth analysis of her interview showed that her experience as a second-generation daughter with her mother set the stage for her narration of her current experience as mother of her adolescent daughter. Chaya strives to change the relational patterns she experienced and wishes to provide Inbal with a different mothering experience. She seemed to use the opportunity of the interview as a challenge to examine and to review these changes.

The dynamics of Chaya's "dialogue" between the parenting she experienced and the parenting she wishes to provide was reflected in the interesting choice of stories in the RAP interview that centered on similar themes: her recollections of herself as a daughter in interaction with her parents and her current account of herself as a mother in her interactions with her own daughter. Two judges rated the form of Chaya's overall discourse in the interview as relatively high in coherency and reflectivity and also in Holocaust salience. Based on our in-depth analysis, we next set out the aspects that point to change in parenting and those that point to some continuity.

Change in Parenting

Chaya's motivation to differ in her parenting from that of her own parents emerged in at least three core themes in the interview, which seemed to play out in the mother–daughter interactions of Chaya with her mother and with her daughter: 1) raise an independent daughter who stood by her own opinions; 2) children who would share their thoughts, lay things out, and be open with her; and 3) children would have good and pleasant memories and she should not become a burden to her children. With respect to these themes, Chaya declared her wish to provide her children with almost the opposite image of what she experienced with her own parents. We first consider these themes through Chaya's eyes.

Themes of Compliance versus Independence

Chaya's perception of her Holocaust survivor parents is that they lived for their children's sake in a style of "*self-sacrifice*" that entailed the constant demand for the children to repay this debt by complete fulfillment of the parents' expectations.

> CHAYA: *This was the atmosphere at home, that . . . the parents work very hard, and everything is for us, and they do not need anything for themselves . . . I wanted us to be like every normal family that goes out and sits sometimes in a restaurant, goes to the movies, goes on trips, but we hardly had any of that.*

She tells the interviewer that it made her feel as if she was living for her parents' sake in an atmosphere of suffocation and emotional blackmailing. She links her compliance with her parents' self-sacrificing to the unspoken message that she serves as a kind of replacement to those who perished.

> CHAYA: *I was so busy trying to please my parents and to be a good girl, and not to annoy them. I knew that all of the family members were exterminated in the Holocaust, and that you need sort of to be instead of them . . . and above all to be a good girl and not to upset them. You cannot cause them grief; they must not know you did something bad. You have to be a good girl all the time.*

In contrast to her parents, who lived for the children's sake, Chaya tries to stand up for her own rights "*to live*" and to enjoy her life. She feels she deserves to develop a career and to live life as part of a couple, and to go out and "have a good time." She feels this in turn enables her daughter, Inbal, to feel that she has the right to be firm about what *she* wants, and to conduct open negotiations with her mother when disagreements arise. The themes of compliance versus independence in the relationship were central to Chaya's stories about her current interactions with Inbal. She in fact ends these stories by telling of the pleasure she gets from Inbal's ability to assert herself in these encounters with her.

> CHAYA: *I was very happy about Inbal's independent-mindedness, that she is this way; I value her ability to have her own opinion. I'm*

> *happy that she is this way . . . I know that I'm a rather demanding and pressuring mother, but she's able to say to me, "NO. This is not what I want."*

Themes of Familial Communication

The other central aspect of change in parenting that Chaya focused on in her narratives was the nature of parent–child communication. She contrasted her experience of lack of open communication with her own parents to her wish to have open channels of communication with her own children. She indicated her parents' Holocaust experience as being at the root of this lack of communication. Her parents' traumatic past was left unspoken: "*It's like a different chapter in their life, and we never knew what this chapter was.*" Her perception of the home she grew up in is of one where communication centered on the commitment to report to the parents ("duty to report") and emotional communication was absent. Her depiction of these experiences resonated with those we have described in previous chapters. For example, she explains that even when there were conversations "you talk but you don't really tell . . . they did talk, they didn't really tell." There was no place for expression of angry feelings in the shadow of the parents' (unspoken) Holocaust story. Their story remained "frozen" or "fossilized" in the past. She refers to this experience as growing up in "a home that did not have a past, but only had a present and a future."

Contrasting her recalled experiences with her parents, she emphasizes the change from "reporting to the parents" to an invitation to share without pressure, and the legitimacy of sharing problems too. She begins with a general statement: "*They know we expect them (her children) to come to us and lay out things, and also to talk about difficulties, that they always have us as behind then, and we never go in front of them and never behind them, but beside them.*" Asked to focus on her relationship with Inbal, she contrasts herself as a daughter who could not share difficulties ("you had to tell only good things") to her perception of her daughter as sharing more difficulties when things do not work out for her and she needs support. She also works hard to respect Inbal's freedom to choose what to share with her and not to show her frustration when she feels that Inbal prefers to keep things to herself: "*Inbal chooses to share with me only what she chooses to share. Hundreds of times I caught on to things that she didn't share... but I never showed her my anger.*"

The conflict about what to share and not to share with her mother appeared in Chaya's recollected narrative in relation to the issue of sexual development. She contrasts her painful experience with this sensitive issue with the way she thinks her daughter experienced the same developmental milestone (i.e., she is pleased that Inbal could easily share these experiences with her).

The Menstruation Story

Chaya's recollection in relation to her mother:

> CHAYA: *I was about 14–15 when I had my first period. I wanted to tell my mother but I was afraid of her reaction. Instead I told my aunt who had immigrated to Israel before the war, because she was more open and easy to talk to than my mother. But my aunt told my mother and this annoyed my mother. She was angry at me that I hadn't told her about it.*

Chaya's account in relation to her daughter:

> CHAYA: *I remember when Inbal first had her period. She woke up in the morning and she called me and started crying... and I was so happy for her, and even happier for myself, that she wanted to tell me.*

Clearly, the theme of sharing and having the freedom to choose what to share, and with whom, is a sensitive issue for Chaya. She rejoices when her daughter shares things she did not dare to share. In relating the story of her daughter's first menstruation she appears more focused on the fact that the daughter had no inhibitions in sharing with her than on what was happening to her daughter and her being there for the daughter. The story seems to be about what it means to succeed in her quest to give her daughter a different experience from her own with her own mother.

Continuity in Parenting

Despite Chaya's goal to provide her daughter with a different parenting experience, aspects of continuity seem to appear throughout these two versions of parenting. Some are explicit and conscious; others are more implicit and therefore more masked and more unconscious. They are particularly evident concerning the issue of the silence within the family about the Holocaust.

Holocaust-Related Themes

Chaya did not know about her parents' experiences during the Holocaust, only the fact that all the family perished and that her father had children who did not survive. Hand in hand with this lack of open communication about the Holocaust, she felt that the Holocaust was always present in the home. The home, she said, was like a "fortress." The parents' friends were all Holocaust survivors and functioned like a substitute family. At festival dinners all those friends who were "there" (in the Holocaust) were invited to sit around the table. For Chaya, life in the shadow of the Holocaust felt like "a preparation should history repeat itself." She gives a number of examples in which this was expressed in verbal and nonverbal messages from her parents. 1) Everyone was happy that she had the looks of a "shikzah" (non-Jewish), which was like a "charm" or a "ticket to life." 2) Her parents gave the children information in the financial domain, so that they would know "what they have and what they don't." She sensed that this message was intended as preparation for rapid packing of personal belongings. 3) Occupational and career choices need to be made to suit an uncertain world, as one's occupation could make the difference between life and death. 4) A cloud of guilt hung in the air over her parents' life and her own life.

The "story that was not told" is a heavy burden on her shoulders. Now a mother herself, her wish is not to become a burden to her own children. In general, she says, she wants her children to have good memories. This goal of weighing more lightly on her daughter's shoulders, in contrast to the heavy presence of the Holocaust in her own life, leads to some confusion in Chaya's account of the relevance of the Holocaust family background in her daughter's life. Unlike her coherent stories throughout the interview, she narrates a somewhat incoherent story about Inbal's trip to Poland.

The Letter for the Trip to Poland

When Inbal's was about to leave for Poland (see Chapter 12 for the meaning of this kind of visit), Chaya gave her a letter she had written that Inbal was to read when she arrived. Parents are customarily requested to write personal letters to be given to the children to read during the visit, the content being entirely decided by the parents. Chaya tells the interviewer that she wrote about everything that Inbal did not know about her parents in the Holocaust, things that can only be written in a letter. Then on a different direction she says that the letter also served as a special opportunity to tell Inbal about all the good things she thought about her that she had not spoken to her about openly. "*I wrote her a letter... and I asked her to read it on the way. I wrote her everything I was thinking, I wrote her lots of good things that I had in mind... I wrote her everything I had not been told. I really wrote her what I thought about her... and I thought that in that way, it will be precisely there (in Poland) that she would feel a connection.*" Chaya concludes the narrative by mentioning, almost in passing, that Inbal did not open the letter. She says that she fantasizes that Inbal will read the letter only after Chaya dies. The letter, according to

Chaya, will ensure that Inbal is left with good memories of a positive mother–daughter relationship, the opposite of the way she feels about her childhood memories with her parents.

In this rather incoherent narrative the mother seems to package together the things that she was not told about the Holocaust, about who she really is, and what her parents thought of her. The things they hid from her to protect her from the harsh trauma of the Holocaust appear as a barrier to the relationship she experienced with her parents. Chaya fantasizes that in Poland some corrective act can somehow be performed through her relationship with her daughter, and through her daughter reading "the things" she wants to tell Inbal. These things are partly Holocaust related, but also sound more like the mother's reflections on her daughter. This story appears to represent the attempt at a concrete remedy for the trauma: good memories to replace the bad ones that Chaya endures from growing up under the cloud of guilt and the shadow of the Holocaust. What remains puzzling from the mother's story is why the daughter did not want to open the letter. Unfortunately, the interviewer did not ask Chaya directly how she felt about that. She seems reconciled to the idea that her daughter will open it when she dies. Apparently, some things still cannot be opened and cannot be said in the presence of the other.

Death and Grief

Following the tragic death of a friend of Inbal, murdered when a terrorist blew himself up in the middle of an Israeli bus, Chaya is naturally concerned about her daughter being able to express her grief and fears of death. Although Chaya indicated that Inbal shares difficult experiences with her to receive support, with this awful event Chaya was aware that Inbal was withdrawing in her room, grieving for the friend. In this respect Inbal appears to repeat with Chaya her difficulty sharing fears and thoughts about death. As Chaya is aware that she remains outside the support circle of her daughter, she wants Inbal's peers to come over so that Inbal will be able to open up and share with them: "*I wanted her friends to come because I knew that it was important for her to be able to talk. But so far she hasn't spoken with me about her pain. You know – it is death anxiety . . . and she doesn't open up, but I can see when it happens to her.*" Chaya feels that at least she, unlike her own parents, sees what her daughter is going through. We now turn to the daughter–mother relationship through the eyes of Inbal.

Mother–Daughter Relationship through Daughter's Eyes: Inbal

In the RAP interview (with a different interviewer), Inbal narrated encounters with her mother that had occurred in the last school year. Both encounters revolved around conflict of wills between Inbal's handling of achievement-related issues at school and her mother's aspirations and pressure to achieve. In the first relationship episode Inbal informed her mother of her decision to drop one of the science subjects she was taking.

INBAL: *I wanted to drop this science subject that I didn't want to take in the first place, but I took it because it was important for my mother that I study sciences too. We were having lunch and I told her that I didn't want to continue with it, and as I expected she didn't agree. She said I was giving in too easily and why won't I do what I'm told. I had hoped she would understand and support me, but she didn't.*

INTERVIEWER: How did you respond to her reaction?

INBAL: *I felt stressed. I tried to reply to her arguments. She said that I was taking the easy way, and I told her that I wasn't, that I had struggled for almost 2 years; I had tried and I really had put real effort into it. It wasn't because I didn't want to make an effort or because of boredom. I didn't think there was any reason to go on with something that made me feel so bad. I wanted her to understand where I was coming from.*

To the interviewer's further questioning Inbal about her feelings and how the encounter ended, she speaks clearly her disappointment.

INBAL: *You see I think that in some ways I expected her to respond this way, but it disappointed me because I had hoped that maybe she would react differently, that she would understand and support me. Later I even thought about it again – if it was worth sticking to my decision, if it sparked such a response, if it was worth it. But in the end I kept to my decision. She won't be angry with me forever because I dropped a subject in school, and it was important to me.*

In this episode we can see through Inbal's eyes the dynamics of the mother–daughter relationship regarding the theme of compliance versus independence. Inbal feels that her mother expects compliance, and she is disappointed with what she perceives as her mother's lack of support and acceptance of her independent decision. Inbal struggles with the tension of going against her mother's expectations, haven taken the science subject in the first place because of her mother's aspirations for her. This leads Inbal to question her decision to drop it in light of her mother's lack of acceptance. Despite the tension this creates for Inbal, the story ends with her not giving in to her mother's pressure and she carries on with her independent decision.

Going back to Chaya's perspective, interestingly she also referred to this "dropping a science class" encounter as one of the relationship episodes that she told about Inbal in her interview. In describing how she felt during this interaction with Inbal, Chaya shows ambivalence toward what she perceives as her daughter's independent mindedness. To the interviewer's question regarding how she felt with Inbal's insistence on her decision, she replies:

CHAYA: *You see I respected her very much for it. I knew she is making the wrong decision. But, ah, I respected her . . . I hope she cannot hear me right now (she is in the other room). I really respected her independent mindedness . . . I knew she was making a mistake; I didn't like it at all. I think she should be taking science. I tried to convince her but she didn't accept my opinion. I knew all along she did it because we (herself and Inbal's father) expected her to, but I didn't want to force her, or to hurt her. It wasn't worth fighting over.*

This opportunity to compare these two separate accounts of this specific encounter about "dropping a science class" offers us some insight to the dynamics between Inbal and her mother. Chaya, who felt she had no choice but to comply with her survivor parents, actually seems to enjoy seeing her daughter's independent decision. Chaya comments to the interviewer that she hoped her daughter could not hear her revealing to the interviewer that she respected Inbal for the decision, so we can infer that Chaya's explicit message is of not accepting her daughter's decision. Out of her ambivalence, perhaps due to some rigidity regarding the great importance of achievement goals, she does not want Inbal to hear this part (her respect) and she presents her only with the disapproving part. It is unclear why she feels that her respect should be kept a "secret." We can safely say that mother's appreciation of Inbal's independence does not come through to Inbal. For her part, she is disappointed with her mother's lack of acceptance and understanding. In any case, both Inbal and Chaya are concerned not to harm their relationship and express some anxiety over the cost to their relationship of disagreement.

The second encounter with mother that Inbal related also centered on achievement at school. Due to a teacher's mistake in grading an exam, Inbal wrongly received a low mark, and the encounter with mother revolved around Chaya's insistence that Inbal speak to the teacher at once and have the error rectified. Not sharing her mother's concern, Inbal did not hurry to attend to the matter and opposed her mother's pressure that the matter be handled in a certain way. She says she did not understand why it bothered her mother so much, what the rush was. Inbal asserted that she wanted to handle it quietly on her own, and was annoyed about what she saw as her mother's unnecessary interference in her affairs. Through Inbal's response to the interviewer's question on what happened in the end, we clearly learn about Inbal's perception of her mother as opposing her and not trusting her enough.

INBAL: *In the end it (the mistaken mark in the exam) did not affect the final grade on the report card. I showed mother the final grade and she was pleased, but still she insisted that I should have done it her way (spoken immediately to the teacher). It bothered me a bit that she still had to have the last word. It bothers me that she wants me to do things her way. Even if I think differently, her way is better.*

Inbal's stories represent Chaya as more controlling and strict than Chaya represents herself in her interview. Nevertheless, Chaya seems to have some awareness of the inconsistency between her wishing to be accepting of her daughter and encouraging her independence, and her actual controlling responses toward her daughter, especially on issues of academic achievement. In the part of the parenting interview in which she is asked about what she would like to change in her relationship with Inbal, she replies first by referring more generally to herself as a mother, and then more specifically regarding Inbal.

CHAYA: *I wouldn't change much... except... maybe hear them out more rather than my desires for them, or my aspirations. Perhaps I wouldn't force Inbal to do things she doesn't want, such as choosing subjects at school. But overall I wouldn't change much.*

Chaya also showed some awareness of Inbal's difficulty in going against her parents' expectations of her. Although she emphasizes her wish that Inbal be more open with her and feel she has a sympathetic ear, she indicates that Inbal "is not open, she is independent in her thinking." Some confirmation of Inbal's difficulty in sharing what she feels with her parents, especially in situations of conflict, was also apparent in the encounters in her relationship with her father. In his interview her father indeed expressed some concern that Inbal was closed (did not express her feelings) and that she kept things bottled up.

Looking Back on Received Parenting versus Current Parenting: Chaya

Toward the end of the interviews Chaya was asked to reflect on the similarity and difference in her relationship with her own mother and in Inbal's current experience with her.

INTERVIEWER: What would you like her to experience in a similar manner to what you experienced in your relationship with your parents?

CHAYA: *Nothing... nothing. Because even the warmth and love that my parents expressed toward me... I first and foremost experienced it as emotional blackmail; I felt suffocated... I vowed that I would not do that to my children. I can't say that I always succeed, but I'm really on my guard against this emotional blackmailing. I think about the difficulties I had to cope with during my teenage years; I for sure don't wish them for her.*

INTERVIEWER: Are there similarities between the parenting you received and your parenting style?

CHAYA: *There is a similarity in the concern, the caring and devotion and my responsibility toward my children. I often find myself thinking in sentences that my parents spoke, but not in terms of the emotional blackmail. In that respect for sure I don't want to be like them. But in terms of the concern, my children know that there is a rule, no matter where you are or how old you are, once a day you must call your mother. It comes from where I came from. I try to get it across with humor.*

INTERVIEWER: How do you understand the differences?

CHAYA: *First and foremost, I made a decision to be different. It's a different generation.*

Finally, toward the end of the interview, Chaya tried to explain to the interviewer why she finds it difficult to address the questions that ask her to reflect on the parenting that she received.

CHAYA: *Both my parents have died and the whole issue of my childhood is entirely closed because it was so problematic. On the one hand, I think my parents made such efforts to rebuild themselves that I*

> *wouldn't be able to do if I were in their place: to rehabilitate life and rebuild a life from zero, without knowing the language and without support... to really come back from hell and to rebuild a life, and to try to keep your own sanity and the sanity of your children. This is something I only understood when I was 40 years old and after I visited Poland for the first time. But I have really closed the whole chapter of my childhood also because I think I went through difficult childhood and adolescence experiences. Not that I was abused, but the reality was such that... I don't have the strength to open it up and this is why I also remember relatively few stories... I have really locked away my childhood memories.*

Like the sons and daughters whose stories we presented in previous chapters, Chaya voiced astonishment and respect for her parents' ability to remake their lives in the aftermath of the Holocaust. She also expressed guilt and pain for criticizing their parenting as they had suffered so much. Along with referring to her own childhood as difficult and suffocating, she also sees her parents as managing to hold on to their own sanity and their children's sanity, hers included. She attributes this more recent realization to her maturity in adulthood, in understanding the difficulties of being a parent when she herself has to deal with being a parent, as well as to her visit to Poland.

A FATHER'S QUEST FOR CORRECTIVE EXPERIENCE THROUGH PARENTING HIS ADOLESCENT DAUGHTER

Both Yehuda's parents were in Europe during the Holocaust; his father was in hiding and his mother's Holocaust experience is unspecified by him. His interview includes many references to the way he experienced growing up in the family of Holocaust survivors and his need to provide his children with a different experience of parenting.

Change in Parenting through Father's Eyes

Yehuda recalls the years he lived at home as extremely tense and difficult, especially in his relationship with his father. He starts the RAP interview this way.

YEHUDA: *I will start with my father... my father is a Holocaust survivor; he went through the Holocaust during his childhood, from about age 9 to 14, something like that. He was in a bunker... and with his family hid from the Germans, and it left its mark in the whole education sphere and everything related to it.*

Themes of Control and Strain versus Respect and Softness

From the brief sketch of his father's Holocaust background, Yehuda immediately proceeds to describe the pressures he felt at home from his father, especially around school achievement

YEHUDA: *There was this pressure at home about studying... to be someone, to get a profession, and to succeed academically, everything that was part of it. It really was a burden because I had other things on my mind; I didn't exactly want to study all the time. I was into sports very seriously and was a volleyball player and I played in a league... and many of my interactions with my father were around the issue of school and studying. Not that I didn't want to be a good student – but with this pressure it bothered me. If there was parents' day, and I got a mark that was lower than what was expected from me... it was accompanied with punishment. Not to be able to leave the house to go to volleyball practice with the team. It was just always an argument, argument...*

Referring to his experience with his daughter Mia, Yehuda emphasizes his respectful attitude. He describes her in somewhat idealized terms: "*She is really a personality, outstanding student, mature, I have no words, any father would like to have a daughter like her.*" He feels great pride in her accomplishments, but he wants it to be clear that he does not overemphasize academic achievements. As he puts it, "*The most important thing to me is that she is a good person and helps others.*"

Although he emphasizes that there are no control issues between himself and Mia, he recounts a situation where he and his wife told Mia to limit her many activities outside the home.

YEHUDA: *We felt she was spending too many hours out of the house and we told Mia we wanted her to spend more time at home. She was*

> *upset by our insistence. It reminded me of the arguments I had with my parents, so maybe because of this sensitivity from my past I was easier on Mia than my wife. But still, there was a world of difference from the strained relationship I had with my parents.*

Going back to the issues of control in his relationship with his father, he recalled the time his father went as far as to interfere directly with the army's decision regarding the kind of unit into which his son would be drafted. Without Yehuda's knowledge, his father went to the local recruitment office to speak to an army doctor so that Yehuda would not be sent to a combat unit. Yehuda found out, and it angered him immensely.

> YEHUDA: *I wanted to be in a combat unit and to contribute as much as possible, as I was very patriotic, but my father wanted to protect me, and to be sure that I kept out of danger and wouldn't be injured in the army. He wanted me to do something that didn't involve combat. It was very important for me to do what I liked and what I wanted, and not to accept his dictate, or imposition. I wanted to fulfill myself and to prove to myself that I was worth something, to raise my self-confidence, to be an officer and be a commander. I wanted to leave home, where I was suffocating, and start to prove things to myself, to contribute to my country. I was very angry and there was a fight at home, and I was offended personally. This really darkened the relationship and damaged the trust, and it affected the relationship in the future.*

Yehuda's sense of suffocation resonates with Chaya's story and others that were presented in the previous chapters. In this context, the focus is on his current parenting attitudes and experiences with Mia in light of his reflections on his memories of angry feelings toward his parents. "*There are days when I look back and analyze it; I understand it. But as a kid, I think there should have been a different way to go about it and to say things, with the same effect . . . the same thing that was achieved but in another way. Not so harsh and strict. To come and talk about it more rationally.*" This is related to the second theme that emerged, namely, his quest to improve the parent–child communication.

Communication Patterns

The strained communication and lack of open expression of emotions that Yehuda experienced with his parents contrasts with the way he tries as a father to listen to his children and to talk to them gently.

> YEHUDA: *I kept things bottled up inside and I never forget them. My father was very firm, so I didn't see any options. My way was not to fight. There was some verbal fighting, but then I'd withdraw and wouldn't talk, and life would go on . . . I was upset by it and it ate me up from within. With my children I believe in talking more and listening to them. To hear their opinion, not to have an absolute idea of mine, not black and white . . . that this is the way it should be and that's it. Instead I try at least to talk with my children in a more soft way, to talk and try to reason more, and less by acts . . . because I think otherwise you cause harm to the relationship.*

He is pleased when his daughter expresses her emotions, and comes for advice, although he is aware that she shares more intimate conversations "to do with girls' stuff" with his wife. "*I don't feel I can contribute much in that area.*"

Looking Back on Received Parenting versus Current Parenting: Yehuda

During the interview, in talking about the frustration and resentment that he kept within, Yehuda goes back and forth between being able now as an adult to understand his parents better and at the same time feeling that things should have been done differently

> YEHUDA: *I simply know that it was not done out of malice . . . these are things that I understand today. Today I understand how my father grew up without a father after his father was killed, and it was important for him that we have a profession and other things, and*

> *that we'll be decent human beings . . . but his obstinacy, much to my dismay, came from things he went through in his life.*

Throughout the interview Yehuda expresses retrospective understanding of his father's background as an explanation for his own difficult experiences when growing up. He also expresses a strong sense that his father's hardships led to the hurtful experiences that Yehuda says he does not forget. The message not to forget that is passed on regarding the Holocaust seems somehow to re-echo in his feeling of being denied freedom and in his not forgetting these hurtful experiences that darkened the relationship.

In parenting his own children, Yehuda compares their experiences with his and is motivated to provide them with a positive parent–child relationship. The theme of open communication is emphasized in his parenthood in light of the stories of the things that bothered him and he "kept bottled up inside." In response to the question "What makes you happy about Mia?" he answers confidently: "*My relationship with her: that she comes and asks my opinion, or comes and talks with me, tells me . . . For me, this is what causes me the most happiness and satisfaction.*"

Finally, Yehuda's account, like Chaya's, is characterized by the quest for a corrective relationship with his daughter. Unlike Chaya's depiction of areas in which she is less successful, this father appears to idealize the relationship and the accounts he related about interactions with Mia are somewhat general. For example, he describes his daughter as very open, but he does not relate an event that exemplifies the openness. The most emotional story was about escorting her on her first day to a pre–army course, when he felt very emotional about this moment of separation and its meaning in terms of his daughter leaving home and starting a new stage in her life. In his eyes at least, Mia enjoys a respectful and warm relationship with her father. In this case we do not have Mia's account for comparison, but we chose this case because it typified the father's quest for correction and the lack of strain in the father–daughter relationship. Again, like many parents, he wants to do it better for his children; whether he is successful or not is hard to evaluate.

The following case refers to a father-mother-son triad from our study that demonstrates parenting experiences with hurdles on the path to a warm and open relationship.

CHALLENGES ON THE PATH TO CORRECTIVE PARENT–CHILD RELATIONSHIPS

Both Giora and Esti are children of survivors; he is in his early fifties and she in her late forties. Yoav is their second child, and he has an older sister. At the time of the interview, the relationship with their son was under great strain. This gives us an opportunity to take a snapshot of the challenges of parenting adolescents. We will focus on the father–son relationship through the eyes of both. In this case, we also include some of the mother's stories to complete the picture. We first present the themes that emerged in the father's interview in relation to the parenting he experienced while growing up with survivor parents.

Father–Son Relationship: Father's Recollections of His Experience

Giora's recollections from his adolescence are depicted in sharp contrast to the way he perceives the current phase in his son's adolescence (to be described later from his perspective and Yoav's). He gives a general statement of the ease of that phase in his own life: *"I know that I went through my teenage years very easily... Actually I didn't go through adolescence; I was a good boy, so I didn't have any confrontations – not with my father nor with my mother."* Unlike other children of survivors, who expressed some bitterness over having to be a "good boy" or "good girl," Giora does not express any dismay in this regard.

Helping the Hard-Working Father

Like many of our other interviewees, Giora describes his father as working long hours and getting home late, and his mother as being a dedicated homemaker who would cook the food while Giora was out playing with his friends. He recalls that his father, who was a blue-collar worker, would work overtime doing repair jobs that were physically hard. Around the age of 15, Giora would sometimes join his father after school to help him by carrying heavy things and handing him tools, for example. He stresses that he did this at his own initiative; his father did not necessarily encourage it because he wanted Giora to be free to play. Nevertheless, Giora states, "*He (father) was glad that I'd come to help him and I felt that it made him feel good and that I was helpful.*" Yet it is in this context that Giora also recites father's motto: "*Thank you for helping me, but see how hard I am working and you need to study, study, study, so that you won't have to work at such strenuous jobs and for such long hours.*" Giora says he took his father's message seriously as he saw for himself how hard his father worked. He qualifies this by saying he did not feel he was studying for his father's sake but that it made sense to him that he needed to study, and it led him to take school and his later studies seriously. So contrary to the pressure that Yehuda described and the punishments he received for not studying, Giora did not interpret his father's message as controlling him, and he identified with his father's point of view so that he felt an intrinsic motivation to study.

Echoes of His Father's Past

Echoes of his father's past are mentioned in Giora's recollections of his father's frequent requests to him and his brothers not to be noisy and to keep quiet.

> GIORA: *I can hear his request, "Give me some quiet." When we would run around or make a noise this would bother him. Let's say that this is where the Holocaust comes in. My father was a survivor of*

> *Auschwitz and I knew he suffered from different aches and pains that these were from the Holocaust . . . that's why we needed to keep quiet. So from a young age I remember that if he was at home, not to bother him.*

In response to the interviewer's question on how Giora felt around this dictum, "Keep quiet, don't make a noise," he answers rather concretely: "Only that we had to be quiet. So if we were playing with a ball we'd stop, and then start again until next time round when we'd stop again." It can be speculated that that this kind of reminder of father's traumatic past in the daily interactions at home lead to Giora's sensitivity to his father and his commitment to help him. Again, however, Giora did not experience this as pressure from the outside but as arising from his empathy toward his father, who did not take his help for granted.

Current Father–Son Relationship through Father's Eyes: Giora

From the part of the interview concerning his current relationship with Yoav (his son), it becomes clear that Giora is beset by much turmoil. In contrast to his recollection of his smooth adolescence, Giora repeats several times in the interview that adolescence is a difficult stage: "*Yoav is 17 and it's a difficult age, it's extreme . . . in a severe way.*" He says his relationship with Yoav is replete with confrontation. He evidently finds coping with his son's rebellious behavior frustrating, and in his eyes Yoav's attitude is one of indifference. He wonders if this may be part of being at the age of showing your parents that you "don't give a damn." He is bothered that Yoav does not take things seriously and by what he perceives as Yoav's disrespect. He ends by saying, "*I'm already waiting for his teenager years to pass.*"

Comparing the way he experienced parenting their older daughter when she was a teenager he says, "*It is just day and night. A daughter is easy; she behaves well; doesn't do stupid things; she brings only nachat [satisfaction]. She's okay still, and he is mischievous. That's why we're stricter with him."* We can learn from this that Giroa's sense of competence as parent of a teenager is challenged at this juncture in parenting the "rebellious son."

Communication Patterns

The communication patterns that concern Giora at this point center on the need to monitor Yoav's whereabouts. Giora would like Yoav to disclose more about what he does with himself so that Giora can prevent him from doing things that may put him in trouble. Although in general Giora feels he knows his son, this recent period of conflict has left him surprised and has diminished his confidence.

As part of the interview protocol on parenting, the interviewer asked the father what he thought Yoav needed from him. He responded thoughtfully.

> GIORA: *What does he need from me? That's a very very good question. You see, ah, sometimes I think that a bit of, ah . . . warmth, love, hugs. But you see he doesn't let it happen.*

Yet when the interviewer persists in probing what Giora thinks Yoav expects from him at this period of his life, the father exclaims in frustration: "*That I leave the house and come back in 2 years so we won't bother him.*" This contradiction between knowing that what Yoav needs is a hug from his parents and feeling frustrated by Yoav keeping his distance represents the push and pull that parents often experience as the adolescent undergoes the task of negotiating autonomy and closeness with his parents. We now turn to look at the parent–son relationship from the mother's eyes.

Mother–Son Relationship through Mother's Eyes: Esti

The father's portrayal of the rocky relationship is corroborated by the mother's depiction of her current experiences with Yoav. In her interview, which was conducted separately, she expressed a great deal of worry over the present difficulties. *I don't know what will happen in the end, will he complete high school with a full matriculation? But I want him to feel we are on his side, at least to protect him.*"

Esti, perhaps more than the father, is concerned about the heavy cost of the conflict on the quality of their relationship with Yoav. She dreads confrontations with Yoav and feels helpless in the face of his oppositional behavior. She tends to withdraw to her room at the height of the confrontation. She explains that she goes away to avert any risk of escalation: "*I am afraid for him . . . and I prefer to restrain myself and to keep silent.*" Esti wants to be able to maintain a dialogue with her son, but she does not trust herself to be able to reach out to him.

Prior to the present turbulence, Esti recounts that her relationship with Yoav was always very close. She even considers this as possibly intensifying Yoav's withdrawal from them.

> ESTI: *The relationship between us was always very close. It's possible that this rebellion is a stage he's going through because he needs to free himself of his dependence on us. It's possible . . . For example, in the past I would pass by him and stroke his head fondly and that would be fine with him. But lately when I stroke his head I feel him cringe and he freezes, and it really bothers me. I don't know quite how to understand it.*

When asked (independently of his father) to what extent her interactions with Yoav could have happened with her older daughter, her answer was similar to her husband's: her current experience with Yoav is totally different from the smooth relationship she enjoyed with their daughter. "*She played the part of the good girl. There was never any rebellion, no confrontations, there were conversations, and it never was a problem. Either she or we would concede or yield to the other, and life would go on.*"

Now we turn to how Yoav experiences his relationship with his parents.

Parent–Son Relationship through the Eyes of the Adolescent Son: Yoav

Examining the relationship episodes that Yoav told about his current interactions with his parents, we were rather surprised by the gap between the impression we got from his parents' experience of him and the experience through Yoav's eyes. Although Yoav did not necessarily refer to the same events that each parent told independently, his relational narratives also clearly portrayed highly intense conflicts with his parents. Yoav's private inner thoughts and feelings about these conflicts, however, did not confirm his parents' perceptions of his indifferent and disrespectful attitude to them.

In one of his narratives, Yoav described an intense conflict he had with his father, who put sanctions on certain privileges. His lifting them was conditional on Yoav's accomplishing his schoolwork properly and improving his slack attitude to his studies. Yoav protested loudly, but after an unsuccessful attempt to persuade his father to change his mind and restore his rights, he ran away from home. While on the manifest level this incident is consistent with the parents' distress over Yoav's rebellious behavior, we can learn much from what Yoav relates about the meaning of the way this event unfolded from his perspective.

INTERVIEWER: What happened after you ran away?

YOAV: *I went home calmer after a few days and my parents were also calmer. I had a conversation with my father and I saw that he was not indifferent, and I saw that they love me and care about me. He also said it was not a solution to run away. I knew he was right; I knew it wasn't a solution but it still gave me time to calm down, and I think it actually did help in that after we spoke I had a great sense of relief because I had wanted to have this kind of conversation with him (father) for a long time. It was meaningful for me and it had an impact on me.*

INTERVIEWER: In what way was it meaningful?

YOAV: *It made me see that the family was important to me, and before that I had taken them for granted, and after this I saw that I had to make an effort. Also in terms of my studying: I still went to school on the days that I was away from home, so I realized that I went to school not for my parents and not for someone else, but I go for myself. So I understood that also in terms of studying I need to put in more of an effort.*

Despite his running away, one can clearly read how the rebellious son also yearns to overcome the strains in the relationship. His parents do not have the reader's vantage point to see that their son is far from oblivious to their reactions to him, and he does care about the relationship. In this episode, and in others that he related, we got the impression that he even admitted some responsibility of his own for the conflicts with his parents.

Putting together the pieces from the independent interviews with each parent and with Yoav, we see that parents and son expressed in their narratives a wish to reach the other. Yet the two sides sense a barrier between them that prevents their messages from getting across. The father experiences his son as indifferent and feels as if he is against a wall. The mother's fear of confrontations with her son makes her appear in his eyes inconsistent and distant. It is the lack of open dialogue that makes these conflicts so painful for both sides. Only through having the conversation with the father is Yoav able to feel that his parents love and care about him.

Looking Back on Received Parenting versus Current Parenting: Giora

Comparing his current parenting to his parents' style of rearing, Giora sees some similarity in his concern for his children, especially in relation to health issues. His son says to him, *"Stop being so Polish [i.e., worrying so much], and I think it really came from my parents."* Nevertheless, he sees himself closer to Yoav than his parents were to him. Perhaps as a way of speaking about his emotional closeness to his son, or perhaps out of the current frustration with Yoav's behavior, Giora describes how he monitors his son's activities: *"I pay more attention to what he is doing. My parents didn't have time to raise us and we grew up somehow. Today parents have more time, and children need more guidance. And there are more dangers around."* Thus, Giora attributes some of the difference between himself as an adolescent and his son as due to the different times in which they live. His parents worked so hard that they left him to himself and he was fine. He cannot leave Yoav to his own devices because teenagers nowadays take more risks. Therefore, parents have to restrain and monitor them more closely than when he was Yoav's age: *"We were not dangerous."*

Looking Back on Received Parenting versus Current Parenting: Esti

The prevalent pattern of the survivors' sons and daughters, entailing the need to protect the parents and avoid confrontation (Chapter 4), is clearly evident in Esti's recollection of her relationship with her parents during adolescence. Although she viewed her father as generally full of vitality and as trusting her to make her own decisions, she recalls him telling her about his enormous losses. Her painful awareness of his enormous losses leads her to feel that the responsibility rests on her not to fail her parents. *"I didn't argue, didn't fight with them. I gave in; I never gave them any reason to worry. I felt I had to be considerate of them and be a good girl."* Looking back she feels that although she felt independent and that her parents trusted her, she felt too much responsibility. She thinks that perhaps because she had to take on so much responsibility she actually demanded more from herself – even beyond her parents' expectations: *"I carried this responsibility like heavy baggage on my shoulders. It weighed down on me; there was a certain heaviness. The Holocaust was like a cloud hanging over my head."*

In her current parenting with Yoav she is confused as to whether he wants them to set him more limits, or, on the contrary, whether they should leave him alone entirely. On the one hand she feels he is distancing himself, and on other hand she feels he deliberately wants to be in conflict with them. She tries to understand him, and wonders whether confronting him more would help. She is, however, incapable of fighting with anybody. In Yoav's mother's case, the core pattern of lack of ability to handle confrontation with her parents while growing up seems to be replayed with the adolescent son, even though he may actually need her to engage with him at these points of disagreement rather than to distance herself.

Reflecting on her parenting style and that of her parents, Esti closed the interview with a more positive outlook. She says she feels fine overall about the way she is as a parent. She thinks she is going in the right direction, and she enjoys her children. As to the difficult period they are going through with Yoav, she has many questions and she is trying to figure it out. She and Giora talk about it a lot. As she puts it: *"No question that Yoav is now the center of our world."* She feels they are trying to search for ways to face the challenges of this period with Yoav, and she believes they will overcome it: *"Once Yoav is over this lousy adolescent rebellion stage, the good relationship we once had will return and we will have a good relationship."*

CONTINUITY AND CHANGE IN ANXIETY AND COMMUNICATION

Shelly, the second child in the last family we introduce here, is described much like Yoav as a far more rebellious adolescent than her older sibling; in this case the daughter is more rebellious than the son. We present it as an example of continuity in some aspects and change in others. Unlike Yoav and his parents, who are now embroiled in the difficulties in the relationship, Shelly's rebellious period is recounted as belonging to the past. Currently the parent–daughter relationship is close, and marked by a pattern of open communication. Batia, Shelly's mother, impressed us by the way she was able to reflect on her own contribution to the dynamics between herself and her daughter in light of her own upbringing. We first focus on the continuity of the theme of anxiety and the need to protect the children.

Continuity of Anxiety through Mother's Eyes: Batia

Batia described the parenting she received as characterized by her parents need to support, help, protect, and defend their children. Both her parents were survivors, and they underwent such harrowing life-threatening periods that she says she does not know how they could endure it. She asks herself how they could have withstood all the terrors, hardships, suffering, and hunger – all these things. They reached Israel after the establishment of the state. They built a home in this country, a warm home with a pleasant atmosphere, and they wanted their children to feel not only good but also protected: *"They wanted us not to feel all the suffering they had gone through, so this meant protecting and protecting all the time."*

To Protect, to Protect

In parenting her own children, Batia feels that she has absorbed her parents' fears, and therefore she is overly anxious about her children. She talked openly in the interview about her anxieties and the way they affected her relationship with Shelly, her adolescent daughter.

> BATIA: *Although my parents tried to shield me from the fears that they carried over from the Holocaust, I am extremely anxious about my children – that they should be happy, that they should feel good, that God forbid nothing bad should happen. If Shelly goes out with someone and I don't know who it is, I'm afraid. If they drive somewhere and they don't immediately call to say they've arrived I am overwhelmed with fear. Maybe it passed on to me without words*

> *because really I am anxious about everything, and these fears are uncontrollable. I know that I control her out of my anxiety. I know it's no good because I don't let her grow up and she's already 18, and she says "Mother, leave it to me," and I know she's right. But if she's driving somewhere I need to know immediately that she's arrived, even if it's only a 10-minute drive away; I need to know everything is okay; I need to know, to have control.*

Batia told the interviewer that currently this did not hamper the mother–daughter relationship, but when Shelly, around 15, began to be more independent socially and to go out, there were many confrontations and much anger. The mother recalls how Shelly would get angry and protest: "You don't understand, you don't give me any freedom and you wrap me in cotton." Batia is aware that she was too controlling and attributes this to her anxieties: "*I am aware that I need to relax and I need to suffocate them less. I know I don't ease off enough and that it's no good, that it's out of overprotection.*" Interestingly, she used the term suffocation to describe the way she is with her children, a word that was used by some sons and daughters to describe their feelings in regard to their parents (see Chapters 3, 4, and earlier in this chapter).

Looking back at the time Shelly was rebellious and there were fights between them, Batia says that Shelly, who as noted was more rebellious than her older brother, knew how to assert herself. Batia reflects on this period.

> BATIA: *I know I got into fights with her, because I didn't let her grow up, and she wanted to grow up at the pace that suited her. And looking back she was right, because she's a great kid and there was no need for me to restrain her.*

Batia is reflective and relatively coherent about what underlies her protective behavior. "*I am driven to protect, this is something I inherited from my parents, to protect, to protect. I think I internalized the fears of the second generation of the Holocaust, it was in the air, in the unconscious."* She describes to the interviewer her inner struggle between letting go and trusting Shelly, and her overriding fear of danger.

> BATIA: *On the one hand I trust her, but in the way I hold her too tightly it's as if I don't trust her, but I really do and I have confidence in her. I know I show my worrying too much. You know, it's more dangerous now than when we were growing up. Now even taking buses is dangerous because of the bus bombings [the interview was conducted during the period of suicide bombings in 2002], there is kidnapping, and what's happening in the country.*

Change in Communication Patterns through Mother's Eyes

Batia says her parents did not tell her about what they went through during the Holocaust, and they did not talk about the economic difficulties. She never asked for anything beyond what they could give. In her current relationship with her daughter, she portrays Shelly now as open with her.

> BATIA: *She easily shares even intimate details with me. She knows I won't open her personal letters, but if she shows them to me she knows I enjoy her openness and sharing. I think she is open because she can feel the warmth, the love and the feeling that she is important and that I want to help. The times of anger are usually out of love and concern and then she says: "Mom, enough. Stop with the worrying. It's okay. I'm grown up."*

It appears that the open communication about the mother's fears and the mother's willingness to hear this from her daughter, even if not always translated into her actual behavior, makes an open mother–daughter relationship possible. In the past Shelly did not understand her mother's concerns and this led to much anger, but now she does understand. It took time to reach this point, but now Batia says that Shelly knows how to calm her and they both know how to reach each other in a positive way.

Father's Recollections on Communication with His Father: Gershon

Like many of our interviewees, Gershon, Shelly's father, referred to the losses suffered by his own father, the sole survivor of a family of eleven. Only later did the father locate a distant cousin but like others referring to the perished families, he states: "*They were all wiped out.*" He referred to the salience of the Holocaust in his life: "*I know that we live the Holocaust; we live it through and through.*"

Attempts to Get His Father to Talk about the Holocaust

Gershon described his attempts from a young age to ask his father questions, and every time his father would give him another piece of information. Gershon was the youngest in the family, and he dared to ask more questions than his brothers. He says, "*The younger ones are braver and the parents open up.*" He wanted to know about the family and tried to put the pieces together. Gershon described an interesting blend of caution coupled with insistence and daring to ask. The father would be sitting at the table and he could see by the look in his father's eyes that asking questions would throw father back to . . . and he would continue to try gently. He knew he was not going to get an answer; however, sometimes he phrased his questions circumspectly to get an answer, at times directly, and at other times casually. He describes this step-by-step process: "*I asked what his grandfather worked at, and surprisingly he told me. Then I'd try to ask about how many brothers and sisters he had, and I got an answer. It didn't seem to me that he was answering unwillingly, but I was cautious, and I was curious and he answered.*" Gershon would go on asking until the point where his father, would say, "*Enough I don't want to talk about it.*" He respected that; as a child he did not have the courage to "*penetrate the silence forcefully.*"

Although Gershon describes the content of the answers he got from his father as shocking to him, he seems to value these moments of getting to know his father and learning about his past. There is also a sense of pride that he got his father to tell him things his other siblings (who did not dare ask) did not know. He knows his father loved him very much, and he felt they understood each other even though they did not talk very much. Several times he expresses his respect for his father.

Father–Daughter Relationship through Father's Eyes: Gershon

With Shelly, he recalls interactions of warm conversations that end with the daughter releasing her emotions and him hugging her. He sounds empathic toward her, and is able to see things from her perspective. He enjoys talking to her and is eager for heart-to-heart conversations. He says that he imagines that these conversations leave a deep impression on the child because he remembers how meaningful such conversations, being very rare, left such an impression on him as a child, and how important they were for him.

Gershon also refers to Shelly's rebellious phase. He feels that they succeeded in coping with it and navigated the difficulties with her. As a parent he says he examines himself and thinks of where he went wrong and how to improve things. He heavily emphasizes understanding his daughter, being supportive, and involved in an appropriate way. Like the mother, he is impressed with Shelly's openness with them and says that as parents, sometimes they "cannot believe she is so open with us."

Parent–Daughter Relationship through Daughter's Eyes: Shelly

Overall, Shelly's interview corroborates the feeling that she enjoys a positive and open relationship with her parents and family. The episodes she chose describe incidents in which she felt her mother pressuring her and focusing on things she needed to improve. In these situations, Shelly says she feels frustrated that her mother is controlling, has no confidence in her, and does not trust her. She wants her mother to stop pressuring her, to understand her, to see her as responsible, and to leave things up to her. Unlike Yoav, she is open about it and expresses her wish to be trusted, so that she and her mother can openly discuss these points of disagreement. Asked how a particular confrontation of this kind ended, she says: "*She understood that she couldn't pressure me to that extent and that if it doesn't come from me there's nothing she can do.*"

Shelly appreciates her father's wisdom and likes to talk to him. She does not get angry with him nor does she take offense or get into fights with him. Rather, he advises her and she listens to what he has to say. She describes an episode in which she could tell her dad what was bothering her. One gets the sense of open lines of communication and the ability to air even negative feelings. Had we interviewed this family when Shelly was in mid-adolescence, the picture may well have been less positive from the parents' perspective, and perhaps, especially from the daughter's perspective.

ON THE QUEST FOR CORRECTIVE PARENTING: CLOSING COMMENTS

The quest for corrective parenting may be universal, especially in relation to adolescents, as parents promise themselves not to repeat the mistakes they think their parents made with them. In general, parents from different family backgrounds may have different parenting experiences in light of past experiences, with some following routes of correction or partial correction and others, despite their attempts to overcome difficult past experiences, being unsuccessful in breaking away from intergenerational transmission of adverse parenting experiences (Crittenden, 2006; Scharf & Shulman, 2006). From our interviews with parents who grew up in survivor families, we were highly impressed by their quest for corrective parenting experiences in relation to two central themes in the parent–child relationship: autonomy versus compliance and parent–adolescent communication.

Regarding the theme of autonomy, survivors' children having experienced overprotection and having had to protect their vulnerable parents, they struggle to grant their own children optimal levels of autonomy and the freedom to make their own decisions. In cases of successful or partial correction they seem to feel good about their children's ability to be assertive toward them and strive to overcome their own anxieties and their academic aspirations for their children. In cases of strain in the parent–adolescent relationship, their past experiences, marked by avoidance of confrontation, seem to cause them difficulty in managing conflict situations that are part of the challenges that parents face with their adolescent children. Yet even in these cases we were impressed by parents trying to cope; clearly, they put great effort into attempting to overcome the hurdles on the path to corrective parenting.

As for patterns of communication, in light of the lack of open communication in the survivors' families, especially in relation to the parents' traumatic past, their children seem determined to keep open lines of communication with their own children. They stress the contrast between the constrained patterns of communication in their families and the pleasure they take in their children sharing with them and having open conversations. In some cases the communication was portrayed as more open through the parents' eyes than through the adolescent's eyes, perhaps representing the gap between the parents' explicit attitudes and actual behavior.

This kind of "Rashomon phenomenon," in which narratives about events are often significantly different for each person who experiences the same event (Luborsky, Barber, & Diguer, 1992), is not surprising here. In relation to generational change in fathers of preschool children, Bretherton, Lambert, and Golby (2006) suggest that the differences that a parent perceives between his or her parenting and the parenting he or she received as a child may appear more striking to him or her than it might appear, for example, to an outside observer. As they put it, "Fulfilling the simultaneously challenging and rewarding task of parenting reasonably well may require the optimistic belief that one can do as well, and perhaps even better than the previous generation" (Bretherton et al., 2006; p. 205). We suggest that in the case of parents who grew up in survivor families, the parents' quest to heal the echoes of the parental past is a powerful motivator for generational change.

The traumatic past of the parents (the Holocaust survivors) was often mentioned when their children reflected on and interpreted the parenting they received in contrast to their own parenting. The children of the Holocaust survivors were highly motivated to provide their children with parenting that was less protective and was characterized by open communication. For example, they attributed the dictum to be a "good boy" or "good girl" to their parents' massive losses, whereas they saw their child as being free of the heavy load they carried. They also sometimes referred to the intergenerational transmission of problematic parenting, such as the need to protect, yet they felt they could make amendments to overcome these tendencies and that their children had a greater degree of freedom to break away from these problematic patterns and to express their protests openly.

In the adolescents' stories only rarely did the grandchildren of the survivors mention explicitly the Holocaust background of the family. In one case, the attribution of the mother's behavior to being raised in a survivor family was suggested by the daughter's history teacher. Noga refers to her mother's insistence that she leave the door of her room open at all times; even when she has friends over her mother wants the door to stay open. Her mother, she says, *"doesn't agree under any circumstance, even if I am listening to music or watching TV, that I close the door to my room."* Noga says it is something psychological and that is why the doors in their house do not have locks. At school Noga talked about this to her history teacher when they were studying about the Holocaust. Her teacher provided her with an explanation for her mother's seemingly inexplicable insistence on the doors in the house not being closed.

> NOGA: *My teacher explained that the second generation of Holocaust survivors needs to know where their loved ones are. If I close the door she can't see me if she goes past the door, and this drives her crazy because she needs to see the members of the family. Before I talked to my teacher I didn't understand it, because why can't mother understand that I want my privacy, so it annoyed me. Also, mother didn't tell me why I had to keep the door open – she didn't explain it to me. But after my teacher's explanation I understood that their parents passed on to them (the second generation) the feeling that they need to maintain eye contact, to know where people are. After we (Noga and her mother) talked I understood myself better, and she (Noga's mother) also understood herself, it was a good feeling that we talked about why. After that she also became interested to find out other things that were unusual or different in the second generation that you don't find with other people. It was better we talked about it and we understood each other.*

Although in Noga's *Leave the Door Open Story* the explanation for her mother's behavior comes from the history teacher, Noga's ability to have an open conversation with her mother about this explanation leads to positive feelings of understanding and acceptance.

Finally, we would like to refer briefly to the part of our study (Wiseman, 2005) that compared the second-generation mothers and fathers and their adolescent children with a comparison group with no Holocaust background. Although we found few differences between the groups in central relationship themes, the communication theme did distinguish them. Second-generation mothers and fathers wished significantly more than the parents in the other group that the adolescent would "*open up to me and share with me.*" In some ways, the *Open Door* story can represent not only fears of abandonment and the need to control the adolescent but also the wish to have no secrets in the home. Addressing the issue of how the adolescents perceive their parents' parenting style, the findings, based also on self-reports (Goldberg & Wiseman, 2006; Wiseman, 2005), generally show that the third generation perceives the parent–adolescent relationship in the same way as their counterparts from families with no Holocaust background. Note that these findings comparing the adolescents with and without a Holocaust family background were obtained with a relatively small sample (approximately thirty adolescents in each group), suggesting the need to replicate the findings with a larger sample.

Finally, the findings described in this chapter lend support to Hass's (1990) impressions from interviews conducted with children of survivors in North America who declared their attempts not to repeat their parents' overprotective behaviors, by trying to give their own children more freedom and to avoid overprotecting them. Although all parents of adolescents struggle with the challenges of managing conflict and granting autonomy while maintaining harmony and closeness in the parent–adolescent relationship (Steinberg & Silk, 2002), we suggest that second-generation parents, in light of their experiences with their survivor parents, perhaps show a heightened sensitivity in the quest to master these challenges successfully.

12

Growing Up to the Music of Knowing–Not Knowing: Reflections and Clinical Implications

The study of the long-term intergenerational effects of the Holocaust on the offspring of the survivors has been addressed in the clinical and research literature for the last three decades. Much of the debated research has focused on the issue of the prevalence of psychopathology in adult children of survivors. In the more recent terminology of the trauma-related literature the issue of intergenerational effects is considered with respect to "secondary traumatization" in survivors' children and "tertiary traumatization" in the grandchildren. The most recent meta-analyses of studies have shown no evidence of either secondary traumatization in nonclinical samples in the children of survivors (van IJzendoorn, Bakermans-Kranenburg, & Sagi-Schwartz, 2003), or tertiary traumatization in the grandchildren (Sagi-Schwartz, van IJzendoorn, & Bakermans-Kranenburg, in press). These findings were based on sophisticated meta-analytic methodology that summarizes a large number of quantitative studies. These meta-analytic summaries do not, however, include studies that rest upon qualitative-narrative methodology, which are also needed to address such a complex phenomenon as intergenerational effects of trauma (Bar-On, 1995; Bar-On, Eland, Kleber, Krell, Moore, Sagi, Soriano, Suedfeld, van der Velden, & van IJzendoorn, 1998; Chaitin, 2003; Rosenthal, 1998). Our study, thus, relies on a unique combination of an adaptation of the Core Conflictual Relationship Theme (CCRT) method and narrative-qualitative methodology as ways to listen to the echoes of the parents' trauma in the relational stories told by nonclinical adult children of the survivors.

We have chosen to use the term "echoes" as it refers to three key points that underlie our understanding of the relational themes and interpersonal patterns that were manifested in the narratives described throughout our book. First, the use of the term "echoes of the trauma" underscores that we are not dealing with the transmission of the trauma itself (Mikulincer, 2006), but with interpersonal themes and child–parent dynamics in which the echoes of the trauma play out in the recollected relational experiences. Second, the term "echoes" carries with it the aspects of voices and sounds that fit our emphasis on modes of communication of the trauma and its ongoing verbal and nonverbal presence. As we show in our analysis of themes of communication, even when the relational space is wordless, the music of knowing–not knowing is heard either in the foreground or in the background, and sometimes in both. Third, the pitch and loudness of the echoes that we can hear are highly variant and depend on many variables such as the source that transfers the echoes (the survivor), the individual at the receiving end (the child), and the surrounding environment (the sociocultural context). This last point speaks to our contention that the relational themes and emotions that we described shed light on the various ways people subjectively construe and deal with their relational and emotional experiences. In giving voice to their authentic subjective experiences and their "narrative truth" (Spence, 1982), we are not necessarily attributing all their experiences to their parents' traumatic background. Indeed, alternative explanations and insights can be offered and the readers of our narratives may consider other interpretations.

It has been suggested that qualitative-narrative studies are more sensitive to context and are more suitable for studying subjective experiences and the meanings of trauma in the life stories of both the survivors and their descendents (Bar-On, 1995; Chaitin, 2003; Lev-Wiesel,

2007; Josselson, Lieblich, & McAdams, 2007). Our adaptation of the conceptual and methodological framework of the CCRT enabled us to reveal the relational issues and sensitivities that adult children of survivors often have maintained. Even if they have been found to score in the normal range of functioning on standardized questionnaires, they still seem to struggle with important relational issues that may not be captured by more objective measurement tools.

THE RELATIONAL THEMES AND EMOTIONS IN THE NARRATIVES

The narrative analysis of stories that the second generation told revealed the prevalent relational patterns that were played out in their meaningful interactions with their parents. To summarize the main themes in CCRT terms, we can say that the basic wish for closeness and/or the wish for autonomy were often met with parental responses that were perceived by the sons or daughters as overprotective and controlling [response of others (ROs)]. The child perceived the parents' worries and anxieties as a sign of their vulnerability and fragility, leading to a commitment not to inflict further pain on parents who have suffered enough [responses of self (RSs) and derivative wishes]. This led to the dictum "I should protect my parents (mutual overprotection) by giving up my basic wishes and avoiding confrontations at all cost." Thus, in our description we are elaborating on the CCRT method by implying that the RSs are turning into secondary wishes that are closer to the surface (i.e., closer to awareness).

Both the mutual overprotection and avoidance of conflict were also played out in the modes of communication. The child does not ask questions, and parents are careful not to burden their children with their traumatic past. In this wordless interpersonal space the child is careful not to express anger openly. Feelings of guilt go hand in hand with the perception of the parents' vulnerability, and the lack of open communication does not provide opportunities to alleviate the guilt. The anxious parent (who may be simultaneously controlling and losing control) fails to regulate the child's anxiety and to serve as a means of comfort. The child feels it is illegitimate to approach the parent with his or her own anxieties for fear that the parent will not be able to endure additional stress and worries. Under the specific circumstances that involve intrusion of parents' traumatic memories or parents' lack of responsiveness and empathy the child experiences feelings of loneliness. Children of survivors recounted experiences of loneliness in which they felt their parents misunderstood them and they further found themselves unable to understand the parent. In contrast, experiences in which the child felt loved supported and recognized lead to feelings of joy and a sense of mutual understanding.

As parents to their adolescent children, the second generation aspires to provide their children with an empathic and supportive relationship marked by open communication and sharing. The extent to which their quest for corrective parenting is successful often depends on their capacity to break away from the patterns (e.g., mutual overprotection and avoidance of confrontation) that characterized their recollected experiences with their parents. Indeed, they may even learn from their adolescent children how to negotiate conflicts while maintaining close bonds.

SOME CLINICAL IMPLICATIONS

What are some of the clinical implications of this relational picture for practitioners treating individuals and families who suffer from the intergenerational aftereffects of trauma?

One of the advantages of formulating the interpersonal themes and sensitivities by means of the CCRT framework is that they are highly relevant for understanding the dynamics that may develop with second-generation adults who seek psychotherapy. The relational themes that we have identified may alert therapists to the particular CCRT patterns that may emerge from material that is obtained during the history taking stage in the intake and the beginning of therapy. Furthermore, the formulation of the CCRT serves as the basis of therapist interpretations in Supportive-Expressive (SE) psychodynamic psychotherapy (Book, 1998; Luborsky, 1984; Barber & Crits-Christoph, 1995; Vinnars, Barber, Norén, Thormählen, Gallop, & Weinryb, 2005). Much of the therapy work involves patients becoming aware and taking responsibility for self-defeating patterns (Siqueland & Barber, 2002). The therapist works with the patient to understand whether the expected response of other (e.g., expecting the other to lose control) and the response of self (e.g., feeling guilty) are still necessary or useful.

There are also transferential themes to consider. Given the nature of the transference that may develop, it is possible, for example, that it will include the components of the CCRT that were identified in the relational narratives with the parents. Specifically, the transference relationship may be characterized by the patient's wish to be assertive (Wish), his or her perception of the therapist as controlling (RO), and the patient feeling that in response he or she must avoid conflict (RS) with the therapist. The therapist's awareness, perceptiveness, and ability to listen and identify such relational themes can facilitate the understanding of intrapersonal and interpersonal in-session processes. Moreover, the therapist should pay special attention to the second generation's tendency to avoid confrontation because it may be played out with the therapist in a manner similar to the processes involved in "withdrawal working alliance ruptures" (Safran & Muran, 2000). Repairing such withdrawal alliance ruptures with the therapist may offer the patient an opportunity to achieve a better understanding of their relational schemas in close relationships. Furthermore, the therapist should facilitate the expression of frustration with the therapist related to the theme of being controlled.

The patterns of familial communication between the survivors and their children are fundamental to our understanding of the interpersonal patterns and emotions that we identified in the relational narratives. More than 20 years ago, a special issue of Psychoanalytic Inquiry edited by Laub and Auerhahn (1985) was titled "Knowing and Not Knowing the Holocaust." Among others, Jucovy's (1985) contribution, titled "Telling the Holocaust story: A link between the generations," emphasized the communication between the generations about the experiences of the parents during the Holocaust. Based on observations from analytic work with survivors and their children, he stated, "We have learned that certain features of a child's development may be influenced by parental withholding of information and that even well-intentioned revelations of parental experiences may be shrouded in uncertainty, distortion, or mystery" (Jucovy, 1985, p. 31). These ideas possess a clear relevance for both individual and family therapy of survivors of other traumas and their descendents.

In the early 1980s, therapists who treated survivors and their families called attention to the need to break the "conspiracy of silence" (Danieli, 1983, 1984) in cases in which it prevailed in therapy, especially in the form of unconscious collusion with the therapist. For example, Jucovy (1985) stated that the discussion of such cases in their study group had the role of encouraging therapists "to make inquiries and to enter the previously impenetrable world of the Holocaust" (p. 43).

Although based on clinical cases, the work of psychoanalysts also holds relevance for our data on nonpatients. For instance, the "double wall" phenomenon (Bar-On, 1995) that often prevailed between survivors and their children prevented verbalizations and explanations of experiences related to the parents' traumatic past. The lack of opportunity to put these experiences into words sometimes leaves a fertile ground for the flourishing of fantasies that the child develops to fill the gaps. Sometimes this involves the generation of possibilities that are even more appalling than those that actually occurred (Bergmann & Jucovy, 1982; Jucovy, 1985, 1992).

In the last decade, intergenerational communication patterns about the forbearers' traumatic experiences have been explicated with regard to families of trauma survivors of various sorts (Danieli, 1998). Research on the descendents of Japanese American Internment camps (Nagata, 1998), Dutch war sailors and resistance veterans (Op den Velde, 1998), Vietnam War veterans (Ancharoff, Munroe, & Fisher, 1998), torture victims (Daud, Skoglund, & Rydelius, 2005), and others have pointed to the prevalence of a "conspiracy of silence" (Danieli, 1998) in the lives of survivors and their offspring. When the intergenerational consequences of traumatic events also include the stigma of physical repercussions (as in the case of the survivors of atom bombings of Hiroshima and Nagasaki), disclosure about the psychological traumas may be profoundly silenced (Sawada, Chaitin, & Bar-On, 2004). Furthermore, lack of acknowledgment of the genocide and the active ongoing denial of the victimization, as in the case of the Turkish genocide of the Armenians, impedes the ability of survivors and their descendents to process and integrate their traumatic history (Kupelian, Kalayjian, & Kassabian, 1998).

Conflicts between Talk and Silence

The conflicts of the survivors of trauma between the wish to forget and the need to tell their stories interface and correspond to their children's conflicted wishes to know the unspoken stories and feeling that they are too dangerous to know (Auerhahn & Laub, 1998). Ruth Wajnryb, an applied linguist, in her book, *The Silence – How Tragedy Shapes Talk*, describes how almost a half a century after the end of the war (when she was approximately 40 years old) her father put up the only pictures he had of his mother, father, and sister who perished in the Holocaust: "One day they were there, on the wall. He said nothing about them, maybe waiting for me to ask; and I said nothing, waiting for a cue from him" (Wajnryb, 2001; p. 213). The trauma is echoed through the pictures on the wall, but it remains unspoken and unarticulated. It is this kind of survivor–descendent silent discourse that bewilders the child who many years later tries to figure out why they could not ask. Wajnryb, who was born in 1948 in Australia and her grandparents died in the German occupation of Poland, wrote her book after her parents died. She recounts how her young daughter asks her "Who's that?" in relation to a photo of her dead grandmother, who she never knew. It is this kind of "freedom to talk about dead grandparents" in an open conversation that she could not have had as a child of survivor parents (Wajnryb, p. 6). In this example, like others that we found in our own work, we see how the "double wall" (Bar-On, 1995) dynamics are extremely difficult to disentangle, especially in relation to the unspoken mourning of the dead loved ones.

Nava Semel, a daughter of survivors, depicts in her recent novel *The Rat Laughs* (Semel, 2001) the conflicts and fears that are evoked around the telling and listening to the survivors' story. The survivor, who was a hidden child in the Holocaust, agrees to tell her traumatic story to her granddaughter who interviews her for a school assignment. In debating her choice to tell the story to the granddaughter, Semel gives us in the grandmothers' words some idea of what made it so impossible for her to tell the story to the second-generation daughter:

> Why actually the granddaughter? Why not tell the daughter? The daughter of the old woman is already not young and still not old, but she was disqualified as a possible addressee. It is unclear who disqualified her. The old lady preferred to postpone the story, every time with a difference excuse, because at any timing it was as if the story may threaten the life of the addressee, and even put in danger the continuity of birth. The daughter also evaded. Maybe she was afraid that receiving it might rob her of her mother and put in her place a crushed creature, with no face and identity. Actually, the truth is that she attributed to the story supernatural (magical) powers. Whoever will criticize the daughter for her refusal to carry the burden of the reception is missing the element of fear in the story. Without the fear no story would be what it is (Semel, 2001; p. 37; translated by the authors).

The idea represented in the above segment, that the "toxic" elements in the survivors' unbearable stories may affect their children and, therefore, endanger the continuation of the family is a strong one. The grandchildren indeed are often perceived as the proof for the ability to overcome this danger. Not only did the survivors bear healthy children but these children in turn continued the chain of the generations. In Semel's novel, the fear of the potential destructive force of knowing is later echoed in the words of the second-generation daughter:

> Maybe it is better that we do not know, because who knows what it would have done to me – to us – maybe destroy for all of us our life (Semel, 2001; p. 89; translated by the authors).

Dialectical Processes in Knowing–Not Knowing

When we began to test our ideas on patterns of intergenerational communication and interpersonal patterns, we distinguished between two major styles of communication in adult children of survivors. We called the first communication pattern we found "knowing and not knowing" and the second one we called "informative verbal communication" (Wiseman, Barber, Raz, Yam, Foltz, & Livne-Snir, 2002; see Chapter 5). This classification into two groups, derived from participants' responses to a self-report questionnaire of parental communication of Holocaust experiences (Lichtman, 1983, 1984), suggests a typology of Holocaust-related communication. Based on our narrative analysis, however, we have come to realize that even those in the relatively more informative verbal communication style can experience knowing–not knowing-like phenomena. Thus, we suggest that we are actually dealing with degrees of knowing–not knowing that lie on a spectrum of communication styles. In other words, in both groups there are situations or aspects of experience in which the "knowing" is at the forefront, alongside situations or aspects in which the "not-knowing" is at the forefront. It is also important to note that although excessive parental Holocaust-related verbal communication was relatively rare in our sample it also does not preclude experiences of knowing–not knowing.

In other words, part of the essence of the knowing–not knowing experience is that the "knowing" may coexist with the "not-knowing." In fact, the hyphen may represent a dialectical relationship between the "knowing" and the "not knowing." There is an inevitable tension between the "knowing" of the parents' traumatic past and the "not knowing" or being unable to think of what the parents went through. This dialectical stance attempts to hold both sides of this tension between what is known and not known, and what one wants to know and does not want to know. The known is at times unconscious because the individual does not know at least consciously that he or she knows. Looking for example at the *Electrical Hand Drill Story*, we speculate that when Shaul asked his mother for an electrical hand drill he did not know, at least at an explicit level of knowing, the meaning of this particular tool and the meaning of the noise. There was no obvious way for him to know because his mother did not reveal her past and did not explain why she could not hear "that noise." It is possible, however, that there is some kind of implicit knowing that goes on between Shaul and his mother, such that at the same time that there is a "not-knowing" about mother's past there is also a "knowing." Perhaps we can even argue that he insists not because he does not know but because he does know. This can be referred to as an experience in which one does not know that one knows.

The psychoanalyst Christopher Bollas (1987), in his book *Shadow of the Object*, coined the term "the unthought known," to indicate when the child knows something but may not have thought it yet. Because what is known is known without words, there is a kind of unarticulated knowing that has not gone through mentalization and symbolization. In psychotherapy we want to help the patient transform the knowing–not knowing into thought. This process often involves being able to give it words, to feel it, experience the pain, and disown parts of the parent that have been projected onto the child.

The Limitation of Words in Telling the Holocaust Story

Although we emphasize the need to know and to make the story known to the next generations, we must consider the limitations of words and of telling the Holocaust story. Unlike an ordinary autobiographical narrative, in trauma survivors the attempt to narrate a coherent account is fraught with difficulties. Greenspan (1998) suggests that to deeply analyze the processes involved in survivors recounting their stories, one has to understand these accounts as ways in which survivors "make a story" of what is "not a story" (p. xviii). He quotes Elie Wiesel (1978) on the "unbridgeable gulf" between the survivors' memory and its reflection in words: "They tried to communicate their experience of the Holocaust, but all they communicated was their feeling of helplessness at not being able to communicate the experience." Hence, Greenspan suggests that the task of listening to Holocaust survivors involves the attempt "to enter into survivors' struggle for and against words" (p. 6). He refers to listening to the "silence between the words" in the recounting, the telling and retelling.

Henry Szor (2007), an Israeli psychiatrist and psychoanalyst, writes about the intricacies of word and silence in therapy of Holocaust survivors. The survivor fears that his words would be met with disbelief and that the listener will not be able to "bear" the hearing of the witness of the atrocity. Szor refers us to Primo Levi (1986) who wrote in his last book *The Drowned and the Saved* about the thought "even if we were to tell it, we would not be believed" as it was represented in a dream common among the inmates of Auschwitz.

> They had returned home and with passion and relief were describing their past sufferings, addressing themselves to a loved person, and were not believed, indeed were not even listened to. In the most typical (and most cruel) form, the interlocutor turned and left in silence (Levi, translation to English 1988; p. 2).

Since the time Primo Levi wrote these thoughts they still hold truth for many. Yet there have also been efforts to listen and believe.

The second generation is struggling to work out ways to know their parents' personal story. Interestingly, historians have recognized this need to make these memories as real as possible with an emphasis on the personal story of each survivor.

In Yad Vashem (the Holocaust Martyrs' and Heroes' Remembrance Museum in Jerusalem) there has been a shift from the historical to the personal and private. Those who were fortunate to have some real object that remained with them have contributed these objects to make the stories more real. The doll "Zozia" that Yael Rozner, a child survivor, received from her mother who hid her in the basement of a deserted house on the border of the Ghetto is displayed in an exhibition called "There Are No Childish Games" (Perroni, 2002; Rozner, 2002). Most recently, a huge hollow trunk of a tree in which Yakov Zilberstein hid after he escaped the death march in 1945 was brought to Yad Vashem. After 60 years Zilberstein located the old tree trunk in the field of the village were he hid when the Germans searched the home of the Czech woman who hid him. What is remarkable is that now this tree that represents a story of an individual survivor has been situated in the heart of the Garden of the Righteous Among the Nations in Yad Vashem (this beautiful garden at the Jerusalem Holocaust Museum, honors the non-Jews who exemplified high-level principles of humanity by endangering their lives to help save Jews during the Holocaust). The introduction of these new museum items is consistent with the shift in the public discourse and commemoration of the Holocaust from the old emphasis on the collective to the story of the individual survivor (*Haaretz*, October 9, 2007).

As part of this emphasis on the personal stories, there has been a surge of stories written by survivors. Dina Porat, a prominent Israeli historian, indicates that the number of books that survivors have published in Israel has reached over 5,000 (published by publishing companies, and personal or family publishing), and that autobiographical writings of survivors are also found in the United States, Australia, Argentina, Germany, and France (Porat, *Haaretz*, January 24, 2007). She attributes this wave to at least two factors. First, the survivors came of age and began to feel that they were running out of time. Second, a change in atmosphere began in the 1980s with the study of the Holocaust becoming part of the history classes in school as well as the availability of educational and experiential trips to Poland. In this context, we suggest that the idea of "each man or woman has a name," can be paraphrased as, "each man or woman has a story."

Shlomo Breznitz (2000), an Israeli psychologist and child survivor, who wrote his personal story in a book *Memory Fields* (Breznitz, 1993), uses concepts from the psychology of memory to explain the powerful impact of survivors' autobiographies on those who read them or listen to them. He observes in his writing about the "Holocaust Experience as a State of Mind" that only long after the "big stories" saw the light of day could the "small stories" venture out and take their rightful place (Breznitz, 2000). The "small stories" are based on episodic memory rather than on semantic memory and on implicit knowledge rather than explicit knowledge. He suggests that small stories lend themselves to greater experiences of empathy. For the descendents of survivors the "personal story" and the ability to reach empathy are crucial to understanding and acceptance. These interesting changes in the way the Holocaust is remembered in Israeli society and in the world at large can be understood in relation to the social and historical context in which the stories are told. As Wolfgang (2007) put it recently: "Remembering is not solely individual. It occurs in social and cultural horizons."

Intergenerational Holocaust-Related Communication

In considering the Israeli social context, we evidenced a certain degree of change in the atmosphere between the interviews we conducted with children of survivors during 1996–1997 and those we conducted during 2002–2004 with the school-based sample of second-generation parents and their adolescent children. In the 2002–2004 study, the second generation seemed more aware of the presence of the Holocaust in their life. In terms of the intergenerational communication, only a few narrators referred to shifts in the communication patterns now as the parents have aged. Opportunities for changes in the communication about the Holocaust in the family may come about through the grandchildren. Trips to Poland that adolescents take through the school system may potentially provide such opportunities.

In a small sample study (supervised by HW), Zussman-Regev (2003) interviewed adolescent grandchildren of survivors about their experience going to Poland to visit the concentration camps, when they were usually accompanied by a group from their high school. She also interviewed the second-generation parent of each high school student about his or her perspective on the impact of the trip on intergenerational communication. The grandchild's trip, including the preparation process, seemed to provide an opportunity for survivors to tell their story to the grandchild and for the grandchild to listen to the personal story. It appears, however, that the style of communication between the second generation and the survivors is less amenable to change as a consequence of the event of the grandchild's trip. The discrepancy in the nature of the survivor–grandchild communication and that of the survivor–child communication can be illustrated by the interview with David (second generation) and Danny (third generation).

Danny, the grandchild (age 17 and a half) who was interviewed after he returned from the youth trip to Poland, describes the process of the opening of lines of communication between his grandfather and him:

> DANNY: *Every year grandfather opens up more and more. Up to 5 to 6 years ago, he did not agree to tell at all. All this time I tried to draw out from him gradually, slowly, slowly, and every year I hear more and more. Every time he would say that "before I go on the trip he will tell me more," so when the time for the trip came he already had no excuse.*

Although Danny says his grandfather wanted him very much to take the trip, the decision was clearly his own. Indeed, since he was a young child he said to his grandfather that when he grows up he will go on the trip to Poland, as he wants to see what his grandfather went though and where he was during the war. In response to his expressed "need to know," the interviewer asked him to reflect on why it is important for him to know. He answers: *"It is like a mission from grandfather, pass the knowledge on so that the next generations will know, and it is also part of my private history."*

The meaning of the trip for the grandfather and the link between the generations became particularly salient during the trip, as expressed through the ongoing cellular phone communication between the grandchild and his grandfather. Danny says that his grandfather does not usually call him but during the trip he kept calling him for brief 15-minute conversations. He further reported that there were times his grandfather cried. The emotional connection and the meaning of the crying for the grandchild suggest some sense of working through the mourned losses: *"The minute grandfather cried, it gave me the feeling that I am doing something grandfather always dreamt about, something big. But I did not take the trip for him."* The theme of the connection to the grandfather's traumatic past through this experience, takes on a real, visceral, and concrete feeling. The grandfather remembered the block ("Lager") number in which he was held, and Danny describes his feeling when he entered one of those: *"It is a different feeling knowing that maybe your grandfather was in this block; it is darkness and it is fear from everything, and closure; it is a feeling you cannot describe. I personally intend to take the trip again, I hope with my children, and then it is another full circle for them and for me to see my next generation there."*

In the interview with David (Danny's father), he says he is satisfied seeing what he perceives as Danny's ability to experience the trip deeply while simultaneously maintaining his boundaries. He is also impressed by his resilience.

DAVID: *It is my success and my wife's (success) as well as his own character that we have a child who is built well, he is sensitive enough, but also he does not go into it and gets crushed from it, but he gets up and continues. Experiences it deeply, and comes out of it and continues forward.*

This may suggest that the father (the son of the survivor) can count on his son to move forward, whereas he himself is perhaps more afraid and vulnerable.

David tells the interviewer that there was never any direct verbal communication about his father's Holocaust experience. Like many of our interviewees, however, he too says that from the time he remembers himself he always knew that his father was a Holocaust survivor even though he could not identify a time when such knowledge was fist acquired (see also Prince, 1985). This knowing–not knowing experience was linked in his mind to hearing his father crying and his rage attacks, whose presence "you cannot hide." David heard some facts about the past only indirectly, when mother talked about it with other people. Once he was with his mother at the doctor's office when the mother told the doctor that his father was in Auschwitz and that "he saw his brothers burning in front of his eyes." There was never a time when David was told the story. The survivor began opening up to his grandchild who began to ask questions and it is through Danny (his son) that David hears more about his own father's story. It is striking that in adulthood the second-generation child still maintains an indirect, echoing mode of communication such that until this very day when the survivor sits to tell his personal story of survival to his grandchild, the son says: *"I always sit on the side . . . I am never in a direct conversation. But I encourage my children to ask and to talk to their grandfather."*

From this example we can see how difficult it is to change the modes of trauma-related communication between the children of survivors and their parents. The working-through is often left up to the third generation (one additional generation removed from the trauma).

Working through Knowing–Not Knowing Processes

Processes of working-through can take place spontaneously or in the context of psychotherapy. In our 2002–2004 study, there were a few cases, in which there was a recent shift in the parent–child communication patterns. Dina referred to the silence that characterized her relationship with her father while she was growing up and the fact that he rarely spoke of his traumatic experiences. Now that her father has aged, however, he has begun to write his life story, and this includes stories from the Holocaust. Dina and her husband have facilitated the process by teaching him how to type and use the computer. She also proofreads his stories and regularly sits with him to go over what he writes. She feels that this has drawn them closer. He has opened up to her, and more deeply shares his emotions with her. She views this as a mutually novel and reparative experience for both of them and, as she puts it, "This has done wonders for both of us." The writing–reading process, and their communication around it, has facilitated empathy and the feelings of sharing. The writing of the stories may serve the role of a creation of "a third," in a way that resembles what occurs in therapy between patient and therapist relating through the shared space between them.

According to Ogden (1994), the psychoanalytic process is assumed to reflect the interplay between three subjects: the therapist, the patient, and the "analytical third" (Ogden). The analytical third is a third subject that is composed by the unique joint contributions of patient and therapist. The therapist's contribution is inevitably influenced by this analytic third and thus inevitably reflects something about both therapist and patient (Safran & Muran, 2000). In the context of working with descendents of trauma, therapists may need to work especially hard to maintain an observational stance that enables them to attend to their own inner associations and emotional reactions.

In psychotherapy with descendents of trauma, the psychotherapist is offering a holding relationship to the patient in which he or she can take the risk of the psychological journey of searching and unraveling the known–not known parts of their parents' story that were never before verbalized in the family. The supportive, safe, and empathic stance of the therapist is essential for making this difficult journey. Perhaps with the therapist for the first time the child of survivors can try to open up areas that were closed with the parents for fear that they would breakdown if he or she were to ask them questions directly. With the therapist, who can withstand the toxic elements in the traumatic stories with all the senses involved (images, noises, smells, and tastes), the process of making the elements nontoxic can begin to take place. During this search the therapist must refrain from assuming that he or she "knows" part of the story because it is important to keep the search as open as possible to avoid any premature closure on meaning. The enabling of this kind of active search into the parents' story is also necessary to start differentiating between the parents' story and the child's own story and identity.

The not known has a grip on the individual in a way that he or she remains stuck due to owning parts that may not be their own in their emotional life or in acting out. This impedes separation–individuation processes and authentic relatedness. What is not known cannot be integrated. Working through takes place by verbalization and making the unthought thought, or in Bion's (1970) terms "thoughts without a thinker" can become mentalized. By transforming the wordless space into a space with words and thoughts that give meaning, the children of survivors can free themselves from the transmission of traumatic experiences from parents to their descendents.

Treating adult children of survivors in psychoanalysis, Kogan (1995, 2002, 2007) has suggested ways in which analysts can help their patients understand the origin of enactments connected to their parents' traumatic past to transform "enactment into mental representation." Kogan's insights into the role of the therapist in helping patients discover the details of their parent's history seem to hold truth for other forms of psychotherapy and for treating offspring of other traumas. As she puts it: "The construction of an unbroken narrative – one that fills the gaps in the child's knowledge, that makes it permissible to mention the unmentionable . . . enables the offspring of survivors to gradually gain some comfort from the split-off knowledge, which has been accompanied by the unacknowledged affects and fears" (Kogan, 2007; p. 104).

Therapists working with patients who grew up in families that had experienced extensive trauma need to be aware that such patients may experience difficulties in expressing their wishes in a direct verbal manner (Wiseman & Barber, 2004). These kind of interpersonal processes, in which the patient has difficulty expressing his or her emotions verbally and directly, may play out in both individual psychotherapy and group psychotherapy with the members of the group. When these kinds of processes occur, the therapist's awareness of the knowing–not knowing processes echoed in verbal and nonverbal expressions may enable the therapist to participate with the patient in a different kind of dialogue. In this kind of open and empathic dialogue, the therapist will help the patient to make the nonverbal into verbal and to shift from knowing–not knowing to self-narration, identity, and authentic relatedness.

In repairing failures of intersubjectivity, psychotherapists need to provide a relational space in which the unthinkable trauma can be expressed and known. Open communication about the trauma, mutual sharing, and empathic close relationships can create a healing bridge between the generations of trauma.

APPENDIX

A. THE SECOND-GENERATION STUDY

The interviewees in this book are those who comprised the group of Holocaust Survivor Offspring (HSO) in our BSF-funded study on Central Relationship Patterns (Wiseman & Barber, 2000; Wiseman, Barber, Raz, Yam, Foltz, & Livne-Snir, 2002). Here we provide information on the procedure, namely, the recruitment of the participants, the Relationship Anecdotes Paradigm (RAP) interviews, the Core Conflictual Relationship Theme (CCRT) ratings, and the narrative qualitative analysis. Details on the demographic background of the participants are presented in Table 1.

Recruitment of the Participants to Our Second-Generation Study

The participants were randomly sampled from lists provided by the Israel Population Registry that included Jewish men and women born in Israel between 1946 and 1966, whose parents migrated to Israel from Eastern European countries after 1945 (i.e., their parents were residing in Eastern European countries during the war). Sagi-Schwartz with their large research project on three generations (Sagi-Schwartz, van IJzendoorn, Grossmann, Joels, Grossmann, Scharf, Koren-Karie, & Alkalay, 2003), which was conducted in Israel around the same period, were the first to get permission for this procedure of receiving such lists for the purposes of conducting controlled studies on families

TABLE 1. *The Second-Generation Study: Demographic Characteristics of the Participants*

Characteristic	HSO (N = 56)	HSO's Mother	HSO's Father
Gender			
Men	30 (54%)		
Women	26 (46%)		
Holocaust experiences background			
Survivors of Nazi concentration camps		56 (100%)	21 (38%)
Were in Europe during the war			17 (30%)
Were outside occupied Europe			7 (13%)
Migrated to Israel before 1939			11 (19%)
Age (in years)	39.74 (3.95)[a]	69.23 (5.16)[a]	72.04 (5.70)[a]
Passed away		12 (21%)	27 (48%)
Education (in years)	15.12 (2.49)[a]		
Marital status			
Married with children (%)	94.2		
Number of children	2.75 (.87)[a]		

[a] Mean (SD) at the time of the study.

of Holocaust survivors. We were fortunate that this procedure paved the way for our study. The sampling and recruitment procedure involved two stages. First, we randomly sampled from these lists of potential HSO. Second, we approached these potential participants through a phone interview to request relevant information regarding the specific Holocaust background of their parents. To be included in our study, we sought men and women whose mothers were survivors of a Nazi concentration camp. This inclusion criterion was intended to reduce the heterogeneity in the parents' Holocaust experiences (Danieli, 1983). If the HSO met these criteria, we then asked them to participate in our study, which involved a personal interview and completing a booklet of questionnaires. Of those who met the inclusion criteria, 52 percent agreed to participate in the study. This moderate response rate most likely reflects the time pressures of the busy work and family life of this age group, as most participants had young children at the time of the study.

Procedure for the RAP Interviews

The RAP interviews (see Chapter 2) were conducted in the participants' homes (except in a few cases in which the participants preferred to be interviewed in an office at the university). All the interviewees gave informed consent for their participation in the study. They signed a consent form before they completed the study protocol and were assured that their anonymity would be maintained. The interviews were audiotaped and fully transcribed.

CCRT Training and Rating Process

The CCRT judges in the Second-Generation Study were seven graduate students in clinical psychology and counseling psychology with at least 1 to 2 years of practicum experience. They were all trained in the CCRT method, including a number of training sessions with Jacques Barber, who oversaw the process. At the end of training, they all reached a level of acceptable agreement. After starting to rate the materials, they held regular meetings to refine certain categories and to correct for drift in the use of the categories. Two raters were trained to bracket the transcribed RAP interview material into relationship episodes (REs), indicating the beginning and ending of each RE, and they also indicated the referent of each RE. All RAP interviews were rated by two (of the seven) independent judges (see Wiseman & Barber, 2000; Wiseman, Metzl, & Barber, 2006).

The Narrative Qualitative Analysis

In addition to rating the RAP interviews on the formal CCRT standard categories (Barber, Crits-Christoph, & Luborsky, 1998), we engaged in a narrative qualitative analysis (Lieblich, Tuval-Mashiach, & Zilber, 1998) of all the interview material. Two primary judges and two additional judges read all the transcribed RAP interviews and made independent notes on the themes and emotions that emerged in the relational narratives. The final analysis of the relational themes and emotions was conducted by the two primary judges in two rounds, each with one of the two other judges. This process involved the judges scrutinizing all the notes and arriving at core relational themes and emotions (see Hill, Thompson, & Williams, 1997; Hill, Knox, Thompson, Williams, Hess, & Ladany, 2005).

B. THE PARENTING ADOLESCENTS STUDY

The interviewees who were included in the study that is presented in Chapter 11 were drawn from the Israel Foundations Trustees-funded study on "The Experience of Parenting Adolescents among Second Generation Holocaust Survivors" (Wiseman, 2005; Wiseman, Goldberg, Remez, & Ben Shmuel-Zetelny, 2005). Here we provide information on the procedure, namely, their recruitment to our study and the interview procedure. In addition, we provide examples of questions from the "Parenting Adolescence Experiences Interview." Details on the demographic and Holocaust background of the participants are presented in Tables 2 and 3.

Recruitment of the Participants to the Parenting Adolescents Study

The sample for this study was a high school-based sample of Israeli-born adolescents from intact families. The recruitment procedure involved a brief screening questionnaire that was administered through the high schools to identify potential adolescents from families with and without a Holocaust background. On the basis of this initial screening, letters were sent by mail to potential participants asking them to participate in the study. Following the letters, the potential families were contacted by phone by the research coordinator. In this conversation, the coordinator explained that the participation in the study required the agreement and consent of the whole triad,

TABLE 2. *The Parenting Adolescents Study: Demographic Characteristics of the Participants*

Characteristic	Adolescent (N = 33)	Adolescent's Mother	Adolescent's Father
Gender			
Boy	15 (45%)		
Girl	18 (56%)		
Holocaust background			
Second generation[a]		33	19
Third generation[b]	33		
Age (in years)	16.95 (85)[c]	47.48 (5.84)[c]	49.25 (4.53)[c]
Intact families (%)	33 (100%)		
Education (in years)		16.23 (3.18)[c]	15.72 (3.47)[c]

[a] The definition of being a child of survivors ("second generation") was being a child of a parent who survived the Holocaust (mother, father, or both) who was in Europe during the years of World War II (van IJzendoorn et al., 2003; Solomon, 1998).
[b] The adolescent was defined as a grandchild of survivors ("third generation") according to the criterion of having at least a mother who is a daughter of a parent who survived the Holocaust.
[c] Mean (SD) at the time of the study.

that is, mother, father, and the adolescent that was contacted through the school. The coordinator spoke to each individually, and only in cases in which all three members of the triad agreed to participate were scheduled the interviews. Of the families that were contacted 60 percent agreed to take part in the research.

Procedure

The interviews were conducted at the family home separately for the mother, father, and adolescent within each family and by different interviewers. All the interviewees gave informed consent for their participation in the study. Upon completing the consent form, each parent underwent the Parenting Adolescence Experiences Interview (see examples of questions later) and the adolescent underwent a RAP interview (Wiseman et al., 2005). The interviews were audiotaped and were fully transcribed.

TABLE 3. *Information on Holocaust Background of the Grandparents*

	HSO Mothers		HSO Fathers	
	Grandmothers	Grandfathers	Grandmothers	Grandfathers
Holocaust experiences background				
Concentration camps	7	11	4	3
Labor camp	7	10	2	4
Hiding	6	6	0	1
Partisans	2	2	2	2
Other	4	4	6	4
Grandparents' background[a]				
Both were survivors	21 (64%)		11 (57%)	
Only mother was a survivor	5 (15%)		2 (11%)	
Only father was a survivor	7 (21%)		2 (11%)	
Missing data			4 (21%)	

[a] Percentage within HSO mothers or within HSO fathers.

Examples of Questions from the Parenting Adolescence Experiences Interview *(Chapter 11)*

*1. To what extent does ____ share her/his experiences and feelings with you? Can you tell me more about that?

When ____ is sad or moody about something, what does she/he do? What do you do?

When ____ is angry at someone or about something, what does she/he do? What do you do?

To what extent do you feel that you understand her/him and what he/she is going through?

*2. What do you expect from ____ in her/his relationship with you?

*3. Are there similar things between the relationship you had with your parents during your adolescence, and the relationship you have with your adolescent daughter/son? Are there differences?

Which of the things you experienced with your parents would you like to pass on to your relationship with ____?

Which of the things you experienced with your parents would you not like to pass on to your relationship with ____?

**4. In your opinion, what does your child need from you? What do you think he expects from you during this period of his life?

**5. Try to think of your parenting style compared to your parents' parenting style. In what ways is your parenting style similar to the parenting style of your father and mother? Are there any aspects of your parenting style that you wish were more similar to theirs? Please give an example.

In what ways is your parenting style different from the parenting style of your father and mother? Please give an example.

How do you think these differences came about, in your opinion?

(*) Questions 1, 2, and 3 are reprinted with permission from the Parenting Representations Interview – Adolescence (PRI-A; Scharf & Mayseless, 1997/2000).

(**) Questions 4 and 5 are from the Parenting Adolescence Experiences Interview (Wiseman, 2005) that was adapted in part from Scharf and Shulman (1998).

REFERENCES

Adelman, A. (1995). Traumatic memory and the intergenerational transmission of Holocaust narratives. *The Psychoanalytic Study of the Child, 50*, 343–367.

American Psychiatric Association. (1994). *Diagnostic and statistical manual of mental disorders* (4th Edition). Washington, DC: American Psychiatric Association.

American Psychiatric Association. (2000). *Diagnostic and statistical manual of mental disorders* (text revision). Washington, DC: American Psychiatric Association.

Ancharoff, M. R., Munroe, J. F., & Fisher, L. (1998). The legacy of combat trauma: Clinical implications of intergenerational transmission. In Y. Danieli (Ed.), *International handbook of multigenerational legacies of trauma* (pp. 257–279). New York: Plenum.

Andersen, P. A., & Guerrero, L. K. (1998). Principles of communication and emotion in social interaction. In P. A Andersen & L. K Guerrero (Eds.), *Handbook of communication and emotion: Research, theory, applications, and contexts* (pp. 49–96). San Diego, CA: Academic Press.

Aron, L. (1996). *A meeting of minds: Mutuality in psychoanalysis.* Hillsdale, NJ: Analytic Press.

Asher, S. R., Hymel, S., & Renshaw, P. (1984). Loneliness in children. *Child Development, 55*, 1456–1464.

Auerhahn, N. C., & Laub, D. (1998). Intergenerational memory of the Holocaust. In Y. Danieli (Ed.), *International handbook of multigenerational legacies of trauma* (pp. 21–41). New York: Plenum.

Baider, L., Peretz, T., Ever Hadani, P., Perry, S., Avramov, R., & Kaplan De-Nour, A. (2000). Transmission of response to trauma? Second-generation Holocaust survivors' reaction to cancer. *American Journal of Psychiatry, 157*, 904–910.

Bakan, D. (1966). *The duality of human existence: Isolation and communion in Western man.* Boston: Beacon Press.

Barber, J. P., & Crits-Christoph, P. (1995) (Eds.), *Dynamic therapies for psychiatric disorders (Axis 1)*. New York: Basic Books.

Barber, J. P., Crits-Christoph, P., & Luborsky, L. (1998). A guide to the CCRT standard categories and their classification. In L. Luborsky & P. Crits-Christoph (Eds.), *Understanding transference: The Core Conflictual Relationship Theme method* (pp. 43–54). New York: Basic Books.

Barber, J. P., Foltz, C., & Weinryb, R. M. (1998). The Central Relationship Questionnaire: Initial report. *Journal of Counseling Psychology, 45*, 131–142.

Barber, J. P., Foltz, C., DeRubeis, R. J., & Landis, R. (2002). Consistency of interpersonal themes in narratives about relationships. *Psychotherapy Research, 12*(2), 139–158.

Barber, J. P., Luborsky, L., Crits-Christoph, P., & Diguer, L. (1995). A comparison of Core Conflictual Relationship Themes before psychotherapy and during early sessions. *Journal of Consulting and Clinical Psychology, 63*, 145–148.

Barlow, D. H. (2004). Fear, anxiety, and theories of emotion. In D. H. Barlow (Ed.), *Anxiety and its disorders* (2nd. ed.). New York: Guilford Press.

Barocas, H. A., & Barocas, C. B. (1973). Manifestations of concentration camp effects on the second generation. *American Journal of Psychiatry, 130*, 820–821.

Bar-On, D. (1995). *Fear and hope: Three generations of five Israeli families of Holocaust survivors.* Cambridge, MA: Harvard University Press.

Bar-On, D. (1996). Attempting to overcome the intergenerational transmission of trauma. Dialogue between descendants of victims and of perpetrators. In R. Apfel & B. Simon (Eds.), *Minefields of their hearts: The mental health of children in war and communal violence* (pp. 165–188). New Haven: Yale University Press.

Bar-On, D. (1999). *The indescribable and undiscussable: Reconstructing human discourse after trauma.* Budapest: Central European University Press.

Bar-On, D. (2006). *Tell your life-story: Creating dialogue between Jews and Germans, Israelis and Palestinians.* CEUP. Hamburg: Koerber (2004) (in German). Ben-Gurion University Press (in Hebrew).

Bar-On, D. Eland, J., Kleber, R. J., Krell, R., Moore, Y., Sagi, A., Soriano, E., Suedfeld, P., van der Velden, P.G., & van IJzendoorn, M. H. (1998). Multigenerational perspectives on coping with the Holocaust experience: An attachment perspective for understanding the developmental sequelae of trauma across generations. *International Journal of Behavioral Development, 22*(2), 315–338.

Baumeister, R. F., Reis, H. T., & Delespal, P. (1995). Subjective and experiential correlates of guilt in daily life. *Personality and Social Psychology Bulletin, 21*, 1256–1268.

Baumeister, R. F., Stillwell, A. M., & Heatherton, T. F. (1994). Guilt: An interpersonal approach. *Psychological Bulletin, 115*, 243–267.

Baumeister, R. F., Stillwell, A. M., & Heatherton, T. F. (1995). Personal narratives about guilt: Role in action control and interpersonal relationships. *Basic and Applied Social Psychology, 17*, 173–198.

Ben-Dor, O. (director). (1988). *Because of that war* [Motion picture]. Israel: Manor Producers.

Bergmann, M. S., & Jucovy, M. E. (1982). *Generations of the Holocaust.* New York: Basic Books.

Bion, W. R. (1970). Attention and interpretation. London: Tavistok.

Blatt S. J. (2004). *Experiences of depression: Theoretical, clinical and research perspectives.* Washington, DC: American Psychological Association.

Blatt, S. J., & Blass, R. B. (1990). Attachment and separateness: A dialectic model of the products and processes of development throughout the life cycle. *The Psychoanalytic Study of the Child, 45*, 107–127.

Blatt, S. J., & Blass, R. B. (1992). Relatedness and self-definition: Two primary dimensions in personality development, psychopathology, and psychotherapy. In D. L. Wolitzky, J. W. Barron, & M. N. Eagle (Eds.), *Interface of psychoanalysis and psychology* (pp. 399–428). Washington, DC: American Psychological Association.

Block, J. (1971). *Lives through time.* Berkeley, CA: Bancroft Books.

Block, J. (1993). Studying personality the long way. In D. C. Funder, R. D. Parke, C. Tomlinson-Keasey, & K. Widaman (Eds.), *Studying lives through time: Personality and development* (pp. 9–41). Washington, DC: American Psychological Association.

Blos, P. (1962). *On adolescence: A psychoanalytic interpretation.* Oxford: Free Press of Glencoe.

Blumenthal, N. N. (1981). Factors contributing to varying levels of adjustment among children of Holocaust survivors (Doctoral Dissertation, Adelphi University). *Dissertation Abstracts International, 42/04*, 1596.

Bollas, C. (1987). *The shadow of the object: Psychoanalysis of the unthought known.* London: Free Association Books.

Book, H. E. (1998). *How to practice brief dynamic psychotherapy: The CCRT method.* Washington, DC: American Psychological Association.

Borkovec, T. D., Robinson, E., Pruzinsky, T., & DePree, J. A. (1983). Preliminary exploration of worry: Some characteristics and processes. *Behaviour Research and Therapy, 21*, 9–16.

Borkovec, T. D., & Sharpless, B. (2004). Generalized anxiety disorder: Bringing cognitive behavior therapy into the valued present. In S. Hayes, V. Follette, & M. Linehan (Eds.), *Mindfulness and Acceptance: Expanding the cognitive-behavior tradition.* New York: Guilford Press.

Bowlby, J. (1969/1982). *Attachment and loss: Vol 1. Attachment* (2nd. ed.). New York: Basic Books.

Bowlby, J. (1973). *Attachment and loss: Vol 2. Separation.* New York: Basic Books.

Bowlby, J. (1980). *Attachment and loss: Vol 3. Loss.* New York: Basic Books.

Bowlby, J. (1988). *A secure base.* New York: Basic Books.

Bradford, L., & Petronio, S. (1998). Strategic embarrassment: The culprit of emotion. In L. K. Guerrero & P. A. Andersen (Eds.), *Handbook of communication and emotion: Research, theory, applications, and contexts,* (pp. 99–121). San Diego, CA: Academic Press.

Bretherton, I. (1990). Open communication and internal working models: Their role in the development of attachment relationships. In R. A. Thompson (Ed.), *Nebraska Symposium on Motivation: Vol 36. Socio-emotional development* (pp. 57–113). Lincoln, NE: University of Nebraska Press.

Bretherton, I., Lambert, J. D., & Golby, B. (2006). Modeling and reworking childhood experiences: Involved fathers' representations of being parented and parenting. In O. Mayseless (Ed.), *Parenting representations: Theory, research, and clinical implications* (pp. 177–207). New York: Cambridge University Press.

Bretherton, I., & Munholland, K. A. (1999). Internal working models in attachment relationships: A construct revisited. *Handbook of attachment: Theory, research and clinical applications* (pp. 21–44). New York: Guilford Press.

Breznitz, S. (1993). *Memory fields.* New York: Knopf.

Breznitz, S. (2000, April). The Holocaust experience as a state of mind. *Paper presented at the Interdisciplinary Conference on Remembrance of the Holocaust: Each Generation and its Story.* University of Haifa, Haifa, Israel.

Brom, D., Kfir, R., & Dasberg, H. (2001). A controlled double-blind study on children of Holocaust survivors. *Israel Journal of Psychiatry and Related Sciences, 38,* 47–57.

Brown, T. A., Barlow, D. H., & Liebowitz, M. R. (1994). The empirical basis of generalized anxiety disorder. *American Journal of Psychiatry, 151,* 1272–1280.

Buber, M. (1936/1947). *Between man and man* (trans. R. G. Smith). London: Routledge & Kegan Paul.

Buchan, J. (1998). *Transparent Child.* Tel Aviv: Zmora-Beitan. (In Hebrew.)

Canary, D. J., Spitzberg, B. H., & Semic, B. A. (1998). The experience and expression of anger in interpersonal settings. In P. A. Andersen & L. K. Guerrero (Eds.), *Handbook of communication and emotion: Research, theory, applications, and contexts* (pp. 190–213). San Diego, CA: Academic Press.

Casella, L., & Motta, R. W. (1990). Comparison of characteristics of Vietnam veterans with and without posttraumatic stress disorder. *Psychological Reports, 67*, 595–605.

Cassidy, J., & Berlin, L. J. (1999). Understanding the origins of childhood loneliness: Contributions of attachment theory. In K. J. Rotenberg & S. Hymel (Eds.), *Loneliness in childhood and adolescence* (pp. 34–55). Cambridge, UK: Cambridge University Press.

Chaitin, J. (2002). Issues and interpersonal values among three generations in families of Holocaust survivors. *Journal of Social and Personal Relationships, 19*, 379–402.

Chaitin, J. (2003). "Living with" the past: Coping and patterns in families of Holocaust survivors. *Family Process, 42*(2), 305–322.

Cierpka, M., Zander, B., Krannich, S., Reich, K., Ratzke, K., Homburg, H., Staats, H., & Seide, L. (1992, June). *Differences of conflictual relationships themes of male and female students.* Paper presented at the Annual meeting of the Society for Psychotherapy Research, Berkeley, CA.

Collins, W. A. (1995). Relationships and development: Family adaptation to individual change. In S. Shulman (Ed.), *Close relationships and socioemotional development* (pp. 54–128). Westport, CT: Ablex Publishing.

Connolly, M. B., Crits-Christoph, P., Barber, J. P., & Luborsky, L. (2000). Transference patterns in the therapeutic relationship in supportive-expressive psychotherapy for depression. *Psychotherapy Research, 10*, 356–372.

Crits-Christoph, P., Luborsky, L., Dahl, L., Popp, C., Mellon, J., & Mark, D. (1988). Clinicians can agree in assessing relationship patterns in psychotherapy: The Core Conflictual Relationship Theme method. *Archives of General Psychiatry, 45*, 1001–1004.

Crits-Christoph, P., Luborsky, L., Popp, C., Mellon, J., & Mark, D. (1990). The reliability of choice of narratives and of the CCRT measure. In L. Luborsky & P. Crits-Christoph (Eds.), *Understanding transference: The Core Conflictual Relationship Theme method* (1st ed., pp. 93–101). New York: Basic Books.

Crittenden, P. M. (2006). Why do inadequate parents do what they do? In O. Mayseless (Ed.), *Parenting representations: Theory, research, and clinical implications* (pp. 388–434). New York: Cambridge University Press.

Danieli, Y. (1983). Families and survivors of the Nazi Holocaust: Some long- and short-term effects. In N. Milgram (Ed.), *Psychological stress and adjustment in time of war and peace* (pp. 405–421). Washington, DC: Hemisphere.

Danieli, Y. (1984). Psychotherapist's participation in the conspiracy of silence about the Holocaust. *Psychoanalytic Psychology, 1*, 23–42.

Danieli, Y. (Ed.). (1998). *International handbook of multigenerational legacies of trauma.* New York: Plenum.

Dasberg, H. (1976). Belonging and loneliness in relation to mental breakdown in battle. *Israel Annals of Psychiatry and Related Disciplines, 14*(4), 307–321.

Daud, A., Skoglund, E., & Rydelius, P. A. (2005). Children in families of torture victims: Transgenerational transmission of parents' traumatic experiences to their children. *International Journal of Social Welfare, 14*, 23–32.

Erikson, E. (1968). *Identity, youth, and crisis.* New York: W. W. Norton.

Ernst, J. M., & Cacioppo, J. T. (1999). Lonely hearts: Psychological perspectives on loneliness. *Applied and Preventive Psychology, 8*, 1–22.

Feeney, J., & Noller, P. (1996). *Adult attachment.* Thousand Oaks, CA: Sage Publications.

Felsen, I. (1998). Transgenerational transmission of effects of the Holocaust: The North American research perspective. In Y. Danieli (Ed.), *International handbook of multigenerational legacies of trauma* (pp. 43–69). New York: Plenum.

Ferguson, T. J., & Stegge, H. (1995). Emotional states and traits in children: The case of guilt and shame. In J. P. Tangney & K. W. Fischer (Eds.), *Self-conscious emotions: The psychology of shame, guilt, embarrassment, and pride* (pp. 174–197). New York: Guilford.

Fonagy, P. (1999). The transgenerational transmission of Holocaust trauma: lessons learned from the analysis of an adolescent with obsessive-Compulsive disorder. *Attachment & Human Development, 1*(1), 92–114.

Freud, S. (1912/1958). The dynamics of transference. In J. Strachey (Ed. and Trans.), *The standard edition to the complete psychological works of Sigmund Freud* (Vol. 12, pp. 99–108). London: Hogarth Press. (Original work published 1912.)

Freyberg, J. T. (1980). Difficulties in separation-individuation as experienced by offspring of Nazi Holocaust survivors. *American Journal of Orthopsychiatry, 50*, 87–95.

Fried, D., Crits-Christoph, P., & Luborsky, L. (1990). The parallel of narratives about the therapist with the CCRT for other people. In L. Luborsky & P. Crits-Christoph (Eds.), *Understanding transference: The Core Conflictual Relationship Theme method* (1st ed., pp. 147–157). New York: Basic Books.

Fried, D., Luborsky, L., & Crits-Christoph, P. (1992). The first empirical demonstration of transference in psychotherapy. *Journal of Nervous and Mental Disease, 180*, 326–331.

Gampel, Y. (1982). A daughter of silence. In M. S. Bergman & M. E. Jucovy (Eds.), *Generations of the Holocaust.* New York: Basic.

Gampel, Y. (1992). Thoughts about the transmission of conscious and unconscious knowledge to the generation born after the *Shoah.* Special issue on

Holocaust trauma: Transgenerational transmission to the second generation. *Journal of Social Work & Policy in Israel*, 5–6, 43–59.
Gibb, B. E. (2002). Childhood maltreatment and negative cognitive styles: A quantitative and qualitative review. *Clinical Psychology Review*, 22, 223–246.
Goldberg, A., & Wiseman, H. (2006, July). *Attachment styles, parental bonding, parental monitoring and risk-taking behavior in adolescents: The case of the third generation of Holocaust survivors.* Poster presented at the International Association for Relationship Research Conference, Rethymno, Crete, Greece.
Greenspan, H. (1998). *On listening to Holocaust survivors – Recounting and life history.* Westport, CT: Praeger Publishers.
Greenwood, J. D. (1994). *Realism, identity, and emotion: Reclaiming social psychology.* Thousand Oaks, CA: Sage.
Grossman, D. (1986/1989). *See Under Love.* London: Cape.
Grossmann, K. E. (1999, April). Discussion. In A. Sagi (Chair), *The developmental sequelae of catastrophic Holocaust childhood experiences across generations.* Symposium conducted in the Biennial Meeting of the Society for Research in Child Development, Albuquerque, NM.
Grossmann, K. E., Grossmann, K., & Schwan, A. (1986). Capturing the wider view of attachment: A reanalysis of Ainsworth's Strange Situation. In C. E. Izard & P. B. Read (Eds.), *Measuring emotions in infants and children* (pp. 124–171). New York: Cambridge University Press.
Gryner, B. F. S., & Luborsky, L. (1998). Positive versus negative CCRT patterns. In L. Luborsky & P. Crits-Christoph (Eds.), *Understanding transference: The Core Conflictual Relationship Theme method* (2nd ed., pp. 55–63). Washington, DC: American Psychological Association.
Guerrero, L. K. (1994). "I'm so sad I could scream": The effects of anger expression on relational satisfaction and communication competence. *The Southern Communication Journal*, 59, 125–141.
Guerrero, L. K., & Andersen, P. A. (2000). Emotion in close relationships. In C. Hendrick, & S. S. Hendrick, (Eds.), *Close relationships: A sourcebook* (pp. 171–183). Thousand Oaks, CA: Sage Publications.
Guttfreund, A. (2000). Our Holocaust. Tel-Aviv: Zmora-Bitan, Publishers. (In Hebrew.)
Halik, V., Rosenthal, D. A., & Pattison, P. E. (1990). Intergenerational effects of the Holocaust: Patterns of engagement in the mother-daughter relationship. *Family Process*, 29, 325–339.
Hass, A. (1990). *In the shadow of the Holocaust: The second generation.* Ithaca, NY: Cornell University.

Hazan, C., & Shaver, P. R. (1987). Romantic love as conceptualized as an attachment process. *Journal of Personality and Social Psychology, 52*, 511–524.

Hazan, Y. (1987). "Second generation of the Holocaust" – a questionable concept. *Sichot – Dialogue: Israel Journal of Psychotherapy, 1*(2), 104–107. (In Hebrew.)

Heinrich, L. M., & Gullone, E. (2006). The clinical significance of loneliness: A literature review. *Clinical Psychology Review, 26*, 695–718.

Herman, J. (1997). *Trauma and recovery.* New York: Basic Books.

Hill, C. E., Thompson, B. J., & Williams, E. N. (1997). A guide to conducting consensual qualitative research. *The Counseling Psychologist, 25*, 517–572.

Hill, C. E., Knox, S., Thompson, B., Williams, E. N., Hess, S. A, & Ladany, N. (2005). Consensual qualitative research: An update. *Journal of Counseling Psychology, 52*(2), 196–205.

Hoffman, M. L. (1982). Development of prosocial motivation: Empathy and guilt. In N. Eisenberg (Ed.), *The development of prosocial behavior* (pp. 281–313). New York: Norton.

Hymel, S., Tarulli, D., Hayden Thomson, L., & Terrell-Deutsch, B. (1999). Loneliness through the eyes of children. In K. J. Rotenberg & S. Hymel (Eds.), *Loneliness in childhood and adolescence* (pp. 80–106). Cambridge, UK: Cambridge University Press.

Izard, C. E. (1991). *The psychology of emotion.* New York: Plenum Press.

Jones, W. H., Kugler, K., & Adams, P. (1995). You always hurt the one you love: Guilt and transgressions against relationship partners. In J. P. Tangney & K. W. Fischer (Eds.), *Self-conscious emotions: The psychology of shame, guilt, embarrassment, and pride* (pp. 301–321). New York: Guilford.

Josselson, R. (1980). Ego development in adolescence. In J. Adelson (Ed.), *Handbook of adolescent psychiatry* (pp. 188–208). New York: Wiley.

Josselson, R. (1988). *Finding herself: Pathways to identity development in women.* San Francisco: Jossey-Bass Publishers.

Josselson, R., Lieblich A., & McAdams, D. P. (Eds.) (2007). *The meaning of others: Narrative studies of relationships.* Washington, DC: American Psychological Association.

Jucovy, M. E. (1985). Telling the Holocaust story: A link between the generations. *Psychoanalytic Inquiry, 5*, 31–50.

Jucovy, M. E. (1992). Psychoanalytic contributions to Holocaust studies. *The International Journal of Psychoanalysis, 73*, 267–282.

Keinan, G., Mikulincer, M., & Rybnicki, A. (1988). Perception of self and parents by second-generation Holocaust survivors. *Behavioural Medicine, 14*, 6–12.

Kellermann, N. P. F. (2001). Psychopathology in children of Holocaust survivors: A review of the research literature. *Israel Journal of Psychiatry and Related Sciences, 38*(1), 36–46.

Kestenberg, J. S. (1982). Survivors-parents and their children. In M. S. Bergmann & M. E. Jucovy (Eds.), *Generations of the Holocaust* (pp. 83–102). New York: Basic Books.

Kiesler, D. J. (1996). *Contemporary interpersonal theory and research: Personality, psychopathology, and psychotherapy.* New York: John Wiley.

Klein, H. (1980). The survivors search of meaning and identity. In *Proceedings of the Fourth Yad Vashem International Historical Conference: The Nazi Concentration Camps* (pp. 543–553). Jerusalem: Yad Vashem.

Kobak, R. (1999). The emotional dynamics of disruptions in attachment relationships: Implications for theory, research, and clinical intervention. In J. Cassidy & P. Shaver (Eds.), *Handbook of attachment: Theory, research and clinical applications* (pp. 21–44). New York: Guilford Press.

Kobak, R., & Duemmler, S. (1994). Attachment and conversation: A discourse analysis of goal-corrected partnerships. In K. Bartholomew & D. Perlman (Eds.), *Advances in personal relationship: Vol. 5. Attachment processes in adulthood* (pp. 121–149). London: Jessica Kingsley.

Kogan, I. (1995). *The cry of the mute children: The psychoanalytic perspective of the second generation of the Holocaust.* New York: Free Association Books.

Kogan, I. (2002). Enactment in the lives and treatment of Holocaust survivors' offspring. *The Psychoanalytic Quarterly, 71*, 251–273.

Kogan, I. (2007). *The struggle against mourning.* New York: Jason Aronson.

Krell, R. (1979). Holocaust families: The survivors and their children. *Comprehensive Psychiatry, 20*, 560–568.

Krell, R. (2000, April). The story of child survivors. Paper presented at the Conference on *Memory and the Holocaust: Each generation and its story.* University of Haifa, Haifa, Israel.

Kupelian, D., Kalayjian, A. S., & Kassabian, A. (1998). The Turkish genocide of the Armenians: Continuing effects on survivors and their families eight decades after massive trauma. In Y. Danieli (Ed.), *International handbook of multigenerational legacies of trauma* (pp. 191–210). New York: Plenum.

Lamb, S. (1986). Treating sexually abused children: Issues of blame and responsibility. *American Journal of Orthopsychiatry, 56*, 303–307.

Laub, D. & Auerhahn N. C. (1985). Knowing and not knowing the Holocaust. Prologue. *Psychoanalytic Inquiry, 5*, 1–8.

Lazarus, R. S. (1991). *Emotion and adaptation.* New York: Oxford University Press.

Leary, M. R., & Meadows, S. (1991). Predictors, elicitors, and concomitants of social blushing. *Journal of Personality and Social Psychology, 60*, 254– 262.

Leon, G. R., Butcher, J. N., Kleinman, M., Goldberg, A., & Almagor, M. (1981). Survivors of the Holocaust and their children: Current status and adjustment. *Journal of Personality and Social Psychology, 41*(3), 503–515.

Levi, P. (1986/1988). *The drowned and the saved.* London: Michael Joseph, Penguin Group.

Lev-Wiesel, R. (2007). Intergeneration transmission of trauma across three generations: A preliminary study. *Qualitative Social Work, 6*, 75–94.

Lichtman, H. (1983). *Children of survivors of the Nazi Holocaust: A personality study.* Doctoral dissertation. Yeshiva University.

Lichtman, H. (1984). Parental communication of Holocaust experiences and personality characteristics among second-generation survivors. *Journal of Clinical Psychology, 40*, 914–924.

Lieblich, A., Tuval-Mashiach, R., & Zilber, T. (1998). *Narrative research: Reading, analysis, and interpretation.* Thousand Oaks, CA: Sage.

Lifton, R. J. (1967). *Death in life.* New York: Simon & Schuster.

Litvak-Hirsch, T., & Bar-On, D. (2006). To rebuild lives: A longitudinal study of the influences of the Holocaust on relationships among three generations of women in one family. *Family Process, 45*(4), 465–483.

Lobdell, J., & Perlman, D. (1986). The intergenerational transmission of loneliness: A study of college females and their parents. *Journal of Marriage and the Family, 48*, 589–595.

Luborsky, L. (1977). Measuring a pervasive psychic structure in psychotherapy: The Core Conflictual Relationship Theme. In N. Freedman & S. Grand (Eds.), *Communicative structures and psychic structures* (pp. 367–395). New York: Plenum Press.

Luborsky, L. (1984). *Principles of psychoanalytic psychotherapy: A manual for supportive-expressive (SE) treatment.* New York: Basic Books.

Luborsky, L. (1998a). The Relationship Anecdotes Paradigm (RAP) interview as a versatile source of narratives. In L. Luborsky & P. Crits-Christoph (Eds.), *Understanding transference: The Core Conflictual Relationship Theme method* (2nd ed., pp. 109–120). Washington, DC: American Psychological Association.

Luborsky, L. (1998b). The convergence of Freud's observations about transference with the CCRT evidence. In L. Luborsky & P. Crits-Christoph (Eds.), *Understanding transference: The Core Conflictual Relationship Theme method* (2nd ed., pp. 307–325). Washington, DC: American Psychological Association.

Luborsky, L., & Barber, J. P. (1994). Perspectives on seven transference-related measures applied to the interview with Ms. Smithfield. *Psychotherapy Research, 4*, 152–154.

Luborsky, L. Barber, J. P., & Diguer, L. (1992). The meanings of narratives told during psychotherapy: The fruits of a new observational unit. *Psychotherapy Research*, 2(4), 277–290.

Luborsky, L., Barber, J. P., Schaffler, P., & Cacciola, J. (1998). The narratives told during psychotherapy and the types of CCRTs within them. In L. Luborsky & P. Crits-Christoph (Eds.), *Understanding transference: The Core Conflictual Relationship Theme method* (2nd ed., pp. 135–150). Washington, DC: American Psychological Association.

Luborsky, L., & Crits-Christoph, P. (1990). *Understanding transference: The Core Conflictual Relationship Theme method.* New York: Basic Books.

Luborsky, L., & Crits-Christoph, P. (1998). *Understanding transference: The Core Conflictual Relationship Theme method* (2nd ed.). Washington, DC: American Psychological Association.

Luborsky, L., Crits-Christoph, P., Friedman, S., Mark, D., & Schaffler, P. (1991). Freud's transference template compared with the Core Conflictual Relationship Theme (CCRT): Illustrations by the two specimen cases. In M. Horowitz (Ed.), *Person schemas and maladaptive interpersonal behavior* (pp. 167–195). Chicago: University of Chicago Press.

Luborsky, L., Popp, C., Luborsky, E., & Mark, D. (1994). The Core Conflictual Relationship Theme. *Psychotherapy Research*, 4, 172–183.

Malpas, J., & Solomon, R. C. (1998). *Death and philosophy.* New York: Routledge Press.

Maor, H. (1994). *The forbidden library.* Beer-Sheva: Avraham Baron Art Gallery, Ben-Gurion University of the Negev.

Mascolo, M. F., & Fischer, K. W. (1995). Developmental transformations in appraisals for pride, shame, and guilt. In J. P. Tangney & K. W. Fischer (Eds.), *Self-conscious emotions: The psychology of shame, guilt, embarrassment, and pride* (pp. 64–114). New York: Guilford.

May, R. (1983). *The discovery of being.* New York: Norton.

Mayseless, O. (2006). Studying parenting representations as a window to parents' internal working model of caregiving. In O. Mayseless (Ed.), *Parenting representations: Theory, research, and clinical implications* (pp. 3–40). New York: Cambridge University Press.

Mazor, A., & Tal, I. (1996). Intergenerational transmission: The individuation process and the capacity for intimacy of adult children of Holocaust survivors. *Contemporary Family Therapy: An International Journal*, *18*, 95–113.

McAdams, D. P. (1985). *Power, intimacy, and the life story: Personological inquiries into identity.* Homewood, IL: Dorsey Press.

McAdams, D. P. (1990). *The person: An introduction to personality and psychology.* San Diego, CA: Harcourt Brace Jovanovich.

McCann, I. L. & Pearlman, L. A. (1990). Vicarious traumatization: A framework for understanding the psychological effects of working with victims. *Journal of Traumatic Stress*, *3*, 131–149.

McKeever, V. M., McWhirter, B. T., & Huff, M. E. (2006). Relationships between attribution style, child abuse history, and PTSD symptom severity in Vietnam veterans. *Cognitive Therapy and Research*, *30*, 123–133.

McWhirter, B. T. (1990). Loneliness: A review of current literature, with implications for counseling and research. *Journal of Counseling and Development*, *68*, 417–422.

Mewborn, C. R., & Rogers, R. (1979). Effects of threatening and reassuring components of fear appeals on physiological and verbal measures of emotion and attitudes. *Journal of Experimental Social Psychology*, *15*, 242–253.

Mikulincer, M. (1994). *Human learned helplessness: A coping perspective*. New York: Plenum Press.

Mikulincer, M. (2006, July). Discussion. In H. Wiseman (Chair), *The relational vicissitudes of trauma in the 'second' and 'third' generation of Holocaust survivors*. Symposium conducted in the International Association for Relationship Research Conference, Rethymno, Crete, Greece.

Mikulincer, M., & Caspy, T. (1986). The conceptualization of helplessness: I. A phenomenological-structural analysis. *Motivation and Emotion*, *10*, 263–278.

Mikulincer, M., & Segal, J. (1990). A multidimensional analysis of the experience of loneliness. *Journal of Social and Personal Relationships*, *7*, 209–230.

Miller, R. S., & Leary, M. R. (1992). Social sources and interactive functions of emotion: The case of embarrassment. In M. S. Clark (Ed.), *Review of personality and social psychology* (pp. 202–221). Thousand Oaks, CA: Sage.

Miron, U. (2004). *A tale of life and death*. Jerusalem: Keter Books. (In Hebrew.)

Nadler, A. (1987). Validity of transgenerational effects of the Holocaust: Reply to Silverman. *Journal of Consulting and Clinical Psychology*, *55*, 127–128.

Nadler, A., Kav-Venaki, S., & Gleitman, B. (1985). Transgenerational effects of the Holocaust: Externalization of aggression in second generation of Holocaust survivors. *Journal of Consulting and Clinical Psychology*, *53*, 365–369.

Nagata, D. K. (1998). Intergenerational effects of the Japanese American internment. In Y. Danieli (Ed.), *International handbook of multigenerational legacies of trauma* (pp. 125–141). New York: Plenum.

Niederland, W. (1968). Clinical observations on the survivors syndrome. *International Journal of Psychoanalysis*, *49*, 313–319.

Ogden, T. (1994). *Subjects of analysis*. Northvale, NJ: Aronson.

Op Den Velde, W. (1998). Children of Dutch war sailors and civilian resistance veterans. In Y. Danieli (Ed.), *International handbook of multigenerational legacies of trauma* (pp. 147–163). New York: Plenum.

Perlman, D. (1988). Loneliness: A life-span, family perspective. In R. Milardo (Ed.), *Families and social networks* (pp. 190–220). Thousand Oaks, CA: Sage.

Perlman, D., & Landolt, M. A. (1999). Examination of loneliness in children-adolescents and adults: Two solitudes or a unified enterprise? In K. J. Rotenberg & S. Hymel (Eds.), *Loneliness in childhood and adolescence* (pp. 325–347). Cambridge, UK: Cambridge University Press.

Perroni, E. (2002). "There are no childish games." About the exhibition in the Yad Vashem Museum in Jerusalem. In E. Perroni (Ed.), *The Play* (pp. 165–168). (In Hebrew.)

Peterson, C., & Bossio, L. (1989). Learned helplessness. In R. C. Curtis, (Ed.), *Self-defeating behaviors: Experimental research, clinical impressions, and practical implications.* (pp. 235–257). New York: Plenum Press.

Pines, D. (1992). The impact of the Holocaust on the second generation. Special issue on Holocaust trauma: Transgenerational transmission to the second generation. *Journal of Social Work & Policy in Israel, 5–6*, 85–105.

Prince, R. M. (1985). Knowing the Holocaust. *Psychoanalytic Inquiry, 5*, 51–61.

Putallaz, M., Costanzo, P. R., & Smith, R. B. (1991). Maternal recollections of childhood peer relationships: Implications for their children's social competence. *Journal of Social and Personal Relationships, 8*, 403–422.

Rakoff, V. (1969). Children and families of concentration camp survivors. *Canada Mental Health, 14*, 24–26.

Raz, A., Wiseman, H., & Barber, J. P. (2002). The CCRT as a tool for understanding core relationship themes among second-generation Holocaust survivors: Two case studies. *Sichot – Dialogue: Israel Journal of Psychotherapy, 16*(3), 257–267. (In Hebrew.)

Reynolds, M., & Brewin, C. R. (1999). Intrusive memories in depression and posttraumatic stress disorder. *Behaviour Research and Therapy, 37*, 201–215.

Rieck, M. (1994). The psychological state of Holocaust survivors' offspring: An epidemiological and psychodiagnostic study. *International Journal of Behavioral Development, 17*, 649–667.

Rieck, M., & Eitinger, L. (1983). Controlled psychodiagnostic studies of survivors of the Holocaust and their children. *Israel Journal of Psychiatry, 20*, 312–324.

Rime', B., Mesquita, B., Philippot, P., & Boca, S. (1991). Beyond the emotional event: Six studies of the social sharing of emotion. *Cognition and Emotion*, 5, 435–465.

Rotenberg, K. J. (1999). Parental antecedents of children's loneliness. In K. J. Rotenberg & S. Hymel (Eds.), *Loneliness in childhood and adolescence* (pp. 176–200). Cambridge, UK: Cambridge University Press.

Rosenthal, G. (1998). *The Holocaust in three generations: Families of victims and perpetrators of the Nazi regime.* London: Cassell.

Roth, S., & Newman, E. (1992). The role of helplessness in the recovery process for sexual trauma survivors. *Canadian Journal of Behavioral Science*, 24, 220–232.

Rozner, Y. (2002). Memories from a hiding place. Play in the shadow of the Holocaust. In E. Perroni (Ed.), *The Play* (pp. 169–184). (In Hebrew.)

Russell, A. (1980). Late effects: Influence on children of concentration camp survivors. In J. E. Dinsdale (Ed.), *Survivors, victims, and perpetrators* (pp. 175–204). New York: Hemisphere.

Russell, D., Peplau, L. A., & Cutrona, C. E. (1980). The revised UCLA Loneliness Scale: Concurrent and discriminant validity evidence. *Journal of Personality and Social Psychology*, 39, 472–480.

Safran, J. D., & Muran, J. C. (2000). *Negotiating the therapeutic alliance: A relational treatment guide.* New York: Guilford Press.

Safran, J. D. (2003). The relational turn, the therapeutic alliance, and psychotherapy research: Strange bedfellows or postmodern marriage? *Contemporary Psychoanalysis*, 39, 449–475.

Sagi-Schwartz, A., van IJzendoorn, M. H., & Bakermans-Kranenburg, M. J. (in press). Does intergenerational transmission of trauma skip a generation? No meta-analytic evidence for tertiary traumatization with third generation of Holocaust survivors. *Attachment and Human Development.*

Sagi-Schwartz, A., van IJzendoorn, M. H., Grossmann, K. E., Joels, T., Grossmann, K., Scharf, M., Koren-Karie, N., & Alkalay, S. (2003). Attachment and traumatic stress in female Holocaust child survivors and their daughters. *American Journal of Psychiatry*, 160, 1086–1092.

Sawada, A., Chaitin, J., & Bar-On, D. (2004). Surviving Hiroshima and Nagasaki – experiences and psychosocial meanings. *Psychiatry*, 67, 43–60.

Scharf, M. (2007). Long-term effects of trauma: Psychological functioning of the second and third generation of Holocaust survivors. *Development and Psychopathology*, 19, 603–622.

Scharf, M., & Mayseless, O. (1997/2000). *Parenting Representations Interview – Adolescence (PRI-A).* Unpublished manuscript, University of Haifa, Israel.

Scharf, M., & Mayseless, O. (2006, July). *Disorganizing experiences within close relationships and their sequelae.* Paper presented at the International Association for Relationship Research Conference, Rethymno, Crete, Greece.

Scharf, M., & Shulman, S. (1998). *Adolescence Experiences' Interview.* Unpublished manuscript. University of Haifa.

Scharf, M., & Shulman, S. (2006). Intergenerational transmission of experiences in adolescence: The challenges in parenting adolescents. In O. Mayseless (Ed.), *Parenting representations: Theory, research, and clinical implications* (pp. 319–351). New York: Cambridge University Press.

Schwartz, S., Dohrenwend, B., & Levav, I. (1994). Nongenetic familial transmission of psychiatric disorders? Evidence from children of Holocaust survivors. *Journal of Health and Social Behaviour, 35*, 385–402.

Schwartz, J. C., & Shaver, P. (1987). Emotions and emotion knowledge in interpersonal relationships. In W. Jones & D. Perlman (Eds.), *Advances in personal relationships* (pp. 197–241). Oxford, England: Jessica Kingsley Publishers.

Segev, T. (1993). *The seventh million: The Israelis and the Holocaust.* New York: Hill and Wang.

Seligman, M. E. P. (1975). *Helplessness: On depression, development and death.* San Francisco: Freeman.

Semel, N. (1985). *A Hat Glass.* Tel Aviv: Sifriat Poalim. (In Hebrew.)

Semel, N. (2001). *The Rat Laughs.* Tel Aviv: Yediot Achronot. (In Hebrew.)

Shafet, R. (1994). Commitment to parents as unsolvable problem in children of Holocaust survivors. *Sihot/Dialogue: Israel Journal of Psychotherapy, 9*, 23–27. (In Hebrew.)

Shapira, A. (1997). *New Jews old Jews.* Tel Aviv: Am Oved Publishers. (In Hebrew.)

Shaver, P. R., & Mikulincer, M. (2002). Attachment-related psychodynamics. *Attachment and Human Development, 4*, 133–161.

Shaver, P., Schwartz, J., Kirson, D., & O'Connor, C. (1987). Emotion knowledge: Further exploration of a prototype approach. *Journal of Personality and Social Psychology, 52*, 1061–1086.

Shiryon, S. (1988). The second generation leaves home: The function of the sibling subgroup in the separation individuation process of the survivor family. *Family Therapy, 15*, 239–253.

Sigal, J. (1971). Second-generation effects of massive trauma. In H. Krystal & W. Niederland (Eds.), *Psychic traumatization* (pp. 55–65). Boston: Little Brown.

Sigal, J. (1973). Hypotheses and methodology in the study of families of Holocaust survivors. In E. J. Anthony & C. Koupernik (Eds.), *The child in his family: The impact of disease and death* (pp. 411–415). New York: Wiley.

Sigal, J. J., & Weinfeld, M. (1987). Mutual involvement and alienation in families of Holocaust survivors. *Psychiatry, 50*, 280–288.

Sigal, J. J., & Weinfeld, M. (1989). *Trauma and rebirth - Intergenerational effects of the Holocaust.* New York: Praeger.

Sigal, J., Silver, D., Rakoff, V., & Ellin, B. (1973). Some second generation effects of survival of the Nazi persecution. *American Journal of Orthopsychiatry, 43*, 320–327.

Silverman, W. K. (1987). Methodological issues in the study of transgenerational effects of the Holocaust: Comment on Nadler, Kav-Venaki, and Gleitman. *Journal of Consulting and Clinical Psychology, 55*, 125–126.

Siqueland, L., & Barber, J. P. (2002). Supportive-expressive psychotherapy. In J. J. Magnavita (Ed.), *Comprehensive handbook of psychotherapy* (Vol. 1, pp. 183–205). New York: John Wiley & Sons.

Slade, A., Grienenberger, J., Bernbach, E., Levy, D., & Locker, A. (2001, April). *Maternal reflective functioning and the caregiving relationship: The link between mental states and mother infant affective communication.* Paper presented at the Biennial Meeting of the Society for Research in Child Development, Minneapolis, MN.

Solkoff, N. (1992). Children of survivors of Nazi Holocaust: A critical review. *American Journal of Orthopsychiatry, 62*, 342–358.

Solomon, Z. (1998). Transgenerational effects of the Holocaust: The Israeli research perspective. In Y. Danieli (Ed.), *International handbook of multigenerational legacies of trauma* (pp. 69–85). New York: Plenum.

Solomon, Z., Kotler, M., & Mikulincer, M. (1988). Combat-related posttraumatic stress disorder among second-generation Holocaust survivors: Preliminary findings. *American Journal of Psychiatry, 145*, 865–868.

Spence, D. P. (1982). *Narrative truth and historical truth: Meaning and interpretation in psychoanalysis.* New York: W. W. Norton.

Steinberg, L, & Silk, J. S. (2002). Parenting adolescents. In M. H. Bornstein (Ed.), *Handbook of parenting* (pp. 33–103). Mahwah, NJ: Erlbaum.

Steinberg, L., & Steinberg, W. (1994). *Crossing paths: How your child's adolescence triggers your own.* New York: Simon & Schuster.

Stern, D. N. (1983). The early development of schemas of self, other, and "self with other." In J. D. Lichtenberg & S. Kaplan (Eds.), *Reflections on self-psychology* (pp. 49–83). Hillsdale, NJ: Analytic Press.

Stokes, J. P. (1987). On the usefulness of phenomenological methods. *Journal of Social Behavior and Personality, 2*, 57–62.

Szor, H. (2007, January). *Word and silence in the therapy of Holocaust survivors – changing perspectives.* Paper presented at the International Conference on The Holocaust as the Paradigm of Psychic Trauma in the 20th Century, Tel Aviv, Israel.

Tangney, J. P. (1995). Shame and guilt in interpersonal relationships. In J. P. Tangney & K. W. Fischer (Eds.), *Self-conscious emotions: The psychology of shame, guilt, embarrassment, and pride* (pp. 114–139). New York: Guilford.

Tangney, J. P. (1992). Situational determinants of shame and guilt in young adulthood. *Personality and Social Psychology Bulletin, 18*, 199–206.

Thorne, A. (1995). Developmental truths in memories of childhood and adolescence. *Journal of Personality, 63*, 593–616.

Thorne, A., & Klohnen, E. (1993). Interpersonal memories as maps for personality consistency. In D. C. Funder, R. D. Parke, C. Tomlinson-Keasey, & K. Widaman (Eds.), *Studying lives through time: Personality and development* (pp. 223–253). Washington, DC: American Psychological Association.

Trossman, B. (1968). Adolescent children of concentration camp survivors. *Journal of the Canadian Psychiatry Association, 13*, 121–123.

Vangelisti, A. L., & Sprague, R. J. (1998). In P. A. Andersen & L. K. Guerrero (Eds.), *Handbook of communication and emotion: Research, theory, applications, and contexts* (pp. 123–154). San Diego, CA: Academic Press.

van IJzendoorn, M. H. (1992). Intergenerational transmission of parenting: A review of studies in nonclinical populations. *Developmental Review, 12*, 76–99.

van IJzendoorn, M. H., Bakermans-Kranenburg, M. J., & Sagi-Schwartz, A. (2003). Are children of Holocaust survivors less well-adapted? A meta-analytic investigation of secondary traumatization. *Journal of Traumatic Stress, 16*, 459–469.

Vinnars, B., Barber, J. P., Norén, K., Thormählen, B., Gallop, R., & Weinryb, R. M. (2005). Supportive-expressive psychotherapy in personality disorders: An outpatient randomized controlled trial. *American Journal of Psychiatry, 162*, 1933–1940.

Wajnryb, R. (2001). *Silence: How tragedy shapes talk.* Crows Nest, N.S.W.: Allen & Unwin.

Waldinger, R. J., Seidman, E. L., Gerber, A. J., Liem, J. H., Allen, J. P., & Hauser, S. T. (2003). Attachment and core relationship themes: Wishes for autonomy and closeness in the narratives of securely and insecurely attached adults. *Psychotherapy Research, 13*, 77–98.

Waldinger, R. J., Diguer, L., Guastella, F., Lefebvre, R., Allen, J. P., Luborsky, L., & Hauser, S. T. (2002). The same old song? Stability and change in relationship schemas from adolescence to young adulthood. *Journal of Youth and Adolescence*, *31*, 17–29.

Wanderman, E. (1976). Children and families of Holocaust survivors: A psychological review. In L. Steinitz & D. Sozonyi (Eds.), *Living after the Holocaust: Reflections by the post-war generation in America* (pp. 115–123). New York: Bloch Publishing.

Wardi, D. (1992). *Memorial candles: Children of the Holocaust.* London: Routledge.

Weiss, E., O'Connell, A. N., & Siiter, R. (1986). Comparisons of second generation Holocaust survivors, immigrants, and nonimmigrants on measures of mental health. *Journal of Personality and Social Psychology*, *50*, 828–831.

Wiesel, E. (1978). *A Jew today.* New York: Random House.

Wilczek, A., Weinryb, R. M., Barber, J. P., Gustavson, J. P., & Asberg, M. (2004). Change in the core conflictual relationship theme after long-term dynamic psychotherapy. *Psychotherapy Research*, *14*, 107–125.

Wiseman, H. (1995). The quest for connectedness: Loneliness as process in the narratives of lonely university students. In R. Josselson & A. Lieblich (Eds.), *The narrative study of lives: Interpreting experience*, *3*, 116–152.

Wiseman, H. (1999, May). *Central Relationship Themes among Second Generation Holocaust Survivors.* Invited guest lecture, Center for Psychotherapy Research, University of Pennsylvania Medical Center, Philadelphia, Pennsylvania, USA.

Wiseman, H. (2005). *The Experience of Parenting Adolescents among Second Generation Holocaust Survivors: Recollections of experiences with their parents and current parent-adolescent relationship.* Final Scientific Research Report: Israel Foundations Trustees Grant (2002–2004).

Wiseman, H. (2007). *On failed intersubjectivity: Recollections of loneliness experiences in offspring of Holocaust survivors.* Manuscript submitted for publication.

Wiseman, H., & Barber, J. P. (2000). *Central Relationship Patterns in Second Generation Holocaust Survivors.* Final Scientific Research Report: Part II. United States–Israel Binational Science Foundation (BSF).

Wiseman, H., & Barber, J. P. (2001, March). *On the wish to avoid conflict: Core conflictual relationship themes among second generation Holocaust survivors.* Paper presented at the Joint Meeting of the Society for Psychotherapy Research (SPR) European and UK Chapters, Leiden, Netherlands.

Wiseman, H., & Barber, J. P. (2004). The Core Conflictual Relationship Theme approach to relational narratives: Interpersonal themes in the context of intergenerational communication of trauma. In A. Lieblich,

D. P. McAdams, & R. Josselson (Eds.), *Healing plots: The narrative basis of psychotherapy* (pp. 151–170). Washington, DC: American Psychological Association.

Wiseman, H., & Barber, J. P. (2007). Intergenerational communication about the Holocaust and interpersonal patterns among second generation Holocaust survivors. In Z. Solomon & J. Chaitin (Eds.), *Childhood in the shadow of the Holocaust: Child survivors and second generation* (pp. 394–417). Tel-Aviv: Hakibbutz Hameuchad Publishing house Ltd. (In Hebrew.)

Wiseman, H., Barber, J. P., Raz, A., Yam, I., Foltz, C., & Livne-Snir, S. (2002). Parental communication of Holocaust experiences and interpersonal patterns in offspring of Holocaust survivors. *International Journal of Behavioral Development, 26*(4), 371–381.

Wiseman, H., Goldberg, A., Remez, H., & Ben Shmuel-Zetelny, M. (2005, June). *Continuity and change in relationship themes in mother-daughter narratives: Merging the CCRT and attachment perspectives.* Paper presented at the 36th Annual Meeting of the Society for Psychotherapy Research, Montreal, Canada.

Wiseman, H., Hashmonay, R., & Harel, J. (2006). Interplay of relational parent-child representations from a psychoanalytic perspective: An analysis of two mother-father-child triads. In O. Mayseless (Ed.), *Representations of parenting: Theory, research and clinical implications.* New York: Cambridge University Press.

Wiseman, H., Mayseless, O., & Sharabany R. (2006). Why are they lonely? Perceived quality of early relationships with parents, attachment, personality predispositions and loneliness in first-year university students. *Personality and Individual Differences, 40,* 237–248.

Wiseman, H., Metzl, E., & Barber, J. P. (2006). Anger, guilt, and intergenerational communication of trauma in the interpersonal narratives of second generation Holocaust survivors. *American Journal of Orthopsychiatry, 76*(2), 176–184.

Witte, K. (1998). Fear as motivator, fear as inhibitor: Using the extended parallel process model to explain fear appeal successes and failures. In P. A. Andersen & L. K. Guerrero (Eds.), *Handbook of communication and emotion: Research, theory, applications, and contexts* (pp. 423–450). San Diego, CA: Academic Press.

Wolfgang, F. (2007, May). *Remembering the Holocaust as a communicative process.* Paper presented at a conference "The Holocaust survivor: A psychosocial-psychological view on life during and after massive traumatization." Ray D. Wolfe Center for the Study of Psychological Stress, University of Haifa, Israel.

Wood, L. A. (1986). Loneliness. In R. Harre (Ed.), *The social construction of emotions* (pp. 184–208). Oxford: Blackwell.
Zlotogorski, Z. (1983). Offspring of concentration camp survivors: The relationship of perception of family cohesion and adaptability to levels of ego functioning. *Comprehensive Psychiatry, 2*(4), 345–354.
Zussman-Regev, I. (2003). *Intergenerational communication about the Holocaust from the perspectives of the second and third generation in families that the grandchild experienced the journey to Poland.* Unpublished master's thesis, University of Haifa, Haifa, Israel. (In Hebrew.)

INDEX

Printed in the United Kingdom by TJ Clays Ltd.